Development

KEY CONCEPTS IN THE SOCIAL SCIENCES

Published

Development

Anthony Payne and
Nicola Phillips

polity

First published in 2010 by Polity Press

Polity Press
65 Bridge Street
Cambridge CB2 1UR, UK

Polity Press
350 Main Street
Malden, MA 02148, USA

ISBN-13: 978-0-7456-3067-0
ISBN-13: 978-0-7456-3068-7(paperback)

A catalogue record for this book is available from the British Library.

Typeset in 10.5 on 12 pt Sabon
by Toppan Best-set Premedia Limited
Printed and bound in Great Britain
by MPG Books Limted, Bodmin, Cornwall

For further information on Polity, visit our website: www.politybooks.com

Contents

For Steve and Jill

Preface

The question of what it is that we study as students of development is one which has preoccupied us for many years – what development is, what we mean by the term, how it should be studied, what the field looks like, how it used to look, and what its future should be. When we were approached by Polity Press to write this book for its 'Key Concepts' series, it seemed like an ideal moment for us to try to distil and consolidate what had cumulatively been many hours of conversation and discussion over a good decade or so, in many different parts of the world, and probably over several bottles of wine! Our collaboration over this time had produced a joint conviction that the study of development needed to be rehabilitated by rooting it firmly in the broader intellectual enterprise of political economy, and it is this prospectus that we seek to lay out and justify in this book. Indeed, as we shall show, it is only relatively recently that the study of development and the study of political economy have come to be seen as residing within separate fields. It was not so 'in the beginning', one might say, and thus our aim here is more properly to argue for a *re*-rooting of the study of development in political economy and to set out one way at least of working through the implications of such an undertaking.

As with all books, our debts in terms of intellectual inspiration, encouragement and direct assistance are considerable. Our ideas owe much to formal and informal interactions with a large number of colleagues and friends, some working in the field of development, some working more broadly in the field of political economy, some just friends. We note too the contribution of many students to whom we have tried to teach 'development' and who, as good students do, have asked us plenty of probing and thought-provoking questions. We are grateful in a practical way to Louise Knight and Rachel Donnelly at Polity for their exemplary editorial shepherding of this project and very useful suggestions along the way. We hope that the book will seem easy to read and will make sense to its readers. Above all, we hope that its publication will lead to a renewed focus on the study of development within political economy. This is much needed in present times.

Anthony Payne and Nicola Phillips
March 2009

Introduction

The concept of development has never been in greater need of analysis and clarification than in the present era. Indeed, a point has been reached where it urgently needs to be unpacked by informed, rigorous thinking. The reasons for this are twofold and connected: on the one hand, the word has come to be extraordinarily widely used in public discourse, probably more so than ever before in its history; on the other hand, it has perhaps never been deployed so glibly, and in general so little questioned and understood, as in the early years of this century.

The first claim is easy enough to substantiate. One has only to recall the titles of many major international organisations, from the United Nations Development Programme (UNDP) and the United Nations Conference on Trade and Development (UNCTAD) to the International Bank for Reconstruction and Development (IBRD) and the Organisation for Economic Cooperation and Development (OECD). The World Trade Organization (WTO) has also lately sought to bring to fruition a so-called Doha 'Development' Round. The United States has within its governmental structure a body called the Agency for International Development (USAID); the United Kingdom has a specialist ministry called the Department for International Development (DfID); whilst for its part the European Commission has long had a Directorate-General for Development. What is more, a conference of over

150 heads of state meeting under UN auspices in New York in September 2000 enjoined the world to pursue a series of 'Millennium Development Goals' (MDGs), and another large gathering of political leaders meeting in Johannesburg in August–September 2002 deliberated under the rubric of the World Summit on Sustainable Development (WSSD). It is also the case that civil society more than matches government in its embrace of the concept: witness the work of the World Development Movement (WDM), the Catholic Agency for Overseas Development (CAFOD), Development Alternatives with Women in a New Era (DAWN) and sundry other development-oriented non-governmental organisations. What is it that all these diverse bodies can be trying to achieve?

The second claim is a matter of judgement. Nevertheless, the argument can powerfully be made that the concept of development is now deployed more and more unthinkingly in public discourse, often being put up simply as a slogan or as a signifier of support for something that is deemed, straightforwardly, to be a 'good'. H. W. Arndt noticed this tendency back in 1987. He observed that 'anyone who asked articulate citizens in developed or developing countries what they meant by this desirable objective of "development" would get a great variety of answers'. In fact, he offered a rather revealing list of the diverse things they might say, as follows:

> Higher living standards. A rising per capita income. Increase in productive capacity. Mastery over nature. Freedom through control of man's environment. Economic growth. But not mere growth, growth with equity. Elimination of poverty. Basic needs satisfaction. Catching up with the developed countries in technology, wealth, power, status. Economic independence, self-reliance. Scope for self-fulfilment for all. Liberation, the means to human ascent.

Arndt added, somewhat sardonically, that 'development, in the vast literature on the subject, appears to have come to encompass almost all facets of the good society, everyman's road to utopia' (Arndt 1987: 1). In the intervening twenty years, during which even more has been said and written about development, the essential truth of this observation has become ever more manifest. Everybody, or nearly everybody, is 'for' development; they are 'for' it generally because they think that most other people are too, though few bother to define the term, and even fewer ponder or probe what it is that they are talking about.

It should be the case that the scholarly literature can be excused such criticisms, and, in part, it clearly can. There undoubtedly exists a great deal of incisive and thoughtful writing about development by scholars deeply committed to their chosen field of enquiry. However, most scholars who study development work in the self-proclaimed field of 'development studies' seek to defend that field strongly from the scrutiny and critical attention of social scientists from other quarters. This is unfortunate. There is no denying at all that development studies has had an heroic history. Indeed, we have argued previously that 'in its heyday it was an exemplar of all that was best about the social sciences – interdisciplinary, focused on big questions, engaged with them, political in the most generous sense of that word' (Payne 2004: 2). But that phase in the history of this sub-field has passed, and development studies, for all of its continuing merits, is no longer quite such a vibrant field of enquiry and debate – as some of its adherents openly admit. In fact, more than two decades ago David Booth (1985) declared that an 'impasse' had been reached in the field, a claim which quickly became the new orthodoxy. What is more, the harsh truth is that, despite the self-conscious efforts of Franz Schuurman (1993) and others to break out beyond the impasse, no basis on which to organise this theoretical advance has been found that has proved to be acceptable across the sub-field. In consequence, contemporary development studies, although still a sizeable academic enterprise in many Western countries, is at the same time an uncertain and under-confident discipline.

We believe, and will seek to demonstrate in this book, that the way forward is to move away from the notion of a specialist field devoted to the study of development. We shall not therefore proceed to unpick this field by considering in turn different (anthropological, economic, geographical, political, social) concepts of, or approaches to, development. We shall instead adopt a different and perhaps bolder method, endeavouring to re-ground the contemporary analysis of development fully and squarely within the wider, and indeed even older, intellectual tradition of political economy.

This is not the place to set out a comprehensive review of the academic discipline of political economy. Other studies over the years have done that very well (Staniland 1985; Gill and Law 1988; Frieden and Lake 1991; Caporaso and Levine 1992; Watson, 2005). The point to highlight and build upon is that within political economy lately much 'critical' (or new, or heterodox, or counter-hegemonic) thinking has come to prominence. Drawing inspiration in the broadest sense from the critical theory of the Frankfurt School and within the field of political economy from the founding work of Robert Cox, this approach self-consciously set out to be 'critical in the sense that it stands apart from the prevailing order of the world and asks how that order came about' (Cox 1981: 129). In Cox's particular formulation, it was a theory of history concerned not just with the past but with a continuing process of change; it was directed to the social and political complex as a whole rather than its separate parts; and it contained within its ambit the possibility of identifying the outlines of alternative distributions of power from those prevailing at any given time. It was also, classically, 'a method of historical structures' (Cox 1981: 137), with the latter conceived as configurations of forces that do not determine actions but nevertheless create opportunities and impose constraints. In other words, it is argued within critical political economy that agency-oriented concepts must of necessity be embedded within structural concepts. In another statement made several years ago, a group of us suggested that the defining feature of a critical (or, as we preferred to call it, 'new') political economy methodology should be that it would reject 'the old dichotomy between agency and structure, and states and markets, which fragmented classical political economy into separate disciplines' and recognise instead the need to 'develop an integrated analysis, by combining parsimonious theories which analyse agency in terms of rationality with contextual theories which analyse structures institutionally and historically' (Gamble et al. 1996: 5–6). We stand by that prospectus and aim to put it to work in this historical account of the key political economy concept of development.

On the basis of this explicitly political economy perspective we set out a particular approach to the analysis of development. It has three distinguishing features.

- The first defines development as the object of strategy. The argument here is really a reminder of the importance of agency. It only makes sense to think of development as the intended goal of somebody or something. There has to be an actor that is putatively being developed. In psychology that actor might be an individual whose personality and human attributes can or cannot develop fully. In political economy, at least until recently, that actor was invariably a national polity/economy/society seeking to develop in accordance with its ambitions and its opportunities. In the contemporary era, development is pursued by actors in a variety of spatial settings (such as cities, or regions defined in both sub-national and supra-national fashion, or indeed perhaps even the globe as a whole), which thereby find themselves drawn into the development discourse. Equally, the focus on who or what is putatively being developed has shifted from an exclusive concern with nation-states and countries to encompass individual people and social groups, which may or may not be defined by their location in a national society/polity.
- The second feature recognises and seeks to uncover the contested ideological dimension of all such development strategies. The argument here is in turn a reminder of the extent to which human beings are bound to disagree about the content of development, about what exactly it might mean for a country (or a city or a region, or a group of people) to be said to be developing. The particular ideological associations that inevitably underpin different concepts of development have long been in dispute, precisely because definitions of the 'good society' vary. Liberals are thus not likely to see development in the same way as conservatives and socialists. Particular conceptualisations of development thus inevitably sit within broader theories of development. That is obvious enough, but it is nevertheless something that needs both to be emphasised, and recovered, in analysis.

- The third feature locates all theories of development in their historical contexts and sees them as being always historically conditioned. The argument here is ultimately epistemological, in that it rejects the view of those who think they can specify the meaning of development in some scientific sense. In our view, by contrast, ideas about development cannot but be shaped, and consequently limited, by time and place. They emerge out of particular historical situations and they change as a result of particular historical events. The story (indeed, more precisely, the many, many stories) of development can therefore only be told historically in full awareness of the changing usage of this ubiquitous term over a long period of time.

There is one other aspect of the approach we take to our material which, if not entirely novel, is rather different from most accounts in this area of debate. In many books seeking to review the concept of development it is presumed that development theory did not begin until 1945, with the emergence of the so-called 'developing countries'. It would, however, be more accurate to say that it was development as a political project – that is, as a programme of change that 'developing countries' should be encouraged to pursue by the already 'developed countries' – that took off in that optimistic post-Second World War period. Indeed, the project can genuinely be said to have run on ever since, right up to and beyond the setting of the Millennium Development Goals at the beginning of the new century. We have also reached a point too, where the distinction that used to be so firmly drawn between 'developed' and 'developing' countries no longer makes any sense in a world composed of 192 countries with vastly differing levels of wealth and resource endowment (Payne 2005a). But this is not actually the key point to stress here. It is rather that the 'developed countries', if that is what they are or have been, must themselves have also experienced development in an earlier historical epoch, and thus have been the focus of the first development theories. It does not matter from this perspective that these were not thought of at the time as being *development theories*, for on this reading that is what they actually were. The divorce of the study of political economy from the study of development is in fact a

recent phenomenon, generated in good part by the emergence
of a specialised sub-field of 'international political economy'
in the United States in the 1970s, focused almost exclusively
on the analysis of interactions amongst the core advanced
capitalist countries of our time (Phillips 2005b). In this book,
therefore, we begin the story of development not with the
espousal of a self-conscious development programme post-
1945, but rather with an account of those classical theories
of political economy that arose alongside and in response to
the initial moves towards development of the 'first mover'
developed countries.

However, even this broadening of our lens will probably
not be enough for those analysts who argue that 'Western
civilisation' in fact had 'Eastern origins'. The contention is
that we need to look to the East, not the West, for the early
developers and, by implication, for the earliest development
theories. In one sense, this is quite an old argument, but it
has lately been restated by John Hobson with great verve and
compelling use of a mass of historical evidence – his argument
is thus one with which we need to engage, at least momentar-
ily. Hobson seeks to undermine the orthodoxy that 'it is the
"autonomous" or "pristine" West that has alone pioneered
the creation of the modern world' (Hobson 2004: 1). By
contrast, he argues:

> First, the Easterners created a global economy and global
> communications network after [the year] 500 along which the
> more advanced Eastern 'resource portfolios' (e.g. Eastern
> ideas, institutions and technologies) diffused across to the
> West, where they were subsequently assimilated, through
> what I call oriental globalisation. And second, Western impe-
> rialism after 1492 led the Europeans to appropriate all manner
> of Eastern economic resources to enable the rise of the West.
> In short, the West did not autonomously pioneer its own
> development in the absence of Eastern help, for its rise would
> have been inconceivable without the contributions of the East.
> (Hobson 2004: 2–3)

As already indicated, Hobson is generally persuasive as
regards the broad historical record and even more convincing
in his argument that Eurocentric accounts err by asking a
biased question at the outset, namely, 'what was it about the

West that enabled its breakthrough to capitalist modernity?' It can be agreed that such an interrogation will not do as a starting point if the aim is to produce empathic world history which appreciates that 'modernisation is a continuous process and one in which regions have taken part in leap-frogging fashion' (Goody 1996: 7). However, from our perspective, the real point to make is that what Hobson deems to be Eurocentric explanations of the rise of the West did give birth to the first theories of development, precisely because of European political power and its associated capacity to project its account of events around the world. In its origins, development theory may well have been Eurocentric, but that cannot mean that we should not recognise when and where this type of thinking began.

Accordingly, Chapter 1 of this book explores those classical theories of development that sought to explain the beginnings of European capitalism in the eighteenth and nineteenth centuries, focusing in particular on the writings of Adam Smith, Karl Marx and Max Weber. Chapter 2 focuses on theorists of 'catch-up' development, contrasting nationalist with communist versions and focusing principally on United States, German and Soviet experiences. Chapter 3 reviews the glory days of development theory, namely, the contest between modernisation theory, on the one hand, and dependency and world system theory, on the other, which dominated the debate from 1945 to the mid 1970s. Chapter 4 looks at a similar contest that dominated the 1980s and 1990s – the rivalry of neoliberalism and neostatism. Chapter 5 moves on to consider a range of alternative theories – the various human development, gendered, environmental and postmodern critiques of all forms of development theory – that also emerged in the latter years of the twentieth century and often acted as the counterpoint to the neoliberal/neostatist rivalry. Chapter 6 brings the story up to date by considering the key directions being taken in development theory in the early twenty-first century, including the turn of neoliberalism towards notions of governance and social capital, discussion of the implications of the rise of China, new debates surrounding poverty and inequality, and, of course, the significance for development theory of the reality of contemporary globalisation. The Conclusion reflects once more upon the three distinguishing features of the approach to the study of development proposed in this introduction and carried through into the analysis contained in the body of the book, and shows, finally, how the concept of development can – and indeed should – sit at the heart of a vigorous 'new political economy'.

1
Classical Theories

Classical theories of development address that long drawn-out period of interlocking economic, political and social change, extending from the sixteenth right through to the nineteenth century, during which key parts of Europe entered the modern age of capitalism and industrialisation. Unsurprisingly, given the extent and the complexity of the transition that was unfolding, the attention of a series of highly original thinkers was engaged and a variety of readings of these momentous events was assembled. In the process, classical political economy was born. As we indicated in the Introduction, the theories that were proposed to account for these changes were not self-consciously described at the time as theories of development. But that hardly obscures the fact that they were seeking to identify the essence of the fundamental shift in the pattern of economic, political and social organisation that was gradually taking place in Europe. In the language of the present book we would say that they were all trying to explain Europe's initial move towards what later came to be called 'development'.

In fact, the theories that came to the fore in this period are absolutely vital to our purpose in this study, because in retrospect we can see that they set the parameters of the whole subsequent intellectual debate about development. It would not be true to say that they left nothing else to be said, but it is the case that they have reverberated through the minds of successor generations and set out the formative themes of what emerge as fundamental overarching perspectives in the study of development and indeed political economy as a whole. They fall into three categories of thinking, referred to here as classical liberal economic theory, classical historical materialism and classical economic sociology.

Classical Liberal Economic Theory

In its initial form political economy addressed the running of large family households or estates, but, as trade and commerce between nations grew and modern state structures began to be built in Europe in the seventeenth and eighteenth centuries, it came to focus centrally upon the economic and political organisation of the emergent nation-state. The earliest economic analyses of this type in the period were 'routinely practical in orientation' (Preston 1996: 53). In England mercantilists took the view that the gains in trade achieved by some nations represented losses for others, with success being measured by the accumulation of wealth primarily in the form of precious metals. They argued that the state should assist its merchants as much as possible in their competition with the merchants of other countries, and therefore supported the regulation of commerce via guilds and monopolies in order to cultivate a trade surplus in the national interest. They believed that the national interest would always be different from the sum of individual interests (Heckscher 1935).

In France, by contrast, the so-called physiocrats challenged the mercantilist notion that wealth was constituted by precious metals and could only be built up by achieving and sustaining a positive balance of trade. They insisted instead that agricultural production was the true foundation of economic value. The group's leading figure, François Quesnay, writing in the 1750s, defined as productive every activity that produced a surplus over the necessary expenses of production and argued accordingly that wealth could best be maximised in France by shifting agriculture away from the predominant, but hugely inefficient, share-cropping mode of production towards larger-scale cultivation backed up by significant capital investments (*'avances primitives'*). The physiocrats were, however, willing to see the policies they favoured implemented by an alliance of the French monarchy and the French landowning classes, with the result that they came quite quickly to be regarded as a conservative movement out of kilter with the spirit of the times which were increasingly being shaped by the rising political strength of commercial interests (Fox-Genovese 1976).

The turn to theoretical elucidation within political economy actually came in Scotland in the person of Adam Smith. Brought up within the scholarly tradition of the Scottish Enlightenment, which was characterised by a focus on moral philosophy and thus a perception that human beings were at heart social animals, Smith set out a fully-fledged model of an economy that developed according to the working of the market mechanism. In so doing, he set the benchmark for all subsequent liberal economic theory. Smith's great work, *An Inquiry into the Nature and Causes of the Wealth of Nations*, was published in 1776. The title is significant: Smith did not speak specifically of economic development, but he very much took the view that the object of political economy was to generate a theory of the growth of national wealth. This was Smith's sense of what development was. He defined 'the annual produce of the land and labour of a society' as 'the real wealth' (Smith 1976: Vol. 1: 12), thereby rejecting decisively mercantilist claims about the importance of the accumulation via trade of a surplus of precious metals and building instead on physiocratic notions of production. In his view, wealth was created by human labour working on natural materials with the purpose of producing useful objects. It was also therefore seen as something that could flow in a variety of directions and in that sense Smith's definition of national wealth 'resembles today's GNP [gross national product] to a remarkable extent' (Vaggi and Groenewegen 2003: 107).

For Smith the key to the growth of national wealth – which he described as the 'natural progress of things towards improvement' – was the emergence of a division of labour enshrined in the context of a market (Smith 1976: Vol. 1: 343). The creation of a physical surplus of subsistence goods, of food essentially, set the division of labour in motion because it enabled the initiation of manufacturing, of doing something more with the spare subsistence goods. People then began to specialise in the production of a single commodity and, by so doing, increased their productivity. Societies grew wealthier as they came to be characterised by a more complex social division of labour. This in turn facilitated a more extensive technical division of labour. Smith famously cited the example of the pin factory wherein ten workers, each specialising in an aspect of the overall production process, turned out 48,000 pins a day, thousands of times more than each could have produced on their own by carrying out themselves all the tasks required to produce a pin. In his judgement, the division of labour was not the product of human wisdom, but was rather the consequence of 'a certain propensity in human nature . . . the propensity to truck, barter, and exchange one thing for another' (Smith 1976: Vol. 1: 25). Crucially, this gave rise, in turn, to the notion of the market, an institutional structure within which buyers and sellers met and reached agreements on price that signalled to the whole emerging economy how economic behaviour should most rationally be organised. Indeed, he specifically argued that, the larger the market, the more the pin factories and other similar manufacturing enterprises would produce, the more revenue would be generated and the more the market as a whole would be opened up. In general, Smith's vision of economic growth was extraordinarily optimistic: he saw its generation as genuinely cumulative, one part of the process leading inexorably to the next, and so on.

Markets, moreover, were deemed to be self-regulating. Smith (1976: Vol. 2: 687) discerned the existence of an 'obvious and simple system of natural liberty', within which – by means of a remarkable paradox – the pursuit of one's own interests also ensured the well-being of all and a steady increase in general prosperity. In his words:

> Every individual is continually exerting himself to find out the most advantageous employment for whatever capital he can command. It is his own advantage, indeed, and not that of society, which he has in view. But the study of his own

advantage naturally, or rather necessarily, leads him to prefer
that employment which is most advantageous to the society.
(Smith 1976: Vol. 1: 454)

This supposition operated at every level of the economy, from
factory owner to labourer. For Smith noted that 'it is not
from the benevolence of the butcher, the brewer, or the baker
that we expect our dinner, but from their regard to their own
self-interest. We address ourselves, not to their humanity, but
to their self-love' (Smith 1976: Vol. 1: 26–7). The market not
only induced individuals to consume and produce in ways
that rationally adjusted their activities to their demands, but
simultaneously also promoted the 'public interest' of increased
national wealth. It did so via the operation of 'an invisible
hand' (one of Smith's most celebrated phrases) that somehow
led the individual to contribute to an end, the collective good,
'which was no part of his intention' (Smith 1976: Vol. 1: 456)
and thereby created order spontaneously.

   Smith was arguing here for more than just the economic
superiority of free market economics. In Anthony Arblaster's
neat formulation, he was 'a moral as well as an analytical
individualist' (Arblaster 1984: 239). He believed that self-
motivated free individuals led moral lives and that the pursuit
of national wealth along the lines he advocated could
contribute to moral perfection. Smith's ethical stance has
provoked disagreement amongst commentators, with some
identifying contradictions between his moral and his economic reasoning and in effect discerning two Adam Smiths
(Jones and Skinner 1992; Winch 1996). Although his views
in this regard are quite complex, the extent of the clash
between an altruistic Smith and a selfish Smith can easily be
exaggerated. In an earlier work called *The Theory of Moral
Sentiments*, published in 1759, he set out an ethic of individual action within a community. In his view the principle
of sympathy – the ability to share to some degree the sentiments of others – dominated all other human passions and
served to hold society together. A man could imagine himself
as an 'impartial spectator', could examine the principles of
his conduct accordingly, and could thereby 'humble the arro-
gance of his self-love and bring it down to something that
other men can go along with' (Smith 1969: 162). This is a

vision of 'man in society', rather than 'man as fundamentally
selfish', and in that sense it does feed through to his subsequent economic arguments. As one analyst has put it, 'the
"invisible hand" ... regulates the self-interest of free individuals in their material interaction to produce a public
interest, just as the "impartial spectator" regulates the contest
between passion and duty. Together, they make a self-
regulating society possible' (Doyle 2001: 1404).

For all of the force of his convictions about the efficacy of
the market and his pioneering contribution to the making of
early liberal economic theory, Adam Smith did not ignore
the role of the state. In his view the state should do what the
market could not do so well. To be precise, the state had
three (but only three) duties: external defence; internal order,
security and justice; and 'erecting and maintaining those
public institutions and public works, which ... though most
advantageous ... are such that the profit could never repay
the expense to any individual or small group of individuals'
(Smith 1976: Vol. 2: 723). By the latter he meant mainly
the building of roads, bridges and canals, although he did
also say that young people, especially those from poor
backgrounds, would need the assistance of the state in acquir-
ing some necessary education. Public goods were an appropriate call upon general taxation, although it was preferable
that local revenues or charges on beneficiaries be exploited
first. 'Were the streets of London to be lighted and paved
at the expense of the treasury', he asked at one point, 'is
there any probability that they would be so well lighted and
paved as they are at present, or even at so small an expense?'
(Smith 1976: Vol. 2: 730–1). He did not need to give
his answer.

Smith's theorising undoubtedly focused on the domestic
constitution of economic growth, but he also had a strong
sense of the international political economy and drew a direct
connection between his theory of wealth and international
trade. One of the early chapters of Volume 1 of *The Wealth
of Nations* was in fact called 'That the Division of Labour is
limited by the Extent of the Market' (Smith 1976: Vol. 1:
31). According to Smith, trade benefited economic development in three ways: it offered a chance to exchange goods
that a country produced efficiently for those it did not; it

created a vent for surpluses that would otherwise be wasted or would cause a glut in the domestic market; and it encouraged an even more specialised division of labour and thus greater productivity. He opposed completely the mercantilist view of trade, arguing that it made commerce 'which ought naturally to be among nations, as among individuals, a bond of union and friendship . . . the most fertile source of discord and animosity' (Smith 1976: Vol. 1: 493). In general too, he was hostile to colonies and tariffs, on the grounds that they acted to privilege certain sectors and groups within the economy at the expense of the wealth of the nation viewed as a whole. Interestingly, however, neither was totally condemned, for colonies extended the market and facilitated a more extensive division of labour, whilst tariffs might usefully be called upon to subsidise temporarily a risky new line of trade or even protect national security. Smith was not a naïve supporter of free trade. He certainly believed that foreign trade was to the mutual advantage of all trading nations, but he recognised that the gains were not likely to be equal (Myint 1977). Wealthy nations had the greatest interest in trading amongst themselves because of their rich markets; poor nations, on the other hand, did not automatically benefit, for they needed first of all to build up production to the point where it could begin to be traded.

In sum, Smith was a very wide-ranging thinker. As Andrew Gamble has argued, classical political economy always comprised three key discourses:

> a practical discourse about policy, concerning the best means of regulating and promoting the creation of wealth, and maximizing revenue for the public household; a normative discourse about the ideal form which the relationship between the state and the economy should take; and a scientific discourse about the way in which a political economy conceived as a social system actually operates. (Gamble 1995: 518)

In his estimation Smith was pivotal less because of the originality of his theoretical insights than because of the fact that he managed 'to combine all three discourses in an arresting social vision'. In good part because of Smith's huge influence, liberal economic theory continued to display this multifaceted identity throughout its classical period, advancing further through the writings of David Ricardo, most of which were produced between 1815 and 1823, and climaxing with the publication in 1848 of John Stuart Mill's *Principles of Political Economy*.

The contributions of Ricardo and Mill are not unimportant, but from our perspective they can be more briefly reviewed. It is their views on trade and protection that bear most directly on thinking about development. Both were somewhat more purist in their liberalism than Smith. For example, Ricardo was much more hostile than Smith to the possible use of protection to promote national security or sustain domestic agriculture. He also advanced a different theory of international trade. Whereas Smith had focused on the gains from trade that derived from 'absolute advantage' (that is, a situation where a country produced an item of goods with less labour input per unit of output than its potential trading partner), Ricardo proposed the notion of 'comparative advantage', wherein a country could specialise in a line of production in which it was merely less inferior than in others in terms of relative cost differences and still trade to mutual advantage with technologically superior countries. This purported to show that a country might need to enter into international trade even if it could produce commodities at the lowest cost, for what was deemed to be crucial was not cost *per se* but rather the cost ratios of competing commodities (Blaug 1986). In the hypothetical example offered by Ricardo, Portugal had an advantage in both wine and cloth production over England, as it used 90 labour hours in making wine (compared with England's 120) and 80 hours in making cloth (compared with 100 hours in England). Even though Portugal had an absolute advantage in both, it still made sense in his view for Portugal to specialise in wine production because it was relatively better than England in the production of that item. England should be left to concentrate on cloth, with both countries trading their surpluses of each and gaining through such specialisation (Ricardo 1981: 133–41).

Mill too was critical of most of the cases where Smith had partially embraced protection, especially in relation to agriculture, but he did alight on one particular situation in which he thought protectionist measures were defensible 'on mere principles of political economy', and that was 'when they are imposed temporarily (especially in a young and rising nation)'. His reasoning was that an economically powerful nation might have the advantage in an industry simply because its people had acquired skills and experience by being the first producers. Mill thus originated the so-called 'infant industry' argument, which we will encounter in various incarnations in the coming chapters. It should be noted that he deployed it most cautiously, arguing that such protection should be 'confined to cases in which there is a good ground of assurance that an industry which it fosters will after a time be able to dispense with it' (Mill 1848: 487), and later reneged upon the idea of tariff protection in favour of direct grants to infant industries (Harlen 1999). Nevertheless, the general point stands: all the classical liberal economic theorists made some exceptions to their core *laissez-faire* principles.

Classical Historical Materialism

At this point Karl Marx enters into the story of development theory, formulating an enormously wide-ranging body of theory that has come to be known as historical materialism. Marx arrived at this core philosophical position by a complex route. He was born in the Rhineland region of Germany in 1818 and was educated in an era in which philosophy was the dominant academic discipline and the work of G.W.F. Hegel the overriding preoccupation of philosophers. Hegel's method was idealist in character, which is to say that he placed the power of ideas at the centre of his conception of the world, arguing in effect that the whole of human history should be understood as the maturation of the human mind or spirit. He famously discerned a dialectical process of thought by which contradictions were seen to merge themselves into a higher truth, or synthesis, that both comprehended and united them. The young Marx associated with the left-wing 'Young Hegelian' movement in Berlin and initially shared the orthodoxy that rational criticism was all that was needed to bring about change. However, like many others in this circle, he was greatly influenced by Ludwig Feuerbach's controversial reversal of the idealist premise of Hegel's philosophy in favour of the argument that existence – the state of being in the material world – preceded thought. Marx retained Hegel's dialectical means of enquiry, but he appropriated Feuerbach's essential materialism in recognising that philosophical critique at the level of ideas had to be complemented by a more practical grasp of the material forces at work in the real world. At this point in his life Marx moved to Paris, where he not only came under the sway of French socialist ideas but also met his lifelong friend and collaborator, Friedrich Engels, who introduced him to British political economy and urged him to turn his focus on to this field. Marx took this advice and identified 'classical political economy' as the main intellectual target of his future work, coining the term in doing so. But, interestingly, he did not reject classical political economy as a whole, drawing on several of its key concepts and findings even as he unquestionably sought to undermine it ideologically.

In his early Paris writings Marx set out the basis of a distinctive philosophical position. The core text of this period, which was prepared during 1844 (but not actually published till 1932), has come to be called *The Economic and Philosophical Manuscripts*. In it Marx referred to Adam Smith as the 'Luther of political economy' (Marx 1964: 147) because he believed that Smith had correctly identified human labour devoted to the production of things as the source of man's creativity and potential advancement. But, in Marx's view, where the liberal theorists had gone wrong was in taking as natural the characteristics of the economic and political system of their day. They operated with an unhistorical notion of development which assumed that human beings were indeed the egotistical seekers after satisfaction presumed in all utilitarian political thought, never questioning whether such a characteristic might actually be an acquired attribute derived from an historically specific system of production. Marx in effect accused the classical political economists of abstracting from and generalising about the society they lived in and knew, and thus of failing to provide the essential explanation of labour. He proposed an important contrasting view within which human beings were understood as making themselves (and therefore their societies) in and through labour undertaken creatively in a social setting. Indeed, it was generally the case that economic phenomena were always also social phenomena: economies were thus also societies. In this analysis the classical political economists erred because they eschewed what could not be treated as purely economic. As Marx put it:

> Political economy thus does not recognise the unemployed worker, the working man so far as he is outside this work relationship. Thieves, tricksters, beggars, the unemployed, the starving, wretched and criminal working-man, are forms which do not exist for political economy, but only for other eyes, for doctors, judges, grave-diggers and beadles, etc.; they are ghostly figures outside its domain. (Marx 1964: 137–8)

In short, the critical innovation at the heart of Marx's philosophy was his insight that human beings do not live and produce simply as individuals, but only as members of a specific form of society.

Marx devoted much of the rest of the *Manuscripts* to an exposition of his concept of alienation, which was the term he used to frame the way the division of labour within the industrial capitalism of his time had degraded this fundamental human characteristic into mere work. He suggested that alienation manifested itself in four ways. First, the worker lacked control over the disposal of his products, since under the terms of a market economy goods were produced for exchange and thus promoted the interests of the seller rather than the worker. Second, the worker was alienated within the very act of the work, because it did not offer intrinsic satisfaction but instead became just a means to an end, thereby destroying the human creativity of the labour. Third, the worker was cut off from having a social relationship with his fellows, since such relations under capitalism had become reduced to the operation of the market. Fourth, the worker was detached from his 'species being', since alienated labour reduced human activity to a mechanical adaptation to, rather than active mastery of, nature. Admittedly, none of these ideas was fully articulated within these early texts. Marx's style was often cryptic and the *Manuscripts* were more a set of notes than a finished treatise. Nevertheless, the basic elements of Marx's overall philosophy of development were laid out here, in that the capitalism of his day, the mid nineteenth century, was presented as a social order that had failed to achieve the creative potential of human beings and thus required major structural reorganisation of its productive system. As Anthony Giddens summarised the argument many years ago, 'the character of alienated labour does not express a tension between "man in nature" (non-alienated) and "man in society" (alienated), but between the potential generated by *a specific form of society* – capitalism – and the frustrated realisation of that potential' (Giddens 1971: 15–16; his emphasis).

Marx's mature conception of historical materialism grew out of these initial reflections on the way human beings make their lives in routine productive activity. Best viewed as a broad approach to social scientific analysis, historical materialism was first set out by Marx and Engels in *The German Ideology* (written in 1845–6 but also not published in full in the lifetime of either author), and then elaborated in the preface Marx wrote to *A Contribution to the Critique of Political Economy*, published in 1859. Marx proposed that two aspects of material life were crucial to understanding historical change – namely, the forces and the relations of production (the combination of the two defining the so-called mode of production). The former were the material means, instruments and techniques of production, raw materials and labour power; the latter were the social relations existing between those persons involved in the productive process. Classes emerged where the relations of production involved a division of labour that allowed for the appropriation of surplus production by a minority grouping which, in so doing, exploited the mass of producers. Classes did not relate to source or level of income, or to functional position in the division of labour, but were constituted by common relationships of groups of individuals to the ownership of property within the mode of production.

Controversially, and to some degree confusingly, Marx also deployed the metaphor of economic 'base' and cultural or political 'superstructure'. For example, he wrote in the above mentioned preface that:

> The sum total of these relations of production constitutes the economic structure of society, the real foundation, on which rise a legal and political superstructure and to which correspond definite forms of social consciousness. The mode of production of material life conditions the social, political and intellectual life processes in general. It is not the consciousness of men that determines their being, but, on the contrary, their social being that determines their consciousness. (Marx 1968: 181)

This last formulation has generated considerable debate about exactly how, and to what extent, the economic base determines the superstructure, with positions ranging from the strongly determinist, to the notion that the 'fit' between the two dimensions can be conceived quite loosely, to the idea that the superstructure in some way 'reacts back' upon the base (McLellan 1971; Worsley 1982). Moreover, it is not even completely clear what constituted the economic base of society in Marx's view: was it the forces of production *or* the relations of production *or* both? The many ambiguities at work here are obvious and can be traced back directly to uncertainties in Marx's own thinking.

Although again there exist passages that seem to argue differently, Marx repeatedly suggested in his many writings that the nature of the productive forces changed over time and thereby forced forward social, economic and political change. What happened was that:

> At a certain stage of their development, the material productive forces of society come into conflict with the existing relations of production . . . From forms of development of the productive forces these relations turn into their fetters. Then begins an epoch of social revolution. (Marx 1968: 181–2).

This period of revolution was only ended when the relations of production had finally been transformed to bring them into line with – indeed to suit – the new forces of production. As Marx and Engels proclaimed in *The German Ideology*:

> [H]istory is nothing but the succession of the separate generations, each of which exploits the materials, the capital funds, the productive forces handed down to it by all preceding

generations, and thus, on the one hand, continues the traditional activity in completely changed circumstances and, on
the other, modifies the old circumstances with a completely
changed activity. (Marx and Engels 1965: 60)

By means of these insights they sought to identify the major
historical examples of modes of production and to account
for the seismic social shifts by which one was transformed
into another. In several passages of varying historical depth
they thus wrote about the transitions from slavery to feudalism and from feudalism to capitalism, as well of course as
speculating prospectively about the transition from capitalism to communism which they deemed to be the inevitable
consequence of the contradictions that were working their
way through the mode of production in which they lived.

From the perspective of development theory it is Marx's
description and explanation of the origins of capitalism that
is obviously of the greatest interest. This was set out most
fully in 1867 in the first volume of *Capital: A Critique of
Political Economy*, the hugely ambitious work that Marx
intended to be his *magnum opus*. In his account, the basis of
feudal society was conceived (in fairly standard fashion) as
small-scale peasant agriculture underpinned by a system of
serfdom wherein the peasant producer surrendered a certain
amount of his produce to the lord. Commercial and manufacturing centres emerged within towns in Europe from as
early as the twelfth century and unquestionably weakened the
old landowning aristocracy, even bringing an end to serfdom
in some countries. But, for Marx, there was no possibility of
capitalism developing while the majority of the labouring
population consisted of a more or less independent peasantry.
The process of 'primary (or primitive) accumulation' – the
initial formation, in other words, of the capitalist mode of
production – only took off in late-fifteenth-century England
when a weakened feudal aristocracy began to drive large
numbers of peasants from the land, thereby expropriating
them from their means of production and 'hurling' them onto
the labour market as the first 'mass of free proletarians'
(Marx 1970: 718). Moreover, in Marx's view, once capital
accumulation began, it became a systematic compulsion,
drawing even the old aristocrats into becoming capitalist

farmers employing wage labour and producing for commodity markets. By the final stages of the process independent peasants had all but disappeared, feeding instead the voracious appetite of new industries in the towns for a ready and available proletariat.

Historians have subsequently challenged many aspects of Marx's account of the genesis of capitalism in England and in Europe more generally, but that is not really the issue here. The important point is that in *Capital* Marx set out a novel explanation of the way capitalist development was initiated as and when new forces of production arose, of how it came into conflict with the existing relations of production of a dying feudal era, and of how it brought into being, via that conflict, a social order much more suited to the widespread adoption of these new productive techniques.

It is sometimes asserted that Marxian historical materialism thereby also discerned general laws of history that chart the path of development through which all countries must pass. Certainly, in one of their most famous sketches of how capitalism would develop worldwide, namely, *The Communist Manifesto* of 1848, Marx and Engels had no hesitation in portraying capitalism as 'a universalising system, a mode of production that would sweep all other modes aside and by its own momentum encompass the entire world' (Barnett 2001: 992). They linked the geographical expansion of capitalism with the discovery and colonial conquest of new markets and observed that:

> The bourgeoisie, by the rapid improvement of all instruments of production, by the immensely facilitated means of communication, draws all, even the most barbarian, nations into civilization. The cheap prices of commodities are the heavy artillery with which it forces the barbarians' intensely obstinate hatred of foreigners to capitulate. It compels all nations, on pain of extinction, to adopt the bourgeois mode of production; it compels them to introduce what it calls civilization into their midst, i.e., to become bourgeois themselves. In one word, it creates a world after its own image. (Marx and Engels 1985: 84)

Other parts of Marx's voluminous writings also support this general view (Larrain 1989: 35). However, after 1848 Marx engaged in much more intensive study of societies outside of Western Europe, notably, India, China and Russia, and added a number of other complicating features to his analysis. For example, the 'Asiatic mode of production' was not one of the stages of societal development highlighted in *The Communist Manifesto*, but it was explored by Marx in a number of articles he wrote in the *New York Daily Tribune* beginning in 1853, and was placed before slavery, feudalism and capitalism in the 1859 preface to *A Contribution to the Critique of Political Economy*, implying at least the possibility of plural paths to development. For the most part Marx thought that the Asiatic mode of production possessed no intrinsic dynamic of change and could thus be said to be static in historical terms, although he oscillated in attributing responsibility for this lack of developmental capacity to the excessive powers of a despotic state and the stifling nature of communal rural production (Hobson 2004: 13). Either way, his view seems to have been that oriental societies could only be projected onto the road to capitalist development by means of the disruptive but historically progressive impact of European imperialism. And yet there are still other parts of Marx's *oeuvre* where he appeared to argue strongly against such a universalising view of development. For instance, in a letter written to Vera Zasulich in 1881, he contended that arguments about the 'historical inevitability' of capitalism were expressly limited to the countries of Western Europe (Marx and Engels 1975: 319). Similarly, he complained that a Russian critic who had insisted on 'transforming my historic sketch of the genesis of capitalism in Western Europe into an historico-philosophic theory of the general path of development prescribed by fate to all nations, whatever the historical circumstances in which they find themselves' was both 'doing me too much honour and at the same time slandering me too much' (Marx and Engels 1975: 293).

These are matters that have long consumed scholars of Marx (Avineri 1968; Melotti 1977) and cannot be resolved here, if at all. Marx lived a long life and wrote a huge amount that bears provocatively on theorising about development. He cannot be dismissed just because he did not espouse a consistent or straightforward view of the 'stages' of societal development across the whole world.

Classical Economic Sociology

Classical development theory is constituted in its final form by a nascent version of economic sociology. The great figure here is Max Weber, often seen as one of the founders of the modern study of sociology. Yet one must be careful with such labels: Weber thought of himself as an historian and a political economist and only came in retrospect to be seen as a sociologist. He was brought up in Berlin in the 1870s and read law, economics, history and philosophy at the universities of Heidelberg, Göttingen and Berlin, before going on to hold a series of academic posts in other German and Austrian universities. Weber's career spanned the period from the establishment of Bismarck's newly unified Germany to the collapse of that order at the end of the First World War, and there is no doubt that his thinking was deeply shaped by his engagement with the problem of German economic and political development, in particular the necessity, as he saw it, for progressive political leadership to assume control of the German state. At the same time, working in this period in this milieu, Weber could not but encounter Marx's work, with the result that his research and writing has sometimes been presented as a conscious and sustained debate with Marx about the nature of capitalism. According to this oversimplified version, Weber ultimately succeeded in overturning the economic foundations of Marxism by identifying and emphasising the role of ideas in history. The reality is much more subtle, for Weber never had the chance to read the writings of the young Marx in *The Economic and Philosophical Manuscripts* since these were not published until after his death in the 1930s. He certainly challenged some of the more mechanistic readings of Marx that circulated in Germany in the 1880s and 1890s, but he also took seriously many of the points made by Marx in his discussion of the historical origins of capitalist development. It is more sensible to proceed analytically on the basis that Weber was above all 'a passionate German nationalist' (Preston 1996: 102) whose concern with the development of capitalism in his country gradually came to be subsumed in a wider set of theoretical questions about the nature of capitalism in general. His contribution to development theory should thus be assessed predominantly in its own terms, rather than in direct relation to Marxist methodological principles, which he sought not so much to repudiate as to fill out and supplement (Zeitlin 1968).

Weber's first significant work was a study of agricultural labour in eastern Germany, published in 1892. He noted the existence of two types of workers on the great Junker landed estates to the east of the Elbe – bonded labourers tied to their employers by essentially medieval contracts, and wage labourers hired on a day-to-day basis in conditions of employment similar to those of an industrial proletariat – and drew a stark contrast between the acceptance of traditional patterns of deference still displayed by the former and an attitude of economic individualism that had come to be acquired by the latter. He showed too that, even though the overall life conditions of the wage labourers were generally worse, bonded labourers wanted nevertheless to exchange their security for the 'freedom' and 'independence' enjoyed by the wage labourers. Weber's conclusion was that these 'illusions' were central to the understanding of human activity. He certainly conceded that the new mode of thinking of German agricultural workers related to the kinds of economic and social changes that were taking place, but he also stressed, as Giddens has put it, that it was '*not merely* an outcome of the economic circumstances of the day-labourers', representing instead 'a part of an ethic which is itself helping to break down the old traditional structure of the landed estates' (Giddens 1971: 124, our emphasis). What Weber was doing here was creating space in the historical process for the intervention of human action driven by value commitments. He developed the theme further in his inaugural professorial lecture given in Freiburg in 1895 when he asserted the primacy of the political interests of the German state over the economic interests of the declining landowning classes (Giddens 1972; Beetham 1985).

Weber thereafter broadened his analysis of the dynamics of capitalist change in Germany to consider these issues on a more general plane. In particular, he published *The Protestant Ethic and the Spirit of Capitalism* in the form of two long journal articles in 1904 and 1905. They were subsequently published as a book and became his most famous work. In this study Weber tackled one of the most fundamental questions in the history of development, namely, why capitalism was initiated first of all in Europe from the seventeenth century onwards. He identified as critical the emergence of a 'spirit of capitalism', defined as ideas and habits that favoured the rational pursuit of economic gain, and argued that it was above all Protestant beliefs and codes of behaviour that served to influence large numbers of people to engage in work in the secular world, creating their own enterprises, trading and accumulating wealth for investment.

The steps by which Weber reached this conclusion are interesting. He began his analysis by seeking to unravel the anomaly that, whereas religious devotion and a concern with material advancement had hitherto usually been seen as opposing inclinations, 'business leaders and owners of capital, as well as the higher grades of skilled labour, and even more the higher technically and commercially trained personnel of modern enterprises' were 'overwhelmingly Protestant' (Weber 1958: 35). He then went on to argue that the unintended by-product of certain types of Protestant ideas – notably Calvinism – was a favouring of self-denial and the rational pursuit of economic gain and other worldly activities. The distinctive feature of Calvinism was the central place allocated to the doctrine of predestination in its theology. Strictly speaking, God decreed that some members of the 'elect' were predestined to everlasting life. This was immutably fixed, which meant that good works, although encouraged, could not of themselves guarantee salvation. Weber believed that this doctrine put great strain on most believers and he suggested that in practice many Calvinists modified it, in effect interpreting success in work as a sign of being amongst the elect. As he rather bluntly observed, 'in practice, this means that God helps those who help themselves' (Weber 1958: 115). The upshot was that believers pursued lives of unremitting work, forsook the pleasures of their success, invested rather than spent their money, and thereby helped to launch early capitalist development in Europe. To reiterate: these early entrepreneurs were not deliberately seeking to bring about momentous changes in their society – they were impelled by religious motives – but they nevertheless acted as catalysts for the spread of a new 'manner of life', not just to be found in 'isolated individuals alone' but in 'whole groups of men' (Weber 1958: 55).

However, it is important not to exaggerate the ambition of Weber's argument. He claimed that the analysis contained in *The Protestant Ethic* disposed of 'the doctrine of naïve historical materialism', whereby Calvinist beliefs could be regarded merely as ideological reflections of extant economic conditions (Weber 1958: 55). In this view, the Reformation was not historically necessary; it was not required by capitalism. That said, all that Weber highlighted was the existence of a telling connection between the rationalisation of modern economic life and certain intrinsically irrational value commitments. Weber had a completely different philosophy of social science than Marx (almost the antithesis in fact) and he did not try to advance an alternative overarching theory of development on the basis of one, slightly sketchy, study of Protestantism. Instead, he devoted himself to a massive programme of research investigating and comparing 'the economic ethics of world religions'. He completed major studies of Confucianism and Taoism in China, Hinduism and Buddhism in India, and ancient Judaism, but died before he could complete his overall project. His findings in these works are far too extensive to reduce to simple summaries. It is true to say that he found no equivalents in China and India to the distinctive mentality of ascetic Protestantism that had, in his view, so effectively stimulated the capitalist spirit in Europe. He talked instead of the prevalence of quietist cultures of acceptance. Nevertheless, it would be 'misleading to regard Weber's studies of India and China as constituting, in any simple sense, an *ex post facto* "experiment" in which the relevant material factors . . . are held constant, and the "independent" influence of the content of ideas is analysed' (Giddens 1971: 178). Indeed, the most important theme that emerges from the wide range of comparative studies undertaken by Weber is that the particular combination of 'material' *and* 'ideational' explanations of development was always both complex and different in every case. This point needs firm emphasis because it serves to correct over-simplistic, ideationally determinist readings of *The Protestant Ethic*.

Obviously, in general, it cannot be denied that Weber set great store by the significance of religious ideas and practices for the analysis of other cultural, economic, social and political aspects of life. But, as Ivan Oliver has rightly reminded us:

> These ideas were always ... intertwined with so much else that he regarded as indispensable to the understanding and explanation of Western civilization and the distinctiveness of that civilization from those of the East. ... [T]he religious roots of Western capitalism formed part of an account of a vast range of pertinent 'factors' (the term is inadequate, conveying as it does a sense of separable entities where Weber sought to emphasize their convoluted interdependence). (Oliver 2001: 1683)

This argument is there too within *The Protestant Ethic* for those willing to see it, for the truth is that the essay has to be almost wilfully misunderstood to justify the claim that Weber considered Calvinist thought to have been *the* sole cause of capitalism's emergence. Nevertheless, the breadth of his approach did increase with maturity (Bendix 1959). Already strongly present, as indicated, in the comparative religious studies, this notion of the 'convoluted interdependence of factors' sat ultimately at the very centre of Weber's thinking, as revealed in two important posthumous publications: first, *Economy and Society: An Outline of Interpretative Sociology*, published in 1921; and second, *General Economic History*, published in 1923. For example, in the closing sections of the latter work, Weber outlined a series of presuppositions for the existence of capitalism, citing such features as rational capital accounting, freedom of the market, calculable law, formally free labour, adequate technology and the use of financial instruments such as shares. He also highlighted a wide-ranging set of influences that affected the particular shape that capitalism took, including the nature of commercial policy, the impact of speculative crises, the role of colonialism, the rise of the modern bureaucratic state and the character of economic policy (Collins 1980). In short, Weber saw a whole range of issues as potentially decisive for the growth of modern capitalism, even if he had not been able to explore all of them adequately in his writings. Rather like Marx's *Capital*, Weber's voluminous final texts are full of hints rather than completed arguments: they were, after all, unfinished pieces of work.

In the final analysis, Weber conceived of the growth of development as a process characterised by the rationalisation of the conduct of life in general and of economic activity in particular. This marked 'the disenchantment of the world' (Gerth and Mills 1947: 155) – the encroachment of rationality at the expense, variously, of belief in magic, superstition, mysticism, charisma and tradition. Put another way, it represented the victory of bureaucratisation, of goal-oriented action over value-oriented action. Weber had no doubt but that modern rational capitalism was the most efficient and advanced economic system yet developed by humankind. For methodological anti-positivist reasons he did not see rationalisation as an inevitable evolutionary trend, but he nevertheless worried that the spread of technical rationality threatened the very ethic of liberal individualism that he had discerned as the animating spirit of capitalism. He described the cumulative outcome of the process in the gloomiest of terms, telling German politicians in 1919 that they faced a 'polar night of icy darkness and hardness' (Gerth and Mills 1947: 128) in which the rationalisation dynamic increasingly trapped creative, autonomous individuals in an 'iron cage' (Weber 1958: 181) of rule-based control – a controversial and much-cited phrase that Weber in fact first used right at the end of *The Protestant Ethic*.

Unlike Smith and Marx, then, Weber had no confidence at all in the existence of a progressive trend in the history of development and, to that extent, he can be said to have inserted a pessimistic note into the classical debate. However, Weber's thought was not ultimately closed and deterministic. As we have seen, his basic philosophical assumptions gave a central place to the concept of agency. In his view, human beings are never completely caught, not even within the 'iron cage' of rationalisation that he so vividly identified.

Conclusion

We conclude here this overview of what we have called the classical theories of development. These early theories of liberal economics, historical materialism and economic sociology – all of them in fact theories of political economy – are conventionally excluded from accounts of the history of the theory of development. But, as we argued in the Introduction, that exclusion only narrows the purview of the field in an unnecessarily restrictive way. What Smith, Marx and Weber, as well as their many contemporary followers and protagonists, were all grappling with was 'the original transition' (Roxborough 1979: 1), that complex and wide-ranging pattern of change that cumulatively marked the advent of capitalism in Europe. They were the first body of theorists seeking to understand development, which means there is no other place at which to begin a book such as this.

Because they were all addressing a broadly common set of questions, albeit while giving remarkably different answers, there also emerges a real internal dialogue between the three strands of theory. Even though the lives of Smith, Marx and Weber barely overlapped, they did, and still do, talk to each other in a meaningful way. Each unquestionably established a set of benchmarks of huge significance within the intense intellectual debate about capitalism, development and modernity that ran through what might be called, *pace* Giovanni Arrighi (1994), the 'long eighteenth and nineteenth centuries'. Their ideas also feed frequently and fundamentally into subsequent debates about development and we shall certainly have cause to mention their names and their work at several later points in this book.

2
Catch-up Theories

Classical theories were followed by what it is most appropriate to call 'catch-up' theories of development. The critical point is that the initiation of capitalist development in Western Europe changed quite fundamentally the economic and political position of every other country in the world. Some thinkers in some countries saw this immediately, but most did not fully grasp what had happened to the global political economy until much, much later. Nevertheless, all were implicitly threatened by the huge accretions of power that consequently flowed to the first industrialising countries. The rest could no longer be *first* to embark upon development – that beast had already bolted – which meant that the best they could do henceforth was to catch up. In short, a further important phase of development theory emerged from the need to react to, and match, the initial development processes that the classical theories had sought to explain, but now with the awareness at the same time that the task was not simply one of replicating what had already occurred, precisely because the context for development had fundamentally changed since that earlier historical era. This problematic has sometimes been conceptualised as that of 'late development', most notably by Alexander Gerschenkron (1962), who emphasised the distinctiveness of countries seeking to develop in the aftermath of the original transition. Clearly it does not generally help to think of the development debates most associated with the development of the United States, Germany and Russia as being in any serious sense 'late': obviously, there was much thinking about development that emerged even later. As we have indicated, what drove these particular ideas forward, in the context of these particular countries, was the increasingly urgent need to catch up with the Western European countries that had already initiated their transitions to capitalist development.

Catch-up theories of development mostly ran alongside classical theories, intertwining with them and often responding to them in direct ways. They were first articulated in the late eighteenth century, were especially visible and influential in the nineteenth and early twentieth centuries, and were not really transmuted into something else until after 1945. They have been advanced in both nationalist and communist versions, and we consider them here under these two headings.

Nationalist Versions

Nationalist catch-up theory has often been seen as an essentially statist tradition of thought that was the more or less direct successor of early modern European mercantilism (Gilpin 1987, 2001). But there are problems with this reading that have been highlighted by a number of recent writers who have sought to 'bring the nation back' into political economy. They stress that most modern versions of economic nationalism have been significantly more complex than the relatively simple ideology put forward by classic mercantilists. George Crane, especially, has argued that 'most discussions of economic nationalism *per se* tend to ignore the variability and malleability of particular definitions of national identity, assuming instead that identity is exogenously given, deducible from state interests, which, in turn, are determined by inter-state systemic conditions'. For him, 'state and nation may overlap in various ways but national identity is not simply an expression of state interest' (Crane 1998: 55). Accordingly, the focus of analysis must be directed explicitly towards the economic ideas of thinkers inspired by nationalism and different visions of national identity, with the additional recognition that, since 'national identities are so variable and changeable across time and place, we should expect the same of the policies that economic nationalists endorse' (Helleiner 2002: 310–11).

From such a perspective the work of Alexander Hamilton is the obvious point at which to begin the account. Hamilton was the chief author of the *Federalist Papers* – a series of seminal articles that appeared in New York newspapers beginning in 1787 arguing for the ratification of the new United States constitution – and was thus one of the true 'Founding Fathers' of the United States. He went on to become the first ever US Secretary of the Treasury in 1789 and wrote four reports that set out ways of enhancing the nascent national economic power of the United States. The most significant was the 'Report on the Subject of Manufactures', published in 1791. This responded to a request from the House of Representatives for an assessment of the country's manufacturing base and for suggestions on 'means of promoting such as will tend to render the United States independent of foreign nations for military and other essential supplies' (Hamilton 1966: 230). At the time the US had lost its trading ties with the British Empire as a result of its successful war of independence and was confronted economically by the heavy tariffs of other European countries. In the 'Report on Manufactures' Hamilton wrote:

> Not only the wealth, but the independence and security of a country appear to be materially connected with the prosperity of manufactures. Every nation, with a view to those great objects, ought to endeavour to possess within itself all the essentials of national supply. These comprise the means of subsistence, habitation, clothing, and defence. (Hamilton 1966: 284)

As Christine Harlen notes, the 'national security rationale' underpinning Hamilton's thinking was clear: indeed, she cites another document in his collected papers, dating from as early as 1774, in which he had already made the connection between greater US economic independence and security from European attack (Harlen 1999: 740).

On this basis Hamilton criticised Adam Smith's espousal of free trade, arguing that the agricultural protectionism of

England, as enshrined most notably in the Corn Laws, limited the ability of a country like the US to benefit from such a system. It was able to import essential manufactured goods, but was in effect prevented from exporting its agricultural products. Nor did it have the national economic power to alter this situation. He observed that, 'if the systems of perfect liberty to industry and commerce were the prevailing system of nations', then 'the arguments which dissuade a country in the predicament of the United States from the zealous pursuit of manufactures would doubtless have great force'; however, it was the 'opposite spirit' that applied (Hamilton 1966: 262). Given that the United States could not sell its agricultural goods overseas, it needed to create an internal market for agriculture, which could only be done by promoting domestic industrialisation (which would have the further benefit of making the various parts of the country mutually dependent on one another and thus underpinning national unity).

Significantly, Hamilton advocated the use of various governmental measures to bring about industrial development. These measures need to be seen in the round if Hamilton is not to be misinterpreted, as has often been the case, as a largely unqualified supporter of autarky or national self-sufficiency (Carr 1941: 155). Hamilton did support protectionism, but only to foster industrialisation. He wanted to limit tariffs to 15 per cent, thought they should only be deployed on a temporary basis, and favoured limiting their application to new undertakings that might soon become internationally competitive, thereby in effect setting out the first systematic version of the 'infant industry' argument augured by Weber (Bairoch 1993; Chang 2002). He was in fact more attracted to the use of industrial subsidies and also recommended a variety of other means (which would much later come to be called 'industrial policies') by which government could and should promote industry, including bringing in skilled labour from abroad, encouraging imports of machinery, protecting the rights of investors, setting up a banking system to provide investment capital and improving the transport infrastructure. In short, it was not that Hamilton was opposed to free trade in principle or had not been influenced at all by economic liberalism; rather, he argued that liberals 'did not adequately address the problems of how economically and politically weak countries might ensure their national security in a world where free trade did not exist' (Harlen 1999: 739). The United States was just such a weak country at the time that Hamilton was its Secretary of the Treasury, and it is perhaps not surprising that, as 'the economic theorist of the first colony to revolt against a European imperial system' (Gilpin 1987: 180), he should have laid down the intellectual origins of nationalist catch-up development theory.

There is therefore a sense in which Hamilton can be said to have adapted the essence of Adam Smith for American usage. His 'Report on Manufactures' had little immediate effect. But it did influence other emerging American political economists such as Daniel Raymond and Henry Carey and, following the victory of the industrialising (and protectionist) North in the American Civil War in 1865, came to underpin what was called, in explicit contrast to the 'British System' of free trade, the 'American System', broadly defined as 'protection for home industries' and 'internal improvements' (Chang 2002: 28; see also Luthin 1944). By the end of the nineteenth century, however, the idea of entrepreneurship had begun to acquire its 'familiar individualistic and popular character' in US thinking (Kozul-Wright 1995: 88) and Hamilton's theory of development came to be valued more beyond than within the national context that had originally stimulated its appearance. Indeed, it very much spread its wings within Europe by virtue of the marked impact it had on the mind of the man who stands as the leading theorist of nationalist catch-up development, namely, Friedrich List.

List was as German as Hamilton was American. He was born in 1789 in southern Germany and worked initially as a civil servant before being appointed Professor of Administration at the University of Tübingen, during which time he was elected to the lower chamber of the Württemberg Diet and acquired notoriety by actively promoting the case for a German customs union. He was in fact convicted of sedition and eventually exiled to the United States, where he lived between 1825 and 1831. It was in this phase of his life that he came across the work of Hamilton and Raymond and found an audience for his wider ideas amongst the industrialists of the Pennsylvania Society for the Promotion of

Manufactures and Mechanic Arts and the readers of the weekly German language newspaper he edited (Henderson 1983; Notz 1925). His first substantial publication emanated from this experience: it was a book entitled *Outlines of American Political Economy*, published in 1827 and derivative of a series of letters that then appeared as articles in the *Philadelphia National Journal* before being gathered together in book form. It set out all of his core ideas in their earliest form (Spiegel 1971). List returned to Europe in 1832 and served as American consul in Leipzig, where he continued to press for German economic and political union. He wrote *The Natural System of Political Economy* in 1837 for a competition organised by the French Academy of Moral and Political Science, but it did not win and the manuscript initially attracted little attention. However, in 1841 he wrote and published his *magnum opus*, entitled *The National System of Political Economy*, although the event was not sufficient to alleviate his severe economic difficulties and depression, leading to his suicide just five years later.

List's intellectual impact has thus largely been posthumous, but it has been considerable. Jacob Viner, for example, dubbed him 'the apostle of economic nationalism' (Viner 1950: 94). List matters to the history of development theory not just because he disagreed with Smithian liberals on policy grounds (as we shall see, the extent of some of these disputes was actually less than one might imagine), but rather because of his major ontological differences with the way the 'popular school', as he called the liberals, viewed the world. He argued that economic liberalism suffered from no less than three substantial faults, as follows:

> Firstly . . . boundless cosmopolitanism, which neither recognises the principle of nationality, nor takes into consideration the satisfaction of its interests; secondly . . . dead materialism, which everywhere regards chiefly the mere exchangeable value of things without taking into consideration the mental and political, the present and the future interests, and the productive powers of the nation; thirdly . . . disorganising particularism and individualism, which, ignoring the nature and character of social labour and the operation of the union of powers in their higher consequences, considers private industry only as it would develop itself under a state of free inter-

change with society (i.e. with the whole human race) were that race not divided into separate national societies. (List 1991: 174).

The theme running through these criticisms was that liberals ignored the central importance of nations in economic analysis (Szporluk 1988). By contrast, List not only asserted that 'between each individual and humanity . . . stands the nation', but went on to base his 'whole structure' on the 'distinguishing characteristic' of 'nationality' (List 1991: xliii, 141).

Yet even these observations do not capture the full significance of List's contribution to the study of development. He also advanced an innovative and highly sophisticated theory of national productive powers – a key phrase in his lexicon that he used as early as his 1827 work on American political economy. In essence, there existed 'a fundamental difference of perspective on human nature between the classical economists and List' (Winch 1998: 304), with List thinking beyond the mutual pursuit of self-interest to embrace the idea that the preservation of society in its broadest sense was an even more vital and instinctive human goal. He thus included within his notion of productive powers all that Adam Smith conceived as the stock of human capital, but added a further radical distinction between productive and non-productive labour, as set out vividly in the following passage:

> Certainly, those who fatten pigs or prepare pills are productive, but the instructors of youths and of adults, virtuosos, musicians, physicians, judges, and administrators, are productive in a much higher degree. The former produce *values of exchange*, and the latter *productive powers*, some by enabling the future generation to become producers, others by furthering the morality and religious character of the present generation, a third by ennobling and raising the powers of the human mind, a fourth by preserving the productive power of his patients, a fifth by rendering human rights and justice secure, a sixth by his art and by the enjoyment which it occasions, fitting men the better to produce values of exchange. (List 1991: 143–4; his emphasis)

Put differently, productive powers consisted for List of three types of capital: the 'capital of nature', comprising land, sea and natural resources; the 'capital of matter', referring to all materials used in the production process; and the 'capital of mind', which embraces skills, training, education, government initiatives and the like. Wealth was created in his view by the interaction of mental capital with the former two forms. In that connection List did not doubt which made the superior contribution and illustrated his point with a tale of two families, each with a farm and five sons. In his words, the father of one family 'puts out his savings at interest, and keeps his sons at common hard work, while the other employs his savings in educating two of his sons as skilful and intelligent landowners, and in enabling the other three to learn a trade after their respective tastes' (List 1991: 139). The fortunes of the first family, which operated according to the theory of values of exchange (as espoused of course by Smith), would inevitably decline, since the estate would have been tended in the manner it had always been and would eventually have to support five families. By comparison, the fate of the second family, which preferred to abide by List's theory of productive powers, would prosper, since the estate would have been improved and would only be split into two, with the other brothers already having secured incomes for themselves in other professions.

List usefully distinguished between the outcome and the cause of development. It was characterised, just as Smith had said, by an unfolding division of labour, but it was caused by the presence of human capital, measured both in quality and quantity. Development for List was, ultimately, 'a process of augmentation of mental capital' (Levi-Faur 1997a: 363). This is a crucial argument, because it was this vision, much more than a different theory of trade, that opened up the active role for the state for which List's political economy has generally come to be known. According to David Levi-Faur, four features of the process of development brought the state forward within List's thinking and positioned it as the key agent capable of nurturing the productive powers of the nation (Levi-Faur 1997b: 161–5). The first highlighted the case for cooperation across the division of labour in order to achieve ever more complicated objectives and the consequent necessity for effective means of communication within a society. The second drew attention to the greater capacity for social conflict in a complex division of labour and emphasised the way that effective national political institutions could overcome potential tensions. The third recognised the progressive lengthening of investment horizons as economies developed. The fourth acknowledged the cultural nature of national productive powers and the need to maintain the various supportive cultural institutions and practices of a society in good fettle. *All* pointed to a range of activities that only the state could realistically perform, running from the expansion of public education to the improvement of road and rail networks, the protection of patents, the improvement of technology and even the sustenance of a strong sense of national solidarity. It was not that List believed that the state could and should do everything, but he was aware, as he put it, that 'every law, every public regulation, has a strengthening or weakening effect on production or on consumption or on the productive forces' (List 1991: 307).

This brings us to the question of tariffs and List's attitude to free trade. Like Hamilton, List has often been seen, excessively simplistically, as just a protectionist, being widely credited, if that is the right word, with Germany's extension of tariff protection to grains and manufactures after 1879. In fact, List always opposed agricultural protectionism, especially as practised in Britain under the Corn Laws, and, again like Hamilton, favoured limited types of protection, for a transitional period, solely to promote industrialisation and only within countries that had the necessary productive capacity. Indeed, in an aside with distinctly racialist and colonialist tones, he explicitly ruled out the possibility of an industrial future for all tropical countries because they were located in a 'torrid zone', and he was generally sceptical of the development prospects of any country that lacked 'an extensive compact territory, large population, possession of natural resources, far advanced agriculture, a high degree of civilization and political development' (List 1991: 247). He also opposed protectionist policies within any country that had already achieved economic dominance and noted critically, with England in mind, that 'any power which by means of a protective policy has attained a position of manufacturing and commercial supremacy, can (after she has attained it) revert with advantage to the policy of free trade' (List

1991: 9). Interestingly, List specifically opposed the early nineteenth-century trade of British manufactures for US cotton and wool on the grounds that, although seemingly equal, it actually enabled Britain to maximise its national productive powers whilst imposing constraints on US productive powers. He thought that liberals misread what was going on because they worked only with a concept of material capital and thus missed the gains and losses of this exchange from the perspective of mental capital (List 1909: 187–202).

In short, the full panoply of List's views does not justify the reputation that he has acquired in some liberal accounts of his thinking. His ideas have too often been conflated with those of the mercantilists because, like them, he was interested in the deployment of state power. Although he criticised the liberals for what he thought was their misplaced and premature cosmopolitanism, 'he did in fact endorse their long-term goal of a universal society in which there existed free trade and a state of perpetual peace' (Helleiner 2002: 313). The point was that he believed that such a society had to be built politically and this could only be done on the basis of strong nations roughly equal in their power (Tribe 1988). The liberals had erred by assuming 'as being actually in existence a state of things which has not yet come into existence' (List 1991: 102). In the meantime, a system of limited and temporary protectionism was the only way to give weaker countries a chance to build up their productive powers and ready themselves for entry into an ultimate 'union of nations of the earth whereby they recognize the same conditions of right amongst themselves and renounce redress' (List 1991: 103, 272). List described this ambitious end-game as a 'universal republic'.

The point being made here is worthy of emphasis. Hamilton and List have been the most enduring proponents of nationalist catch-up theory because their ideas represented effective syntheses of mercantilist and liberal strands of economic theory. The favoured nostrums of other earlier and more extreme economic nationalists, such as Johann Fichte and Adam Müller, both of whom came from Prussia and genuinely advocated autarchy (Helleiner 2002: 317–9), have largely faded into obscurity. It is significant too that

Hamilton and List also took an empirical, inductive and deeply historical approach to their political economy analyses. Indeed, List is quite properly regarded as the founder of the so-called German Historical School of economics, which flowered in the second half of the nineteenth century and included within its compass the likes of Wilhelm Roscher, Bruno Hildebrand, Karl Knies, Gustav Schmoller, Werner Sombart and, albeit more distantly, Max Weber himself. As indicated earlier, many of their core ideas found ready acceptance in a Bismarckian Germany that was being outcompeted economically by low-cost British imports, and in fact the 'German Historical School' remained the dominant school of development economics in many continental European countries well into the twentieth century. List was a broad-ranging European thinker long before there was a European political economy to think about, and his ideas exerted their greatest influence on this part of the world. But it has also been shown that his views had an impact on the development debate in several other societies, such as Japan (Morris-Suzuki 1989), Canada (Henley 1989–90) and India (Gopalakrisnan 1959). He cannot ultimately be regarded solely as a German, or even European, theorist.

Maybe Hamilton and List said all that could be said on their chosen theme, because, perhaps strangely, other fully-fledged theorists of nationalist catch-up development do not really exist, even though several regimes in different parts of the world sought broadly to follow the prospectus in the hundred or so years between List's death and the end of the Second World War. It is easier therefore to identify political leaders and policy makers who overtly acknowledged their debt to Hamilton and List and arguably made minor contributions to the theoretical development of catch-up political economy by virtue of the particular practical gloss they brought to the general package. We will mention just two such people by way of illustration. The first is Sergei Witte, who was Russia's Minister of Finance between 1892 and 1903 and was responsible in that position for the largely successful implementation of what became known as the 'Witte system'. Influenced by reading List and inspired by a desire to assert Russia's economic interests against those of Germany, its most threatening neighbour, Witte pursued a set of policies characterised by attempts deliberately to 'substitute' (Gerschenkron 1962) remedies for acknowledged weaknesses: 'foreign capital was invoked to substitute for domestic investment; state capitalism for flourishing private enterprise; capital-intensive manufacture for deficient labour supplies; government orders at special prices for the poorly developed market in capital goods' (Trebilcock 1981: 232–3). The second, very different, figure was Sun Yat-Sen, the first president of the Republic of China between 1912 and 1925. Sun was educated in Hawaii where he studied the ideas of Hamilton and other exponents of the 'American system of political economy' (Billington 1992). He also reacted strongly against the damage that he thought had been done to his nation by British-imposed free trade over the course of the nineteenth century and, once in power, planned the national reconstruction of China around Hamiltonian axes: the pursuit of industrialisation behind protective tariffs, the establishment of a national bank and the initiation of major public works projects in relation to railways, roads, canals, harbours and dams, all regulated according to priorities set by the government (Hsu 1933; Wells 2002). As indicated, neither Witte nor Sun Yat-Sen can be said to have made contributions to the theory of nationalist catch-up development of the originality of either Hamilton or, very obviously, List. But their elaborations of the core ideas form part of the story and serve to highlight the genuinely global reach of this approach to development.

Communist Versions

Communist theories of development constitute the other variant of the catch-up approach. However, it is important to note from the very outset that this was not what they were originally meant to do in theoretical terms. For, as we saw in the last chapter, neither Marx nor Engels ever advanced a fully-fledged theory of communist development. They both presumed that communism would only emerge as and when the full potential of the capitalist mode of production had been reached and the inherent class contradictions of that system had rendered it ultimately unviable. As a consequence, they did not spend much intellectual effort at all in trying to think through in detail the political economy of a communist society and they certainly took for granted that it would not lack for basic material well-being. In that sense they did not think that communism would ever need to trouble itself with what classical historical materialist theory had conceptualised as development. That historical task would have been dealt with, as it were, by capitalism at an earlier stage. In practice, however, Marxists since Marx have always had to live and operate within a continuing capitalist world order and have thus not had the luxury, if that is the right word, of thinking and acting within a bountiful 'post-development' world of communism. It is this grave disappointment that has in effect turned 'actually existing' communist theories of development into variations of the catch-up imperative.

The theoretical discussions of relevance here have, for obvious historical reasons, mostly taken place within the former Soviet Union. They began in fact in pre-Soviet Russia in the mid to late nineteenth century as the earliest Marxist revolutionaries engaged politically with the *Narodniki*, or friends of the people, around a set of development questions that Andrzej Walicki (1969) later called the 'controversy over capitalism'. The *Narodnik*, or populist, current of opinion, advanced most eloquently by Alexander Herzen and N. G. Chernyshevsky, held that the traditional Russian village community was preferable to industrial society as a basis for the building of socialism. It was deemed 'to embody values of communal control over individual greed and competition . . . and to operate the socialist principle of land as a social utility – a source of general welfare – rather than as an exploitable commodity' (Kitching 1982: 36). Initially, the argument was that Russia could avoid the pain of capitalist industrialisation and move directly to socialism. But, as railways spread and large factories began to appear, courtesy in part of Witte's nationalist ambitions for Russia, the basic *Narodnik* position had necessarily to shift somewhat. V. P. Vorontsov argued pointedly that capitalist industrialisation in Russia would encounter an impassable obstacle in that it would destroy the handicraft production of the peasantry, and generally damage its purchasing power, but would not be able to create its own alternative domestic market because its statist and highly capital-intensive nature generated employment for only very few workers in relation to the total population (Walicki 1969: 115–26). Nor could Russia, as a 'latecomer', expect to industrialise by exporting to external markets since they had been monopolised by the first countries to develop. In these circumstances Vorontsov confidently reasserted the Russian 'privilege of backwardness' and espoused what was to all intents and purposes a programme of rural development based on state support for peasant and artisan production.

These populist notions were fiercely opposed by orthodox Marxists in Russia, notably Georgi Plekhanov, the so-called 'father of Russian Marxism', and Vladimir Ilich Lenin. Lenin in particular argued that the Russian village was a breeding ground of superstition and backwardness, and in his analysis of *The Development of Capitalism in Russia*, published in 1899, he sought to show not only that capitalism was already advancing rapidly in the country, but that the process was irreversible and would not fail, as the *Narodniki* alleged, because of the limits of the internal market (Lenin 1960–70: Vol. 3). He took the view that capital accumulation created its own market, primarily for investment goods, and further suggested that the ruin of peasant handicrafts and the spread of proletarianisation would of themselves extend, rather than limit, the domestic market. Moreover, in a critical theoretical contribution in the context of Marxism, Lenin stressed that capitalist development was historically necessary in Russia and had indeed to advance much further before socialism could be contemplated. Confronting the practical matter of *What Is To Be Done?*, published in 1902, he adopted the position that, given the relative numbers of workers as opposed to peasants in Russia even at the end of the nineteenth century, the workers should not be encouraged to strive directly for a communist society (Lenin 1960–70: Vol. 5). Equally, though, they should not allow their revolutionary potential to be bought off by temporary concessions from capital; rather, the way forward was their organisation by a proletarian party of professional revolutionaries that would operate in full knowledge of the extent of the opportunities and constraints offered by history to proponents of such a form of change in Russia at that time. In Marxist language, therefore, Lenin espoused a thoroughgoing determinist position and sought to close the 'controversy over capitalism' in the clearest possible terms.

Many of these issues nevertheless reappeared, albeit in slightly different guise, in another extended argument usually referred to as 'the Soviet industrialisation debate' (Erlich 1960), which raged within the Soviet political elite throughout the 1920s. As Björn Hettne has pointed out, this was 'extremely rich' intellectually and can almost be seen as 'a rehearsal' for later post-1945 debates about development (Hettne 1995: 232). At the same time it was closely bound up with personal and political rivalries, and ultimately a bitter contest for ascendancy, within the Communist Party of the Soviet Union. The economic and political context within which this debate took place is thus critically important to our understanding of the theoretical issues raised, and here the crucial question concerns the position into which the Soviet Union had been forced in the years from 1917 to 1924. A little historical background is necessary before we can elucidate the competing positions in the debate.

Following the success of the October Revolution, the Bolsheviks held power but had few detailed plans about the direction in which they wanted to move the economy. As we have already seen, the writings of Marx and Engels were of little practical help. Moreover, the Bolsheviks quickly found themselves fighting, literally for survival, amidst civil war and foreign intervention. Production was falling and food was short. The emergency response of the state was a period of nationalisation, centralised control and rationing, subsequently dubbed by scholars the era of 'War Communism' (Nove 1969: 46–82). This phase lasted until March 1921, by which time the regime was safer but the Soviet economy had almost ground to a halt and a change of direction was manifestly required. There followed the famous turn to the New Economic Policy (NEP), introduced by Lenin himself and based upon a partial return to the principle and practice of market exchange within the Soviet economy. NEP was controversial at the time and its meaning remains highly contested in historical accounts, in good part because Lenin's death in 1924 gave him no chance to clarify by word or deed the conflicting glosses that he and others placed on the change of policy at the time. At the heart of NEP was the notion of forging a link between town and country, industry and agriculture, worker and peasant. But this apparently simple notion, which came to be known in Russian as the *smychka*, begged many important and interesting questions. Did it represent a fundamental, or merely a tactical, retreat from Marxist principles of development? Was it a considered rejection of the excesses of 'War Communism' in favour of the pursuit of a gradualist road to socialism? In which case were Lenin and his comrades not fully aware of the prospect of capitalist social relations being generated if peasants were allowed, indeed encouraged, to sell their surpluses in the market-place? Did Lenin view NEP as a long-term strategy of Soviet development and, if so, how long was the long term? None of these questions can be answered with certainty. NEP itself was broadly successful in generating economic recovery, with idle industrial capacity largely being brought back into production by the mid 1920s. Nevertheless, many inconsistencies of policy remained, along with a residual lack of clarity as to whether development was henceforth to favour the worker or the peasant, or both, in some form of alliance still to be specified. As summed up by Stanley Cohn, NEP had been 'established to buy time, but time was running out' (Cohn 1970: 17).

The essential point was simple: by this stage in the Soviet Union's history it was apparent that future economic growth required the creation of new productive capacity. A few voices, most notably that of G. Sokolnikov, the Commissar of Finance, argued that given the extent of the proportion of the national product generated by agriculture the best returns on investment in the next phase could still be secured from agriculture, with agricultural exports paying for imported capital goods and thus funding industrialisation down the line. This was, however, very much a minority position within the ruling party. The dominant view held that industry meant strength and strength ensured economic and political independence; industrialisation was thus a necessity if the future of socialism was to be secured. It was widely agreed, therefore, that key decisions needed to be taken soon about the method and the rate of capital accumulation that was to be pursued in the cause of Soviet industrialisation. The great debate about industrialisation thus began to take off in the Communist Party in 1924, reached a symbolic climax at the Fourteenth Party Congress in 1925 and ran on vigorously until at least 1928.

For the sake of simplification, the proposals for new policies can be associated with each of the two major factions of the party – the Right and the Left. The Right was led by Nikolai Bukharin, the editor of *Pravda* and the chief theoretician of the party following Lenin's death. He advocated a course that was essentially a modified continuation of NEP, arguing that industry and agriculture should grow together in a balanced fashion and at an optimal rate. In his thinking, industry was dependent on agriculture for the supply of raw materials, for the income with which to buy foreign machinery and for basic demand (because the consumers of its output could only be the peasants); equally, agriculture was dependent on industry for the supply of machinery, fertilisers and consumer goods and needed the growing urban labour force to buy its products. In particular, it was essential that agricultural incomes should increase so that more savings could in future be obtained from agriculture. Peasants should therefore be encouraged, not condemned, and their savings should definitely not be sequestered. Bukharin even urged them in one speech to 'get rich', although he was subsequently forced to withdraw the remark. However, the observation was revelatory in that it showed how far Bukharin's view of the peasantry differed from that of the bulk of the Soviet leadership. The official line was that, apart from a minority who were poor or landless and thus comparable to the proletariat, peasants were mostly small-scale capitalist producers, of whom some, the *kulaks*, had grown to become exploitative, large-scale capitalist producers. By contrast, Bukharin saw the peasant family differently, as being neither inherently capitalist nor socialist in orientation, but in fact peculiarly Russian. The peasants were critical to his strategy of industrialisation because he thought that industry could only sensibly produce the goods the peasants wanted and thus could only grow on the back of peasant demand. This might mean that industrial development in the Soviet Union would be slow (Bukharin spoke at one stage of 'riding into socialism on a peasant nag'), but it would at least be steady and assured, and could be accelerated if the state also channelled resources (voluntarily) from the agricultural to the industrial sector via savings banks. As for socialism in relation to all of this, Bukharin considered that socialism would eventually overcome private enterprise because of its demonstrably greater efficiency.

The Left of the Communist Party was led by Leon Trotsky, Commissar for Foreign Affairs, although it was the faction's economic spokesman, Evgeni Preobrazhensky, who articulated its position within the industrialisation debate most cogently. Based on a series of lectures and speeches given over a number of years, he published his major statement, *The New Economics*, in 1926. In this work he argued that the only effective way to create modern, technologically advanced, capital-intensive industry was simply to go ahead and build it, rather than wait for it to emerge slowly from the build-up of consumer-goods production. This obviously required major investments in fixed capital, which raised the key question of where this was to be obtained from. On this point Preobrazhensky drew on Marx's notion of primitive accumulation in a capitalist economy, whereby external, colonial sources could be exploited to raise capital, but instead coined the term 'primitive socialist accumulation' to refer to the only option open to a new socialist state without colonies, which was to accumulate internally from the non-socialist parts of the economy that still existed. He put it as follows:

> The more backwards economically, petty bourgeois, peasant, a particular country is which has gone over to the socialist organisation of production, and the smaller the inheritance received by the socialist accumulation fund of the proletariat of this country when the social revolution takes place, by so much the more, in proportion, will socialist accumulation be obliged to rely on alienating part of the surplus product of pre-socialist forms of economy. (Preobrazhensky 1965: 124)

He meant of course the peasants. He did not formally exclude accumulation derived from the surplus product of the workers in state industry, but was only too aware of the fact that peasants accounted for much the greatest proportion of the 'pre-socialist' sector of the Soviet economy. He reasoned, therefore, that the state needed to seize control of peasant savings and profits by means of both fiscal and pricing policies, the latter involving a crude exercise of the state's monopsonistic powers to pay low prices for products and resell them at higher prices to urban consumers. The proposed policy was also as much political as economic, for it was fuelled by a strong sense of the extent to which continuing *kulak* enterprise represented continuing capitalist development in the Soviet Union. Preobrazhensky acknowledged that high prices would result from his proposed programme in the short term, but insisted that this problem would disappear once the new factories began to produce in quantity. Finally, he and his supporters repeatedly made the point that this forced and immediate creation of a heavy capital goods industry would ensure the country's security more quickly and effectively than a gradual consumer-goods-led form of industrialisation.

The debate has been presented here in schematic form, largely by reference to the polarised positions of Bukharin and Preobrazhensky. In practice many other economists and party members took part in what was, for its time, an extraordinarily sophisticated theoretical debate about development strategy. The lines of division emerge clearly enough, although it must also be emphasised that the protagonists shared many assumptions about the terms on which they wanted the Soviet Union to catch up (and indeed overtake) the capitalist countries. As Alec Nove has stressed:

> All took for granted the necessity of the retention of sole political power by their party. All took for granted the necessity of industrialization and were under no illusions concerning the limitations of individual peasant agriculture. Peasant cooperation and collectivisation were regarded by all as desirable aims. The difference lay in tempos, methods, the assessment of dangers, the strategy to be followed in pursuit of aims very largely held in common. (Nove 1969: 128)

The other great difference lay in the eventual outcome of the fight for control of the party that was interwoven within the industrialisation debate. At the time of the Fourteenth Party

Congress in 1925 the party followed Bukharin's line. Preobrazhensky's ideas were deemed to be too risky, too threatening to the *smychka* that was still seen to underpin the regime politically. Crucially, Joseph Stalin, the General Secretary, backed Bukharin, although in retrospect, it seems, primarily in order to focus criticism on the political forces in the party that looked to Trotsky for leadership. It can also be seen with hindsight that Bukharin's ascendancy within the Communist Party of the Soviet Union was on the wane even as his prospectus for industrialisation was formally adopted. Stalin later stole and brutally implemented many of the ideas of the Left faction, which brings us to a consideration of the final phase in this account of communist catch-up theories of development, namely, that package of ideas and practices known somewhat uneasily as 'Stalinism'.

Stalin in effect 'resolved' the great debate about industrialisation by means of the assertion of his growing personal power within the party. The critical moment came in the winter of 1927–8 when it became apparent that the peasants were not willing to sell enough grain at the official price. They behaved straightforwardly as 'economic men', hoarding their grain to await higher prices or simply feeding it to their livestock. Defying the party's rules and disregarding the law, Stalin ordered forced confiscations of grain and went himself to the Urals and Siberia to supervise the police operation. He had already isolated and expelled many of the leading figures of the Left, including Trotsky; now he turned on the Right, including Bukharin, condemning as 'right-wing deviationists' all those who sought to avoid a clash with the *kulaks*. In September 1928, in a last attempt at reasoned argument, Bukharin published a paper entitled 'Notes of an Economist' in which he reiterated his case for moderation and balance in development strategy (Bukharin 1979). Yet in April 1929 the Sixteenth Party Congress adopted the maximum version of the First Soviet Five-Year Plan, envisaging massive increases in industrial investment (by 228 per cent) and output (by 180 per cent), whilst by November of that year Bukharin had been expelled from the leading councils of the party. The road was thus opened to the sudden, wholesale collectivisation of Soviet agriculture, by which was meant the requirement that peasants henceforth worked only on state-run collective farms (Lewin 1968). Although the process met with resistance, it was brutally enforced, with many *kulaks* also being exiled for fear that they would dominate the new collective farms from within. The result was that collectivisation, signifying a massive shift of power within the Soviet political economy, was accomplished by as early as 1934. By taking control of agriculture out of private hands and transferring it to the state, it became possible to increase the marketed share of agricultural production and thus put a larger amount of the accumulated surplus into financing industrial development, which surged ahead accordingly. In effect, Stalin outdid even Preobrazhensky, whom he had had expelled from the party in 1927 and deported to the Urals in 1928.

Possessed of almost complete power within the Soviet state, over the next decade Stalin proceeded to introduce the full model of development that has subsequently come to bear his name. It has been said to incorporate the following distinctive features:

> priority to heavy industry, chronic overstraining of resources in planning, a high rate of investment, little or no advancement in consumer standards, partial substitution of social for material incentives, a rapid transfer of labor from agriculture to urban occupations, minimum foreign economic relationships, a high female employment rate, and high priority to education. (Cohn 1970: 23)

Organisationally, the model was characterised by what Gregory Grossman (1963) described as a 'command economy', with production targets planned – in detail and according to the priorities of the state – by Gosplan, the state planning commission, and then transmitted for implementation to producing enterprises. It certainly did not follow that plans could necessarily be carried into practice, but it was nevertheless firmly believed that the state machine had both the duty to plan development and sufficient capacity to make this a worthwhile undertaking. Setting aside some of the particular priorities of Stalin's era, such as the emphasis given to heavy industry, this faith in planning was arguably the most important feature of the model as a whole and the aspect that has had the greatest impact on subsequent theorising about development.

From the perspective of this chapter the most striking feature of the Stalinist model is that it was explicitly conceived in catch-up terms. In a speech entitled 'The Tasks of Economic Executives', made in 1931, Stalin said: 'We are fifty or a hundred years behind the advanced countries. We must make good this distance in ten years or we shall go under' (Stalin 1976: 529). In fact, as Nove, having just cited this remark, went on to observe: 'it so happened that there was just ten years' (Nove 1975: 72) – a pointed reference to the attack on the Soviet Union launched by Nazi Germany in June 1941. The many human sacrifices made during the course of the 1930s in order to build up major new industrial complexes devoted to machine building and arms manufacture bore fruit in a certain way in the capacity to defend the state from invasion that was undoubtedly generated as a consequence. Stalinism brought about the industrialisation of the Soviet Union at a faster pace than could have been imagined in 1917 and, in so doing, preserved the Soviet people from Nazi takeover. Whatever its many failings and excesses, and they were considerable, Stalinism has at least this substantial achievement to its credit. The question has been subsequently raised in academic debate – 'Was Stalin Really Necessary?' – and a good deal of discussion has been devoted to this issue (Nove 1964; Ward 1998). The analysis has, however, been for the most part inconclusive, focusing primarily on the narrower matter of whether or not collectivisation made a net contribution to Soviet industrialisation (Thatcher 2000). In the end, this does not seem to be the most relevant question on which to focus. Stalinism happened and needs to be understood. It should be seen as a climactic phase in the history of Soviet development and the culmination of the considerable communist contribution to development theory.

Conclusion

We argued at the beginning of this chapter that the various theories of development to be examined in the succeeding pages were all shaped by the imperative of catch-up. This is admittedly a somewhat unspecific formulation, defined above all by the necessity of reacting to something else, namely, the early development of the first developing countries. But the phrase nevertheless captures the essence of what has impelled this body of theory. We have distinguished between nationalist and communist versions of the core approach, although it must immediately be conceded that many of the communist variants were also as thoroughly nationalist in inspiration as the founding versions of catch-up theory. Perhaps unsurprisingly, given the nature of the underlying objective, nearly all the theoretical contributions we have examined were advanced by men of affairs, rather than by academics or intellectuals *per se*. List is only a partial exception since he too took part in formal politics. Catch-up theories of development were thus characteristically practical in orientation. They sought not so much to explain development as to bring it about, preferably in a hurry.

We also conclude here that part of the story that does not appear in most historical accounts of the evolution of development theory. We have hitherto focused on development thinking as it related to the development of what after 1945 would come to be termed the 'First World' and the 'Second World' – that is, the core capitalist countries of the 'West' and the core communist countries of the 'East' respectively. In the next chapter we move on to consider the period after 1945, during which development theory came to be seen as a field of study in its own right and the focus of attention was the plight of the so-called 'Third World'.

3
Golden Age Theories

As indicated above, development theory came into its own after 1945. Prompted by the decline of European colonialism following the end of the Second World War, and the consequent creation of several new, ex-colonial states in Africa and Asia, the economic, social and political problems faced by this growing number of generally poor countries generated a busy and fashionable field of intellectual enquiry. It also became a business serviced by a host of new advisers, experts and policy entrepreneurs. What gave this new 'development studies' political salience was its proclaimed focus upon a 'Third World' caught between the competing appeals of a capitalist 'First World' and a communist 'Second World' and the very different paths of development they offered up as alternatives. The new 'developing countries' were caught in the middle of a battle for historical direction and were subjected to pressures and entreaties from both sides in the Cold War. Development studies in effect became Third World studies, the terrain marked out by the clash of two large, yet still diverse bodies of thought known as 'modernisation theory' and 'underdevelopment theory'. This is where books on development habitually begin and how their first chapters are conventionally conceived.

The present chapter will also cover this ground, and in some detail, because it undoubtedly offers rich and interesting fare for a study of thinking about development. But from the outset we have taken a longer and broader view of the lineage of this complex concept and we do not want to detach the 'Third World' from the wider debate, even at the moment when this grouping of countries took centre stage within that debate for the first time. The point often missed in the more conventional accounts is that the ostensible rivalry of modernisation theory and underdevelopment theory took place in the context of a particular historical phase in the unfolding of the global political economy. This was characterised by the ending of world war and the beginning of a thirty-year period of accelerating and apparently easy growth in all the core economies of the capitalist world. It was as if the 'First World' had somehow managed to master the techniques of capitalist development. Eric Hobsbawm (1994) subsequently described these years as a 'Golden Age'. It was a highly appropriate phrase. In this chapter, therefore, we preface our account of modernisation and underdevelopment theories with a discussion of the dominant growth theory of the immediate post-1945 era. This new mode of economic thinking underpinned the whole of the emerging debate about 'Third World' development and needs to be understood before we can move on to consider its detail. We can accordingly think of all of these interlocking ideas as essentially Golden Age theories of development.

Growth Theory

The body of growth theory that emerged after the end of the Second World War was grounded in the general revolution in economic theorising led by John Maynard Keynes in the 1930s. By that decade economic orthodoxy had come to rest upon the work of so-called neoclassical equilibrium theorists like W. S. Jevons, Alfred Marshall, Léon Walras and Vilfredo Pareto. They were the leaders and beneficiaries of the 'marginalist revolution' of the second half of the nineteenth century whereby the sweeping macroeconomic perspectives of classical political economy had been replaced by a new paradigm characterised by increasingly abstract, indeed algebraic, calculations about the marginal utility of different economic choices in conditions of presumed scarcity (Blaug 1986). Even amidst conditions of severe depression, they maintained that employers would hire more labour as and when its price reached a low enough point, arguing in effect that the market-place, if left to its own devices, would always eventually restore equilibrium. Growth was simply not an issue in the neoclassical tradition, causing Blomström and Hettne to dismiss this whole school of thought as 'merely a parenthesis' in terms of the history of development theory (Blomström and Hettne 1984: 12).

Keynes took issue with the prevailing orthodoxy, arguing that economies could move into what he called a depression equilibrium wherein the various factors of production were not deployed to optimum effect. In his *General Theory of Employment, Interest and Money* (1936) he showed that aggregate demand for goods and services in an economy, driven jointly by consumption and investment, was the key to determining the level of employment. Of the two components of demand, investment was the more important because it fed through more effectively into all parts of the economy, generating a 'multiplier effect' and causing the economy as a whole to expand. Crucially, for Keynes, the state could act to encourage investment by manipulating interest rates and could even engage in deficit spending in a depression in order to get economic activity going. He said famously at one point that burying banknotes in old mines and paying private enterprise to dig them up again was better than nothing if the prime objective was to reduce unemployment. Keynes's ideas served in effect to re-legitimise state regulation and planning in the management of capitalist economies. They transformed economic thinking in the free-market world (Ormerod 1994) and were adopted successfully and widely by many Western governments (of all political persuasions) in the years after 1945. Keynes was without question the intellectual founding father of the Golden Age.

As we have seen, Keynes himself was primarily interested in short-term problems of stabilisation in times of depression and high unemployment – he did not focus explicitly on longer-term issues such as growth and development. However, other economists sought to build on his insights by attempting to design policies that would maintain full employment in the new post-war social democracies of the West. In economics, this move has come to be known as 'dynamising Keynes', and gave rise explicitly to growth theory. The main progenitors were Roy Harrod, a British economist from Cambridge University and the author *inter alia* of a biography of Keynes, and Evsey Domar, an American economist from Brandeis University. Although working independently of each other and drawing on slightly different premises, they developed a 'dynamic theory' of growth based on the relationship between savings, investment and output (Harrod 1939; Domar 1947). The resulting Harrod-Domar model subsequently became 'highly elaborated and often esoteric' (Brookfield 1975: 30), but at its heart was a fairly simplistic proposition. In essence, its argument was that economic growth required an increase in the planned national rate of savings in order to generate the extra capital investment that led to growing output. Since the marginal propensity to save was presumed to increase as income levels rose, it was believed that economic growth, once started, would be self-sustaining. The model proved to be serviceable in the context of economic theory at the time and survived with amendments into the 1950s when another American economist, Robert Solow (1956), presented a revised version which challenged the assumption that the same amount of capital would always be needed to produce a given output and thus introduced the notion of technological progress as a further, and perhaps the best, facilitator of long-term growth.

Growth theory was in the first instance a product of 'First World' economics. However, given that in the late 1940s and early 1950s most economists still believed in a 'mono-economics' capable of application equally to 'developed' and 'developing' countries, it was hardly surprising that the key postulates of growth theory were carried over into that growing body of analysis that sought to understand and address the economic circumstances in which the new, ex-colonial countries generally found themselves. Indeed, as Björn Hettne has pointed out, the basic economic problem facing these countries was conceived at the time in precisely these terms, namely, 'how to break loose from the fetters that prevented them marching along the growth path, mathematically symbolized in the Harrod-Domar model' (Hettne 1995:

42). Accordingly, the basic tenets of growth theory were immediately taken on board by ambitious 'Third World' countries, such as India, and fed directly into a report entitled *Measures for the Economic Development of Under-developed Countries*, produced by a group of experts for the United Nations in 1951. They had been asked to come up with policies to reduce unemployment and underemployment in newly independent countries, but redefined their task as one that related more fundamentally to 'economic develop-ment rather than . . . unemployment' (United Nations 1951: 9). In making their recommendations, they very much adhered to the Keynesian spirit of the times by acknowledging the central role of the state in engineering development, by endorsing the case for increased saving rates, and by recognis-ing the need for experts to initiate and manage a process of economic planning.

The task of completing the translation of growth theory into the study of development fell in the main to W. Arthur Lewis, a Caribbean economist from the tiny island of St Lucia. He had been one of the UN group of experts men-tioned above and went on in a highly influential academic article to state the core issue in classic terms:

> The central problem in the theory of economic development is to understand the process by which a community which was previously saving and investing 4 or 5 per cent of its national income or less, converts itself into an economy where voluntary saving is running at about 12 to 15 per cent of national income or more. (Lewis 1954: 155)

He looked at the nature of the typical underdeveloped country, as he saw it, and identified two sectors: one capital-ist, the other traditional. The former was dynamic, reinvest-ing the profits it generated and generally moving the economy forward; the latter did not save and acted only to sustain its current condition. In such a situation the key to growth was for the capitalist sector to move to absorb all the surplus labour that existed in the traditional sector, whereupon it would begin to dominate the economy and growth would be self-sustaining. Lewis quickly followed up this much-cited analysis with a major book called *The Theory of Economic*

Growth (1955). This work was not itself especially original in conception or content, mostly reiterating the close connection between growth, technological knowledge and the need to increase the amount of available capital. However, as one commentator has aptly noted, it did serve to synthesise persuasively 'themes within classical political-economy, material drawn from Keynesian-influenced economic growth theory and descriptive historical and social scientific material related to the condition of the underdeveloped countries' (Preston 1996: 166), and, in so doing, it mapped out the terrain of what by the mid 1950s could genuinely be called a nascent field of 'development economics' (Meier and Seers 1984).

The characteristic metaphors of the field at this time were those of the 'trap', the 'bottleneck' and the 'vicious circle' – with the heavy implication that, if only these could be variously removed or turned around, whether by internal direction or external support, then growth could be started up, pursued in unilinear fashion and continued until sufficient momentum was gained to render it self-sustaining. In a review of the prospects for industrialisation in his own region, the West Indies, Lewis even used the analogy, unlikely for that part of the world, of a snowball! The idea, he said, was to roll your snowball up the mountain, which demanded a considerable initial effort; it was undoubtedly hard to get going, but, once you were there at the top, it became easy and the snowball simply got bigger and bigger as it tumbled downhill of its own accord (Lewis 1950). Other analysts, such as P.N. Rosenstein-Rodan (1943, 1961), talked even more explicitly of the need for a 'big push' in the form of a massive initial investment programme designed to lower costs by means of growing several industries simultaneously, whilst in not dissimilar fashion Albert Hirschman (1958) advocated 'unbalanced' growth as a way of focusing on those parts of the economy with the greatest potential and thus sidestepping the constraint of scarce entrepreneurial resources. Early 'development economics' was thus based firmly on the presumption that the development problem was analogous to the low-level, or depression, equilibrium identified by Keynes in the 1930s and the attendant expectation that it could be 'solved' in broadly the same ways that Keynesian economics had thereafter made growth possible in the industrialised, capitalist West. The notion that structural factors might play a significant part in explaining, and constraining, the economics of development was not considered. That argument came from Latin America, not Anglo-America, and will be picked up later in the chapter when we focus directly on underdevelopment theory.

Modernisation Theory

For the time being we stay on mainstream terrain and move to consider the many responses that began to be made to the ever more obvious limitations of an early development economics based predominantly on the mechanisms of capital formation. As more and more diverse variables appeared to assert their relevance to the discussion of economic issues, sociologists, psychologists, anthropologists, political scientists and assorted others flocked to the debate and development flowered as a new, independent and interdisciplinary research field within an expanding academy. Attention to these issues was most prominent in the United States, stimulated by the advent of the Cold War and the obvious relevance of 'winning over' the new 'developing world' to the achievement of a successful outcome in that existential political conflict. US President Harry Truman made this absolutely clear in his inaugural address of January 1949, when he announced a 'democratic fair deal' for the entire world, professing his optimistic belief that prosperity would 'trickle down' naturally to the poorest countries and regions but also promising the provision of direct US development aid to underpin the process. For two decades after the Second World War US social scientists and their graduate students thus enjoyed generous support from both governmental and private agencies as they poured into Africa, Asia and Latin America to study the severe problems of poverty, instability and change that were undoubtedly being encountered in these regions in the immediate post-war years. They were driven forward in their enquiries by their confident presumption that development involved the passage of the 'Third World' along the same path of progress from tradition to modernity previously travelled by the advanced countries. This imitative process was conceptualised as 'modernisation', defined in a retrospective review by Daniel Lerner, one of the leading early theorists of this type, as a 'process of social change whereby less developed societies acquire characteristics common to more developed societies' (Lerner 1972: 386). The broad set of theoretical constructs used to frame all of these studies thereby came to be known as modernisation theory.

The striking feature of this literature, especially in retrospect, is the extent to which its conceptual schema was at the time made up somewhat on the hoof. The explanation was that in the US there existed no strong prior tradition of enquiry into these parts of the world that might have guided research design and activity and, in so doing, rendered its findings more sensitive to the reality of variegated conditions and experiences (Shils 1963). In addition, the enterprise of bringing together the study of such very different areas, with their diverse histories, geographies and cultures, within a single organising framework was itself entirely novel, as well as hugely ambitious. In these circumstances, as Dean Tipps has noted, it was 'hardly surprising that social scientists engaged in this task should turn for assistance to the familiar intellectual traditions of Western thinking about the nature of social change' (Tipps 1973: 200). Indeed so: but it is very important nevertheless to grasp fully what happened here, because the instinctive reflex highlighted by Tipps served (again) to lodge at the heart of this burst of theorising about 'Third World' development key ways of thinking that had been forged in earlier analyses of the original Western transition to modernity. The particular inspiration here was not primarily economic, but sociological. Even though, as we shall see, modernisation theory did mature into a genuinely interdisciplinary approach to the analysis of development, it remains significant that it grew out of, and built directly upon, the concerns of classical sociology (Harrison 1988).

Within the sociological tradition, the two bodies of thought that were most influential as precursors were the social evolutionism of the eighteenth and nineteenth centuries and the structural functionalism of the mid twentieth century. In essence, evolutionism posited the existence of a long and gradual process of social and cultural change, marked by movement through stages proceeding from the simple to the complex in a fashion analogous to the biological growth of organisms (Bock 1979). Typically, this transition was expressed by drawing a dichotomy between two ideal types of society, as in the contrast drawn by Sir Henry Sumner Maine between status and contract in legal matters, by Herbert Spencer between homogeneous and heterogeneous societies, by Ferdinand Tönnies between *Gemeinschaft* (community) and *Gesellschaft* (association), and by Emile Durkheim between mechanical and organic solidarity (see Nisbet 1969). Progression between the two poles was in each case deemed to reflect growing specialisation and differentiation. By comparison with these writers, Weber's analytical distinctions were much more widely elaborated to allow for a greater range of historical societies, but it has been argued that they also drew attention to a process of rationalisation and disenchantment that at least 'implicitly pointed to the same polarity' (Larrain 1989: 88).

Structural functionalism came much later, dominating thinking in sociology to an extraordinary degree, especially in the US, during the late 1940s and 1950s. The approach was associated above all with the name of Talcott Parsons (1951), who self-consciously saw himself as reinterpreting Weber. He also drew explicitly on Tönnies's *Gemeinschaft–Gesellschaft* dichotomy in setting out no less than five 'pattern variables' that, in his view, described the ideal typical structures of 'traditional' and 'modern' societies – affectivity vs affective neutrality; ascription vs achievement; functional diffuseness vs functional specificity; particularism vs universalism; and collectivism vs individualism. These terms were deployed by Parsons in a highly abstract fashion and do not need to be explained in detail here: the point is that, according to Parsonian structural functionalists, each framed a dichotomous choice that actors had to make in respect of their role orientation. These cumulative choices were deemed to constitute a system and to be the only ones available. In the structural functionalist view they collectively set the key behavioural shifts that took place, and indeed had to take place, in every case of the transformation of a traditional into a modern society.

Early modernisation theory in particular was powerfully shaped by these intellectual inheritances. Their first significant application to the 'Third World' appeared in an edited book published in the early 1950s by Bert F. Hoselitz (1952). It was revealingly entitled *The Progress of Underdeveloped Areas*. The various authors were writing in direct response to Truman's inaugural address and raised a number of themes that subsequently became characteristic of the genre, such as the connection between economic change and other social, cultural and psychological changes; the 'blocking' capacity of tradition; the emphasis on internal factors as being the most crucial in determining whether development took place; and, not least, the potential for Soviet influence to make an unfortunate appearance if American-style development was not successfully initiated. One of the contributors, Marion Levy, set a trend by explicitly using the Parsonian 'pattern variables' to reflect on the impact of introducing Western technology into non-industrialised societies. His conclusions implied that there was a positive relationship between some role orientations within the structural functionalist system and economic growth (Levy 1952). A few years later Hoselitz himself followed suit and argued that economic roles in 'developing countries' were problematic because they were primarily understood in particularistic, functionally diffuse, ascriptive and self-orientated terms. Each needed to be shifted to its polar opposite. However, he also criticised his fellow economists for generally neglecting or underestimating 'the primary social determinants of economic progress' (Hoselitz 1960: 42), making it clear that he defined the social widely enough also to include political factors. His interest in deploying this broader framework of analysis was vital because he helped to establish, and then edited from 1952 onwards, the journal *Economic Development and Cultural Change*, thereafter using its pages as a key vehicle through which to refine and publicise the modernisation paradigm.

From these early days onwards, modernisation theory took off to such a degree and spread to such an extent that we should henceforth more properly refer to the impact of several modernisation theories, held together loosely by adherence to a limited number of sweeping claims. Tipps is again helpful here in that he has sought to discern the common intellectual ground that underpinned all modernisation theories. In so doing, he noted two important methodological similarities: first, 'definitional inclusiveness', whereby the concept of modernisation tended to be 'a "summarizing" rather than a "discriminating" one, as every effort is made to specify its meaning in terms which are sufficiently general to avoid excluding any of the possible ramifications of this "multi-faceted process"'; and, second, the aggregation of all the relevant processes of change to the national level, whereby 'theories of modernization are fundamentally theories of the transformation of national states (which are implicitly taken to be coterminous with the boundaries of whole societies)' (Tipps 1973: 201–2). Yet, beyond these important defining considerations, he was only able to detect agreement on generally quite superficial features – for example, that modernisation was both transformational and progressive, that modernisation in one sphere generated complementary movement in other parts of the social system, that modernisation was classically dichotomous in character, and, finally, that modernisation was always conceived in teleological terms as 'a process of change . . . defined in terms of the goals towards which it is moving' (Tipps 1973: 204). In practice, as they grew in number and range, modernisation theories diversified beyond their base in sociology and sought to extend the range of their analysis to all other aspects of the development process. Although it was always acknowledged that the phenomenon under investigation was genuinely multifaceted in nature, most modernisation analysts actually worked within distinct professional sub-fields, with the result that these other variants tended to display their professional bias by focusing upon the dimension of development associated with a particular social science. Accordingly, it is possible to identify no fewer than four further specialist versions of the modernisation paradigm – based in economics, psychology, political science and geography – and we will say something about each of them in turn.

The most celebrated variant appeared in economics and was associated with the name of W. W. Rostow. A historian working at the University of Texas, Rostow published *The Stages of Economic Growth* in 1960. In the true spirit of modernisation theory he made clear at the outset that economic changes were the result of social and political forces every bit as much as economic forces. Indeed, he explicitly sought to propose an alternative to Marx's theory of history and gave his book the arresting subtitle: *A Non-Communist Manifesto*. He identified five stages of economic growth through which all societies passed – traditional society, preconditions for take-off, take-off, the road to maturity, and the age of mass consumption – driven forward by what he considered to be a 'dynamic theory of production' (Rostow 1960: 3). Traditional society was mainly agricultural, with low productivity and a pre-Newtonian attitude towards the physical world. It was not wholly static, but there was a ceiling to growth determined by lack of technology. The preconditions for growth were established in the second stage as modern science and trade forced dynamic changes in production. Take-off was 'the interval when the old blocks and resistances to steady growth are finally overcome' (Rostow 1960: 7). The rate of investment doubled, profits were ploughed back into new industries and entrepreneurs expanded in number. Growth became self-sustaining. The road to maturity was a long phase where over several decades every aspect of the economy was modernised and new technologies spread widely. This led, finally, to the stage of mass consumption, which was characterised by the full orientation of the economy to the production of consumer durables and services and the expansion of consumption beyond basic needs to embrace welfare and social security. At this point the society in question could be said to have completed its transition from traditionalism to modernity.

In many ways Rostow's theory of stages marked the apogee of modernisation theory. It was strong and self-confident in tone, as well as thoroughly typical in that it derived its inspiration from a particular, and ultimately quite simplistic, reading of Western history. Indeed, he stated baldly at one point that 'it is useful, as well as roughly accurate [sic], to regard the process of development now going forward in Asia, the Middle East, Africa, and Latin America as analogous to the stages of preconditions and take-off of other societies, in the late eighteenth, nineteenth and early twentieth centuries' (Rostow 1960: 139). Yet, at the same time, his schema was never conceived as a purely theoretical exercise.

Even as a scholar, and certainly later when he became Director of Policy and Planning in the US State Department under President John F. Kennedy and chief adviser on Vietnam to President Lyndon Johnson, Rostow was concerned that the United States should support, aid and protect modernisation processes wherever they were occurring in the world. On this count he was unquestionably highly influential, much more so than any other early development economist. Indeed, Harold Brookfield wrote that 'the 1960s can almost be described as the Rostow period in the history of development studies'. He attributed the huge persuasiveness of Rostow's theory to the fact that 'it seemed to give every country an equal chance; it "explained" the advantage of the developed countries; it offered a clear path to progress – without spelling this out in detail; it identified the requirements for advance with the virtues of the West . . . [and] it debunked the historical theories of Marx' (Brookfield 1975: 38).

Another group of modernisation theorists emphasised the psychological dimensions of growth and change, seeking to link differences in human personality to levels of progress. In general, traditional people were thought to be uncreative and authoritarian in personality type, their lives gripped by uncontrollable forces. By contrast, modern societies were characterised by the leadership of innovative personalities capable of initiating change in various spheres. The American psychologist, David McClelland, took these arguments the furthest, arguing that economic development emanated in part from a psychological characteristic that he called 'the need for achievement' (or '*n* achievement') (McClelland 1961). Defined as 'a desire to do well, not so much for the sake of social recognition or prestige, but to attain an inner feeling of personal accomplishment', this attribute was something thought by McClelland to be developed in childhood through exposure to books and stories that emphasised self-help and competition (McClelland 1966: 76). He believed that this psychological trait was exactly what Weber had also seen when he referred to the 'spirit of capitalism' and its linkage to the Protestant ethic. On this basis McClelland investigated a range of historical and contemporary societies in search of *n* achievement, claiming eventually to have shown that concentrations of high-achieving 'business entrepreneurs' were indeed conducive to economic development. Weberian influence can also be detected in a long-running survey of attitudes to modernity carried out by Alex Inkeles and David H. Smith (1974). They argued that 'modern man' (apparently bereft of modern woman) was characterised by a distinct set of attitudes, such as openness to new experience, a change orientation, calculability, faith in science, a more democratic attitude to the opinions of others, and so on. Traditional man, whom they named 'Ahmadullah' (to be compared with 'Nuril', the modern urbanite) in their case-study of East Pakistan, was, by obvious contrast, more or less the exact opposite in make-up and outlook. In sum, then, psychological theories were just as dichotomous in their portraits of the classic ideal types of the traditional/modern poles as other variants of the modernisation paradigm.

For their part, political scientists defined political modernity, which was to be achieved via a process they dubbed 'political development', by direct reference to the liberal democratic models of the West, principally of course the presidential system of the United States. American scholars were once more in the vanguard, led by Gabriel Almond from his influential base as chairman of the American Social Science Research Council's Committee on Comparative Politics, which was the main sponsoring body of much of this type of modernisation work. In 1960 Almond edited a book with James Coleman, called *The Politics of the Developing Areas*, which relied heavily on the package of Parsonian 'pattern variables' and tried, not very successfully, to separate out a specific political system from the social system as a whole (Almond and Coleman 1960). In this endeavour, as Hettne subsequently noted, 'the state was abstracted away' from the analysis altogether (Hettne 1995: 55). Collaborating a few years later with C. B. Powell, Almond moved to set out fully the basis of political development, conceiving of it as an aspect of modernisation marked by three criteria: structural differentiation, sub-system autonomy and cultural secularisation (Almond and Powell 1965). Other writers came up with different lists of key components, but all were extrapolations from the institutional apparatus that had emerged over time and as a consequence of complex historical processes in the leading Western democracies. The criteria thus served to highlight again and again how far traditional political systems had to travel. Initially, modernisation political scientists displayed great optimism in their assessment of the prospects for change – in a revealing phrase Almond later recalled 'the missionary and Peace Corps mood' that prevailed in these circles in the early 1960s (Almond 1970: 21) – although it has to be said that this faded quickly with the benefit of bitter experience. For example, David Apter, having undertaken extensive fieldwork in Ghana, came to identify the need for a 'mobilization system', sustained by an authoritarian political organisation, as the best means by which to accomplish the political transition between tradition and modernity (Apter 1965). Yet even this was seen as only a temporary deviation from the normal, evolutionary path. It was significant, though, that the trend in this particular strand of the modernisation literature moved briskly to focus on crises in political development (Binder et al. 1971) and ultimately on the priority of political order (Huntington 1968 and 1971; see O'Brien 1972).

Lastly, the geographers also had their take on modernisation. In this view 'Third World' countries were isolated, parochial enclaves, cut off spatially from the forces of progress and awaiting change through the spread of innovations. Modernisation was thus seen as a process of diffusion, stimulated in the main by contact situations, such as colonial administrative centres, port cities and trading posts. The pattern of change was marked by a series of lines moving across the map as new attitudes and ideas ran along the various transport systems that existed. Modernisation geographers accordingly invested great efforts in devising quantitative means by which to measure these flows, believing that they were indeed charting the very processes by which the remotest corners of primitive subsistence economies were being brought into the modern world.

As can be seen, modernisation theories were both prolific and wide-ranging. At their best, as Adrian Leftwich has fairly observed, they offered 'a total vision of development, as both process and condition' (Leftwich 2000: 33). They fully recognised that development required more than the accumulation of capital and the injection of technology. They also re-emphasised the classical Weberian insistence that development was at heart a transition. At their worst, however, modernisation theories were crude in their presentation of highly complex situations, often reading Western history in excessively simplistic and rose-tinted ways, and certainly framing many of the particular post-1945 developmental crises they sought to address in far too stark a manner. As a result, they came in for stinging criticism from many quarters (including the various underdevelopment theorists about to be considered) for their ethnocentrism, their equation of modernisation with 'Westernisation' and their obvious ideological commitment to the US cause in the Cold War (see Hoogvelt 1978). Modernisation theories mostly did have a policy purpose close to their core, even if Ankie Hoogvelt exaggerated somewhat in claiming that 'they wrote a kind of "How to develop" manual for less developed countries' (Hoogvelt 1978: 35). More seriously, from an analytical perspective these theories were also caught in a theoretical dilemma whereby they both insisted, on the one hand, that changes had to happen internally as a result of endogenous forces and yet also acknowledged, on the other hand, that the desired changes often needed to be induced from abroad by exogenous forces.

In summary, then, the modernisation paradigm rose to prominence in this phase of the history of development theory in good part because it chimed so well with the dominant mood of the times, especially in the United States at the height of its post-war hegemony. Both its strength and its weakness derived from the same defining feature, namely, its evocation of such strong and simple images with which to try to catch the essence of the many confusing transformations underway in Africa, Asia and Latin America in these years.

Underdevelopment Theory

We turn in the final section of this chapter to a body of thought traditionally considered to have been the great rival paradigm to modernisation thinking in the 1960s and 1970s. It has come to be known at various times as structuralism, neo-Marxism, dependency theory and world systems theory.

We prefer to identify each of these schools as sub-fields of a wider theoretical construct that we think is best described as underdevelopment theory. What all the strands of thought encompassed by this phrase had in common was that they identified the underdevelopment of the 'Third World' as constituting something more than merely its failure, as yet, to achieve the type of development already effected in the developed world.

The need for some new thinking within development studies was clearly identified in a classic article asserting 'the limitations of the special case' published by the British economist, Dudley Seers, in the early 1960s. Seers not only advanced the heretical thought that mainstream economic theory might be applicable only in the context of Western industrial capitalism, but went on to suggest that, historically, the latter was not the norm but actually a special case. He proposed as the way forward the 'modest but revolutionary slogan' that 'economics is the study of economies' (Seers 1963: 27), implying by his use of this telling phrase that different theoretical frameworks were required to understand different types of economies. In this connection he praised the work of a small number of development economists who had lately begun to move their field in new directions. For example, Hans Singer (1950) had attracted attention by questioning the assumption that participation in international trade necessarily benefited all parties. He argued that those countries producing raw materials were subjected to deteriorating terms of trade compared to industrialised countries and that the distribution of gains was therefore likely to be uneven. Contrary to standard free trade beliefs, peripheral countries should not acquiesce in the production of export commodities in which they held a comparative advantage, but should instead seek to change the whole structure of comparative advantage by themselves investing in industrialisation. In similar vein, Gunner Myrdal (1957) had explicitly broken away from the confines of equilibrium theory to advance an institutionalist analysis based on the notion of 'circular cumulative causation', whereby over time the direction in which a socioeconomic system moved became self-reinforcing, either positively or negatively, as institutions adjusted and then bedded in. He also argued that trade often aggravated the economic differences between participating countries and thus generated 'backwash' effects that ran against the 'spread' effects of neoclassical liberal theory. These were steps forward, according to Seers, who, like Singer and Myrdal, had spent some time working for the United Nations during the 1950s, a common experience that probably explains their collective rejection of Western orthodoxy. Seers reported that he had, as a result, come to be hugely impressed by the work of a group of political economists gathered around Raúl Prebisch at the UN Economic Commission for Latin America (ECLA) in Santiago in Chile. As he wrote prophetically in the article mentioned: 'Prebisch lives closer to the seismic fault from which the tremors are emanating' (Seers 1963: 79). This was the first moment at which Latin American scholars had contributed to the evolution of development theory and so we must pay due attention to the ideas of these early Latin American structuralists.

The theoretical novelty of Latin American structuralist thinking lay in it being based not on the formal modelling characteristic of neoclassical economics but on actual patterns of real economic activity – on history. Prebisch had been the Director-General of the Central Bank of Argentina from 1935 to 1943 and had been deeply influenced by the severity of the depression brought upon his country's economy by the collapse of demand for its primary products during the world depression. He observed at first hand the different roles assigned to primary exporters and industrial exporters in the international division of labour of that period and concluded that the relative lack of development of Latin American economies was better explained by reference to their debilitating structural position in the world economy than their alleged internal deficiencies. Indeed, Prebisch (1950) came to doubt whether Latin America even possessed what could be called national integrated economies, as opposed to loose packages of sectors, enclaves and other parasitical forms each with their different modes of behaviour and distinctive roles in the world economy as bequeathed to them by the dominant forces in that system. In sum, his crucial intellectual insight, often described simply as the 'Prebisch thesis', was that the global system was divided into powerful 'central' economies and weak 'peripheral' economies. Moreover, just as Singer had also argued, the terms of trade generally moved in such a way that the centre mostly benefited and the periphery mostly suffered.

On the basis of this analysis ECLA devised and promulgated a radical new strategy of Latin American development. It urged the pursuit of industrialisation based on the substitution of current imports by domestic production, encouraged, at least initially, by protection from foreign competition. It did not deny that foreign businesses could facilitate this process, but it nevertheless had reservations about building in excessive reliance on their activities and decisions. Instead, governments were seen as the natural bases from which to plan and coordinate import-substitution industrialisation (ISI) and the associated regional common market that ECLA later deemed to be an ancillary part of the strategy. Indeed, the shorthand phrase that came to be used widely was 'programmed industrialisation', connoting thereby a greater degree of state intervention than usually suggested by the Keynesian model *per se* (Hirschman 1961; Gurrieri 1987). These measures constituted notable breaks with conventional thinking about 'Third World' development at that time, especially in the United States, where there had long existed a special interest in and anxiety about Latin America (Pollock 1978). But at the same time they were not totally original contributions either, for there was an obvious lineage to the long tradition of economic nationalism associated with List and other theorists of 'late industrialisation' working in Germany, the US itself, Russia and Japan in the late nineteenth and early twentieth centuries (Love 1980). There was another sense too in which ECLA was less radical than it has sometimes been portrayed: its economists continued to have great faith in the capacity of industrialisation to end underdevelopment and generally still believed that the role of capital was crucial to the successful initiation of development. After all, the main critical point they made about the periphery's declining terms of trade was that this damaged local accumulation of capital. By the late 1960s the ECLA model of development was itself considered to be in crisis, still dependent – despite ISI – on foreign capital, decisions and imports (O'Brien 1975; Chilcote 1984). At this point, as Preston has noted, 'the argument moved out of the

structuralist frame used by Prebisch to embrace work
from wider traditions within the social sciences', enabling
a fully-fledged theory of dependency to emerge (Preston
1996: 188).

This other strand of thinking was a critique of classical
Marxist development theory that came to be known as 'neo-
Marxism'. The key argument underpinning this new line of
thought was that Marxist theory had hitherto focused predominantly on the situation of the advanced capitalist world.
As we have seen, neither Marx nor Engels had much to say
of direct relevance to the 'Third World'. Their early followers
chose in the main to preoccupy themselves with the problem
of imperialism, which was always understood within this
canon as a stage in the evolution of advanced capitalism,
albeit with important implications for the prospects of development of the colonies (about which, it should be noted,
Marxist theories of imperialism disagreed) (Lenin 1916;
Luxemburg 1951). In this context, the innovation represented
by 'neo-Marxism' was to try to see imperialism from the
periphery's point of view (Foster-Carter 1974). Its founding
father was Paul Baran, one of the key figures, along with Paul
Sweezy and Leo Huberman, behind the establishment in 1949
of an influential socialist journal in the US called *Monthly
Review*. This group advanced a general theory that saw the
condition of capitalism mid century as being defined by
monopoly, whereby corporations cooperated to control competition and protect a status quo they dominated. This was
viewed as an irrational misuse of the economic surplus, or
total material output, of the capitalist economy (Baran and
Sweezy 1966).

Baran extended this interpretation of the working of capitalism to the underdeveloped world. Drawing indirectly on
the so-called 'drain theory' proposed by Indian writers in the
late nineteenth century – which alleged that Britain appropriated a vast annual tribute from India that not only robbed
India of development potential but also stimulated Britain's
economic growth (Nairoji 1962, cited in Hettne 1995: 79–80)
– Baran explicitly argued in *The Political Economy of Growth*,
published in 1957, that the exploitation of the 'Third World'
was an inherent feature of the growth of capitalism. 'The
backward world', he wrote, constituted an 'indispensable

hinterland' that provided the West with endless opportunities to extract economic surplus to its advantage (Baran 1973: 20). Most colonisers, excepting only those who took control of Australia, New Zealand and North America, acted to inhibit the local accumulation of capital, determining instead to 'take their loot home' (Baran 1973: 274). In the process, the budding industries of the colonies were stifled, their economic surplus was diminished and stagnation set in across the 'Third World', even as the 'First World' grew in consequence. The only recourse available was to break from the world capitalist system altogether and pursue socialist economic planning. It hardly needs to be said that such views were a far cry from the mainstream of contemporary development economics. But it should be added that they also marked a clear break with classical Marxism, which had always tended to argue that capitalism was a necessary stage in the development process. In fact, Baran can be read more as a complement to Lenin in highlighting the historical significance of the territorial division of the world by the major capitalist powers. At any rate, his work represented an important moment in the rediscovery, revival and reinterpretation of the broad Marxist tradition in Western countries in the late 1950s and into the 1960s.

Although its genealogy has sometimes been explicated in too simplistic a fashion (see Cardoso 1977), the claim that dependency theory had this mixed parentage – ECLA structuralism, on the one hand, and 'neo-Marxism', on the other – remains both apposite and insightful (Blomström and Hettne 1984; Kay 1989). It also explains why a variety of subtly different dependency accounts were generated. The Brazilian Theotonio Dos Santos proposed perhaps the most cited definition, as follows:

> Dependency is a conditioning situation in which the economies of one group of countries are conditioned by the development and expansion of others. A relationship of interdependence between two or more economies or between such economies and the world trading system becomes a dependent relationship when some countries can expand only as a reflection of the expansion of the dominant countries, which may have positive or negative effects on their immediate development. (Dos Santos 1970: 231)

Such a conceptualisation emphasised economic relations and can be read as giving priority to external causation. In a later contribution, Dos Santos (1977) distinguished between conditioning and determining factors in explaining that the accumulation process was conditioned by the dependent position of an economy but determined by its own internal laws and processes. In general, the *dependentistas*, as they sometimes were known, placed greater weight on internal factors than did the ECLA school. Indeed, like much modernisation theory, the best dependency theory was sociopolitical, as well as economic, in its orientation, as best exemplified in the mature work of writers such as Osvaldo Sunkel (1969, 1973) and Celso Furtado (1964, 1969), and in the classic text entitled *Dependency and Development in Latin America*, jointly authored by Fernando Henrique Cardoso and Enzo Faletto and first published in Mexico in 1969. In a much-quoted passage in the preface to the subsequent US edition of their book, the authors declared that they conceived

> the relationship between external and internal forces as forming a complex whole whose structural links are not based on mere external forms of exploitation and coercion, but are rooted in coincidences of interests between local dominant classes and international ones, and, on the other side, are challenged by local dominated groups and classes. (Cardoso and Faletto 1979: xvi)

That said, many other writers in the dependency school were not as careful in their formulations (or, for that matter, as interested in class), with the result that the international division of labour was often dissected in terms of a one-dimensional dependency relationship between whole countries or regions that were, to all intents and purposes, explained away by reference to which side of a crude centre–periphery distinction they were deemed to sit (Booth 1985).

Yet, as Seers rightly noted, dependency theory, like so much development theory in general, was 'very much a product of a particular place and particular historical period' (Seers 1981: 13) – in this case, the Latin America of the 1960s. Some of it was written with polemical intent and, as such, cannot be expected to have shown a natural balance and restraint. Understood as an indigenous assertion of voice, it ran the standard gamut of many such schools of thought from the truly excellent in quality to the merely strident. However, the story of dependency theory does not end here. It escaped from Latin America, conquered much of the Western intellectual world, at least for a period, and ultimately perhaps became too successful for its own good. The theory acquired a great populariser in the form of André Gunder Frank, a German economist initially trained in the free-market haven of the University of Chicago but converted to *dependencia* by the experience of working in Latin America from the early 1960s onwards. He attracted attention initially as a fierce critic of the prevailing sociology of modernisation, accusing those espousing the traditional–modern dichotomy of being 'intellectual and political schizophrenics' (Frank 1969: 77). He then moved on to assert, *pace* Baran but using case studies of the economic history of Brazil and Chile, that the world capitalist system was characterised by a metropolis –satellite structure, whereby the metropolis exploited the satellite via a 'chain-like' flow of surplus running from the most remote Latin American village to Wall Street in New York. 'Thus at each point', he concluded, 'the international, national and local capitalist system generates economic development for the few and underdevelopment for the many' (Frank 1967: 8).

What is more, he went on, 'development and underdevelopment are two sides of the same coin' (Frank 1967: 9). This phrase became globally famous and in just a few words served to elevate dependency theory (Frank-style) to paradigmatic status within the mainstream of Western social science (Foster-Carter 1976). In fact, as is so often the case, Frank's detailed work embraced several much more nuanced hypotheses, such as the argument that satellites tended to experience their greatest development when ties to the metropolis were at their weakest, during periods of war perhaps, or as the result of geographical isolation. But his reputation was made (and from a more critical perspective lost also) in that one 'soundbite' and Frank never quite succeeded thereafter in laying to rest the charge that his formulation of dependency was exaggerated and excessively crude. For all that, he remains the quintessential embodiment of the two sources of origin of dependency theory.

Frank also acts as a link to world systems theory (WST), of which he can be seen as an originator. WST had great affinities with the dependency school, essentially extending the latter's insights into a general theory of the world economy, but it had other antecedents too, notably the *Annales* school of French historians, founded in 1929, which typically compared societies over long sweeps of time. Within this lineage the fullest expression of WST was undoubtedly that articulated by Immanuel Wallerstein, an American sociologist working at the State University of New York at Binghamton. He treated world history as the development of a single system and identified four main stages in his history of the modern world system: (i) the emergence of a European world economy during the 'long sixteenth century' from 1450 to 1640; (ii) a mercantilist struggle between 1650 and 1730; (iii) the geographical expansion of the European world economy under British hegemony to become truly a world system from 1760 to 1917; and (iv) the consolidation of the world system under the new hegemony of the United States after 1917 (Wallerstein 1974, 1979, 1980). Wallerstein controversially sidestepped the problem of how to analyse the transition from feudalism to capitalism by defining capitalism not, as Marx had done, by reference to the emergence of a particular mode of production expressed in terms of social relations, but much more simply as 'production for sale in a market . . . to realize the maximum profit' (Wallerstein 1979: 15). He postulated the existence of a world market system within which different types of state (core, semi-periphery and periphery), marked by significant asymmetries of power, manoeuvred for economic advantage. As such, the world system had its phases of expansion and contraction, crisis and change (see Shannon 1989), but it remained one system and worked consistently to constrain the prospects of transformation for 'Third World' countries to no more than the possibility of changing their structural position within the world system from peripheral to semi-peripheral. WST thus firmly closed off some of the more open-ended outcomes, such as 'dependent capitalist development', contemplated by the more sensitive Latin American members of the dependency school.

Other thinkers also contributed to the WST project, broadly defined (Emmanuel 1972; Amin 1976), but

Wallerstein was always viewed as the theory's leading figure and his work therefore attracted the sharpest critiques, especially from the left (see Hoogvelt 1982). The central issue at stake in these particular debates was the question of what was the fundamental defining feature of capitalism. Ernesto Laclau (1971, 1979) took the view that Wallerstein's conception of capitalism as profit-motivated production for the market was confused and inadequate because it ignored the issue of the relations of production. He had forgotten, Laclau wrote, 'what any Marxist knows' (Laclau 1979: 46). Robert Brenner (1977) made much the same point in accusing Wallerstein of advancing a form of 'neo-Smithian Marxism' by virtue of working from a market-based definition of capitalism reminiscent of Adam Smith himself. He thus failed to appreciate that development could only be achieved via the evolution of class relations shifting from one mode of production to another. Indeed, Wallerstein's insufficient attention to and understanding of the centrality of class was a common theme of criticism from Marxists (Leys 1977; Phillips 1977; Petras 1978). These debates were highly intense in the way they were conducted, often coloured by an almost anguished sense that underdevelopment theory, as variously formulated, had not lived up to its initial radical promise. As Colin Leys put it, the emergence of a notion of underdevelopment seemed to many (on the Left, at least) to rescue the development field from the 'arid formulations' and 'intellectual deserts' of modernisation theory (Leys 1977: 93). He, for one, was a convert, applying it enthusiastically to the study of Kenya (Leys 1975), only to renege bitterly on the apparent promise and progressive content of the concept and condemn the whole literature two years later for its 'sense of theoretical repetition and stagnation'. In his view, underdevelopment theory had failed to transcend its origins as a critique of the modernisation school; it had got stuck within that problematic, producing in the final analysis no more than 'a revision of bourgeois development theory, and an ultimately non-radical one at that' (Leys 1977: 94).

For a period, then, the air was thick with the whiff of betrayal. By the time it had cleared it was apparent that underdevelopment theory had moved on in at least three new and diverse directions. The first built directly on the Latin

American tradition and sought to retreat from the excessive systematisation of the dependency concept that had been a feature of its spread around the world in favour of a more focused approach directed at specific societies and the unique manner of their insertion into the world system. It was also readily acknowledged that, in the next phase of such studies, 'internal' factors should be given as much weight in the assessment of causation as 'external' ones. Gabriel Palma articulated this position with the greatest force, arguing that no single, convincing, overriding theory of dependency was ever going to be found, but adding that this did not mean that dependency was not a useful 'methodology for the analysis of concrete situations of underdevelopment' (Palma 1978: 881). He was able to cite Cardoso (1977: 21) in support of this view, noting that the eminent Brazilian political economist had also rejected the vision of ultimately drawing up a formal league table of levels of dependency in favour of calling for 'improvements in the quality of historical-structural analysis', a goal to which he and Faletto had, of course, been committed from the outset. It was revealing perhaps that Cardoso's warning was delivered in a paper specifically devoted to a critique of the 'consumption' of dependency theory in the United States, rather than its deployment within Latin America itself.

The second trend grew out of Laclau's condemnation of the turn away from the core Marxist concept of mode of production made by world systems theory and also sought to restore to the prevailing analysis a greater sensitivity to empirical detail and the specificity of different situations, at least by comparison with what was perceived to be the sweeping style associated with the 'neo-Marxists'. Substantively, this approach addressed the articulation, or interplay, of different modes of production within a single economic system. Drawing on the French structuralist version of Marxism associated with Louis Althusser, its main exponents were anthropologists like Claude Meillassoux and P. P. Rey, writing initially mainly in French, and the British sociologist, John Taylor (1979). The problems of development were henceforth explored not by means of the application of a mechanical centre–periphery model, but rather by reference to the fact that, in the 'Third World', the capitalist mode of production was nearly always articulated with non-capitalist modes of production. As Hettne put it, underdevelopment in this reading was generally viewed as a consequence of 'a stalemate in the process of articulation' (Hettne 1995: 147). What was less clearly set out, however, were the requirements needed for the capitalist mode to come to dominate, and then to replace altogether, other non-capitalist modes of production. As this literature took off, there also emerged a debilitating tendency for the number of apparently existing non-capitalist modes ('colonial', 'statist', 'lineage', 'petty commodity', 'tributary', 'peasant') to grow with each new piece of research (Foster-Carter 1978). In the end, this often highly abstract form of Marxist theorising about development and underdevelopment did not manage to escape from the limitations of the Althusserian structuralist reading of Marx on which it was grounded, and it retreated into being a concern of aficionados only.

The third, most controversial, formulation spinning out of the attack on underdevelopment theory was the bold reassertion of a 'neoclassical Marxist' position represented by the work of Bill Warren (1973, 1980). Warren aimed explicitly to revive Marx's original idea that the advent of capitalism constituted historical progress and thus denied the argument that it had instead brought about the underdevelopment of many previously colonised parts of the world. This was actually a myth that had become dangerously popular, because it served as an excuse, in many parts of the 'Third World'. Deploying a mass of empirical economic evidence, much of it drawn from official sources, Warren claimed that 'substantial, accelerating, and even historically unprecedented improvements in the growth of productive capacity and the material welfare of the mass of the population have occurred in the postwar period' (Warren 1980: 189). In other words, genuinely capitalist societies were emerging in Asia, Africa and Latin America and growing in autonomy all the time, especially as indigenous manufacturing sectors expanded in size and reach. Warren conceded that the process had yet to spread to the poorest countries and readily acknowledged that capitalist growth was being accompanied by many ugly social problems. But was this not precisely the nature of capitalism, as so vividly described by Marx and Engels themselves in their studies of early European development?

Capitalism was not a 'nice' phenomenon; moreover, it had always grown in uneven fashion, which meant that there were serious analytical problems with those bodies of theory that sought to treat the 'Third World' as one bloc. In Warren's hands, therefore, underdevelopment theory unashamedly went back to Marxist basics.

Conclusion

We need now briefly to sum up our review of what we have dubbed 'Golden Age' theories of development. As was noted at the beginning of the chapter, this period from 1945 to the mid 1970s is conventionally described in the history of development theory as being marked by a 'Great Debate' between the modernisation and the underdevelopment paradigms. In reality, there was not as much debate between the two schools (as opposed to within them) as one might suppose or ideally want to have seen. The two approaches were rather more like ships that passed in the night – close enough to be spotted by each other and even to generate some casual abuse across the waves, but never set upon respective courses that either threatened collision or necessitated the sudden dropping of anchor. In practice, they constituted two worlds of scholarship and political activity, with each having its favourite publishing outlets. The world of *Economic Development and Cultural Change* was light years away from that of *Monthly Review*. Indeed, very few journals managed to accommodate both modernisation and underdevelopment work within their pages in even roughly proportionate fashion. While it is the case that most underdevelopment writing appeared somewhat later in time than modernisation theorising, that does not mean it was mainly driven by a desire to respond in some directly adversarial fashion. In fact, Baran's major work on the political economy of growth was published fully three years before Rostow's classic account. The truth is that both bodies of theory ran along mostly according to their own internal debates and pressures.

The two bodies of theory also had two important features in common that we should note by way of conclusion. The first was their joint commitment to many of the key tenets of the growth theories that we began the chapter by discussing. These ideas underpinned both the modernisation and the underdevelopment approaches. After all, the underdevelopment school gave away nothing to its modernisation counterpart in the firmness of its advocacy of the merits of a national, autonomous pattern of economic growth, built in the main upon the successful domestic accumulation of capital. The second common characteristic was that both approaches sought to focus on the apparently distinctive problems encountered by a 'Third World'. This of itself marked an important break with prior forms of development theory. As a consequence, the difficulties encountered by both modernisation and underdevelopment thinking by the end of the 1970s created what Hettne accurately depicted as 'an awkward theoretical vacuum' in the newly specialist field of development studies (Hettne 1995: 104). It is striking, but also perhaps unsurprising in light of the general thesis of this book, that in the 1980s this space was filled by the revival of globalist theories of development that self-consciously went back to earlier statist and liberal mainstream traditions in their efforts to move the field beyond the once dominant theories of the Golden Age.

4
Neoliberal and Neostatist Theories

The critique and ultimate discrediting of dependency theory and its neo-Marxist offshoots represented the start of what was widely described as the 'impasse' in development studies. This was deemed to have taken hold by the 1970s and the means of its resolution was debated fiercely over the next couple of decades. Its most important cause was the manner in which the idea of the 'Third World', on which development theory during the Golden Age had been entirely based, was rendered redundant by the key trend that could be observed in development trajectories across the world – namely, the increasing differentiation and divergence within what had previously been analysed as a single, homogeneous group of countries. In terms of performance, the spectacular rise from the 1960s onwards of Japan and the newly industrialising countries (NICs) of East Asia (Taiwan, Korea, Singapore and Hong Kong) was set against the much less inspiring perform-ance of most Latin American economies and the continued stagnation of Africa. In terms of development strategy, export-oriented industrialisation in East Asia contrasted sharply with inward-looking development strategies in Latin America. The task for development theory was now to under-stand and explain this differentiation, as well as to find ways of defending the field against claims that it had consequently lost its rationale and validity.

The period in question came to be characterised by a trenchant debate between two bodies of theory. The first

consisted of an amalgam of currents in neoclassical economics and associated theoretical tendencies in political science,
which came to be known simply, and pervasively, as 'neoliberalism'. The second can be termed 'neostatism', associated
theoretically with the influences of the 'infant industry' arguments of Hamilton and List, as well as the legacy of Keynesian growth theory in modern economics and its counterparts
in political science and political sociology. The key point is
that both of these theoretical currents had as much to do with
the advanced capitalist economies as with something, or
somewhere, that might once have been called the 'developing
world'. Indeed, they were both first and foremost concerned
with analysing and improving performance and strategy in
the advanced capitalist world, notably in the context of the
growing 'crisis' of the welfare state in Europe and the declining performance of the Anglo-American economies relative
to those organised along more 'statist' lines, such as Japan,
Germany and, later, the East Asian NICs. Yet they also
became central to what, with a hint of defiance, we continued
to call 'development theory'. Neoliberalism was associated
most visibly with the elaboration of the so-called 'Washington consensus' agenda in the late 1980s, and its dissemination
across the so-called developing world by a powerful nexus
of governments, institutions and market actors. Neostatist
theories generated exceptionally fertile debate about the
role of states in development, taking as their cue the East
Asian 'miracle', but extending their attention widely across
other regions.

The Neoliberal 'Counter-Revolution'

The crystallisation of neoliberal economic theory from the
1960s onwards was built on a robust rejection of Keynesian
growth theory and a forceful challenge to the nascent field
of development economics. The theoretical foundations of
this approach were initially laid as a theory of advanced
capitalism and specifically as a critique of the experiences of
Keynesian growth strategies in the advanced industrialised
economies of Western Europe. The critique was extended to

the developing world, taking the form of an attack on the strategies of inward-looking industrialisation that were perceived to have yielded significant development failures, especially in Latin America. The evidence of accelerating inflation, growing state intervention and resurgent political conflict in European countries, coupled with parallel manifestations of the same root problems in Latin America and elsewhere, provided ample ammunition for neoliberal economists as their counter-revolution gathered force over the course of the 1970s and 1980s.

Neoliberalism emerged in this political context as a body of political-economic theory and practice which borrowed the assumptions of the new classical (or more commonly neoclassical) economics that rose to a position of pronounced dominance in the professional economics community from the 1960s onwards – a set of assumptions organised around the central principle of rational choice and the methodological individualism on which it was based. This approach yielded a profound cynicism about politics and, more specifically, states, given its assumption of self-interest as the overriding motivation for individuals' behaviour. To this neoclassical theoretical apparatus was thus attached a political-economic agenda based on the contention that, in David Harvey's words, 'human well-being can best be advanced by liberating individual entrepreneurial freedoms and skills within an institutional framework characterized by strong private property rights, free markets, and free trade' (Harvey 2005: 2). The resulting body of neoliberal theory, associated strongly also with the traditions of Western liberal political thought, came to represent 'a body of settled conclusions immediately applicable to policy' (Toye 1991: 321) and on this basis to consolidate itself as a 'counter-revolution' in both political economy broadly and development theory more specifically.

The theoretical bellwether for the neoliberal counter-revolution took the form of the doctrine of monetarism. Monetarism had its roots in the so-called 'Austrian school' of economics, which was associated most visibly with the work of the economist Friedrich von Hayek. Early monetarist theory was largely disregarded as 'an aberration, a throwback to an earlier period of capitalism, a revival of the discredited doctrines of *laissez-faire*, lacking foundations in the contemporary capitalist world' (Gamble 2001: 129). It was thus initially only slowly, but eventually with astonishing speed, that monetarist versions of neoliberalism made inroads into the Keynesian consensus that had dominated economics since the 1940s. It was the crystallisation of the so-called 'Chicago school' of economics, associated most famously with Milton Friedman, who worked for some thirty years at the University of Chicago, which came to provide the monetarist backbone of the neoliberal counter-revolution. Assisted by the decision of the Nixon administration in 1971 to let the dollar float and thereby bring to an end the fixed exchange-rate regime of the post-war period, the monetarist ideas propounded by the Chicago school achieved clear ascendancy from the mid 1970s onwards in the Anglo-American economies, exemplified by the 'revolutions' undertaken in the United States under President Ronald Reagan and the United Kingdom under Prime Minister Margaret Thatcher. But they were also disseminated confidently to parts of the developing world, notably to Chile, where the so-called 'Chicago Boys', a group of Chilean economists who had been trained in Chicago under the tutelage of Friedman and others, oversaw the first decade of economic policy under the dictatorship of Augusto Pinochet (Valdés 1995).

Briefly summarised, the theory of monetarism took as its starting point a rejection of the received Keynesian wisdom that changes in the money supply would be ineffective as a means of managing economies under conditions of economic depression. In a speech given in 1967 to the American Economic Association, Friedman lamented the manner in which 'the wide acceptance of [Keynesian] views in the economics profession meant that for two decades monetary policy was believed by all but a few reactionary souls to have been rendered obsolete by new economic knowledge' (quoted in Krugman 2007: 28). Friedman set about the task of correcting this misunderstanding, rejecting the Keynesian emphasis on fiscal policy in favour of a renewed monetary approach, in which central banks would keep the money supply growing at a slow but constant rate as the best means of maintaining economic stability. Nevertheless, the key point about monetarism is that it was as much a political strategy as a matter of technical economics: it sought to 'depoliticise' monetary policy by removing it from the control of governments, thereby insulating this central pillar of economic policy from discretionary political interference (Friedman and Schwartz 1963).

As it turned out, monetarist policies fared poorly across the board, failing to prevent recessions as much in the US and UK as in Chile. Consequently, monetarism in its purer forms was a short-lived phenomenon in the broader evolution of neoliberalism. The 'free-market' ideology associated with monetarism fared much better and, by the end of the 1980s, had largely eliminated Keynesian discourse from the mainstream of both the economics profession and global development debates. Yet the political message of monetarism remained fundamental to both. Hayek understood inflation as a function of the political balance of power, in which Keynesian commitments to full employment led to a huge increase in the bargaining power of organised labour (Gamble 2001), an argument which underpinned later responses to union militancy in the Keynesian welfare economies of Europe. In this sense the enduring contribution of monetarism was its political case for a particular kind of relationship between capital, labour and state, regardless of its efficacy as a specifically economic strategy.

The assault on Keynesianism was simultaneously pursued on a second front, namely, in the field of development theory. A second generation of development economists emerged as fierce critics of the first generation associated with Golden Age development theory, motivated both by the perceived theoretical deficiencies of this earlier work and by disillusion with the failures across the world of development strategies formulated on that basis (Meier 2005). Particularly prominent among these second-generation economists were Harry Johnson, P. T. Bauer, Deepak Lal, Bela Balassa, Anne Krueger and Ian Little. Notwithstanding differences in the focus of particular members of this group, the attack was launched on the basis of a series of common convictions, which came to define the neoliberal agenda for both the academic study of development and policy reform in developing countries (see Wade 1990; Colclough 1982; Toye 1993; Leys 1996a).

First, these early proponents of the neoliberal revolution lamented the manner in which development economics had built its intellectual enterprise on an assumed, and highly misleading, distinction between 'developed' and 'developing' countries, and argued instead for a return to a form of 'monoeconomics' built upon the 'universal' principles of rationality which were central to neoclassical economic theory (and, indeed, had provided the early focal point for the critique launched by 'first-generation' development economics). Second, the Keynesian influence on development economics was deemed to have yielded an over-emphasis on large-scale capital formation, and consequently a distorted understanding and diagnosis of the requirements for growth and development. Third, it was argued that government intervention in economies carried unacceptable consequences in the form of economic and political incoherence. On the one hand, states' promotion of ISI in developing countries had resulted in the proliferation of inefficient industries requiring permanent subsidisation, but with few prospects of increasing their international competitiveness. On the other hand, extensive government intervention encouraged large-scale rent seeking, in which economic agents engaged themselves more in lobbying for government subsidies and protection than in competitive productive activities. The results were disabling levels of both corruption and political conflict, which generated significant economic dislocations and hampered the formulation of effective economic strategies. Finally, the Keynesian influence had introduced into developing economies a pronounced anti-export bias, which constituted a crucial barrier to economic development.

For Bauer (1972), development economics was therefore to be written off as not only plain wrong but, moreover, 'intellectually corrupt' (Toye 1993: 75); for Lal, famously, 'the demise of development economics is likely to be conducive to the health of both the economics and the economies of the developing world' (Lal 1983: 180). So it was that the neoliberal counter-revolution brought a disconcertingly swift end to the momentum that had been gathering in the field of development economics over the preceding couple of decades. Albert Hirschman felt it appropriate by 1981 to proclaim the demise of the field, commenting apparently wistfully that 'our subdiscipline had achieved its considerable lustre and excitement through the implicit idea that it could slay the dragon of backwardness virtually by itself or, at least, that its contribution to the task was central. We now know that this is not so' (Hirschman 1981: 23). This is not to say that development economists vanished into thin air, nor indeed that their insights slipped completely into obsolescence. What followed was inevitably a period of both furious reaction to the neoliberal critique and a sustained period of rethinking 'from within' (Colclough 1982; Desai 1982; Sen 1983; Stewart 1985). Efforts to rehabilitate and revitalise the field have continued since that time (Chang 2003; Meier 2005). But it was indisputable that, by the early 1980s, neoliberalism had come to define thinking about development, at least to the extent that it represented the point of reference against which all alternative bodies of theory needed to position themselves.

Yet the neoliberal counter-revolution was not simply about the domestic determinants of economic growth and did not arise simply as the result of theoretical debates in the economics profession. Rather, it emerged from and was propelled by the process of structural change in the global political economy – the conjunction of seismic material and ideological shifts that are usually summarised in the shorthand term 'globalisation'. There is considerable debate about the lines of causality in the relationship between the acceleration of globalisation from the 1970s onwards and the resurgence of neoliberal thought. Yet it is clear that the material 'trigger' for the neoliberal counter-revolution was the rise to prominence of finance capital in the 1970s, to which the political response was the ending of the post-war international regime of fixed exchange rates and the concomitant unleashing of a contemporary phase of globalisation associated with high levels of global capital mobility. The neoliberal counter-revolution thus also represented an agenda for putting in place an ideological and policy environment within which the 'structural hegemony' of global capital (Gill and Law 1989) could flourish.

This 'globalist' emphasis in the neoliberal conception of development not only represented an understanding of how development strategy should be formulated, but it was also central to the implications of the neoliberal counter-revolution for development theory. Aside from questions of their substance, the key shift distinguishing Golden Age from neoliberal theories of development was precisely the movement from a national (and nationalist) to a global (and globalist) frame of reference. Philip McMichael summed up this shift in his contention that, in the contemporary period, development strategies have 'more to do with global positioning than with the management of the "national household"' (McMichael 2000: 150). It is clearly important to remember that development always was conditioned by the manner of countries' insertion into the international political economy: dependency theory and its offshoots taught us at least that much. Yet, prior to the emergence of the neoliberal counter-revolution in the 1970s, mainstream development theory had been marked by a primary concern with national development objectives and an analytical and explanatory focus on internal conditions in particular countries. The era of the neoliberal counter-revolution featured instead a new and distinctive emphasis on participation in the global political economy as the prerequisite for economic growth and development, rather than as the structural brake on them that was perceived by dependency theory.

One of the striking anomalies of neoliberal development theories, however, lay in their conceptualisation of the roots of development *failures*. While the roots of strong economic performance were deemed to lie in the achievement of effective insertion into the global economy, development remained conceptualised as an inherently national process. Development failures were understood to stem purely from endogenous factors, associated in the main with 'incorrect' government policies and institutional deficiencies, compounded by the forms of corruption and clientelism that resulted from excessive state intervention in economic affairs. Consequently, development failures were deemed amenable to remedy by the implementation of 'appropriate' neoliberal policies and the retrenchment of the state (Toye 1993). The neoliberal policy agenda thus constituted a programme of *internal* reform in developing countries, which left untouched the issues of the global environment within which these policies were articulated (Phillips 2005b). This form of 'methodological nationalism' stands uneasily beside the normative globalism of the neoliberal counter-revolution (Gore 2000) and, indeed, accounts for many of the shortcomings of neoliberal development theory that were revealed particularly starkly in the economic crises that erupted in Latin America and East Asia during the 1990s.

So what, then, were the central elements of the neoliberal counter-revolution and the policy reform agenda associated with it? In a nutshell, the substance of neoliberal thinking rested on the prioritisation of capital as money over capital as production (Gamble 2001) and the consolidation of market-led mechanisms of resource allocation as the most effective means of stimulating industrialisation and development. The prescriptive emphasis thus fell on 'getting the prices right' (that is, freeing markets to set prices rather than maintaining systems of 'political prices'), creating competitive markets integrated into the international economy, and positioning the private sector as the engine of accumulation and growth. The core project thus sought fundamentally to redraw the relationship between markets and states in order to preserve the new dominance of money capital in national and international economic organisation and eliminate the disabling political consequences of excessive rent seeking for economic growth. States would, for this purpose, be relegated to roles consistent with the philosophical position advocated by Friedman in a statement which has come to be seen as the emblematic summary of neoliberalism: 'To the free man, the country is a collection of individuals which compose it . . . The scope of government must be limited . . . to preserve law and order, to enforce private contracts, to foster competitive markets' (Friedman 1962: 2).

This neoliberal agenda for 'depoliticising' development was also pursued through the forceful advocacy of outward-looking trade regimes, which would serve all of the core objectives outlined above: domestic markets would be subjected to international competitive pressures and inefficient industries consequently deprived of protection; governments would be less able to impose 'political prices'; and uncertainty for producers and investors would consequently be reduced (Wade 1990: 11). Outward-looking trade regimes would furthermore lead to processes of upgrading and diversification of exports in line with the central Ricardian principle of comparative advantage (Balassa 1982) and one of the main barriers to development would consequently be dismantled. So went the argument for thoroughgoing trade liberalisation in developing economies, deploying the supposedly cast-iron (but, for many, very shaky) case that had been advanced in neoclassical economics for the existence of a direct link between free trade and economic growth (Lal 1983; Krueger 1980; Balassa 1982).

The point at which these influences were definitively brought together and shaped into a blueprint for economic growth came at the end of the 1980s with the elaboration of the so-called 'Washington consensus' – a formulation famously originated by the US-based economist John Williamson. The 'Washington' part of it should be understood not in a restricted sense as the US government, but rather as the global network of elite institutions, governments, policy makers and market actors that had its epicentre in Washington DC. The 'consensus' part referred to the depiction of such theoretical and political unanimity within this elite global network, and indeed the associated professional economics community, that the agenda could be presented from the start as essentially immune to reasonable questioning. Williamson famously dismissed dissenters as 'cranks', arguing that:

> [T]he superior economic performance of countries that establish and maintain outward-oriented market economies subject to macro-economic discipline is essentially a positive question. The proof may not be quite as conclusive as the proof that the Earth is not flat, but it is sufficiently well established as to give sensible people better things to do with their time than to challenge its veracity. (Williamson 1993: 1330)

The Washington consensus consisted of a list of ten policies that were considered to be the definitive statement of what it took, as it were, to develop. Williamson (1990) set these out as follows:

- Maintenance of fiscal discipline (budget deficits should not exceed 2 per cent of gross domestic product [GDP])

- Re-ordering of public expenditure priorities (reduction and elimination of subsidies; prioritisation of spending in education, health and infrastructure)
- Tax reform (broadening of tax base; maintenance of 'moderate' marginal tax rates)
- Maintenance of positive real interest rates (to discourage capital flight and increase savings)
- Maintenance of 'competitive' exchange rates
- Trade liberalisation
- Elimination of barriers to foreign direct investment
- Privatisation of state-owned enterprises
- Deregulation of the economy
- Enforcement of property rights.

In its essence, then, the Washington consensus represented 'the belief that Victorian virtue in economic policy – free markets and sound money – is the key to economic development' (Krugman 1995: 29). As Colin Leys put it pithily, by the end of the 1980s 'the only development policy that was officially approved was not having one – leaving it to the market to allocate resources, not the state' (Leys 1996b: 42). He also went on to highlight the World Bank's own revealing formulation of the neoliberal agenda: 'new ideas stress prices as signals; trade and competition as links to technical progress; and effective governments as a scarce resource, to be employed sparingly and only where most needed' (World Bank 1991: 49). As such, the Washington consensus, as the distilled version of the neoliberal agenda of the 1980s and 1990s, represented a political agenda which aimed to restructure in its entirety the relationship between states, capital and labour, premised on an 'authoritarian and technocratic ideal . . . based on small and highly effective government' (Toye 1991: 326). While clearly the product of a long tradition of Western liberal thought, the contemporary neoliberal agenda thus departed significantly from the approach of Adam Smith and other classical liberal thinkers in its appreciably more minimalist vision of the role of the state in development. What is more, in the extreme versions of Western economic liberalism that informed the neoliberal counter-revolution, what even such an historically significant figure as Smith had to say on the matter of the role of states was no longer credited (Johnson 1999; Johnson and Keehn 1994; Colclough 1991).

The programme of policy reform that came to be encapsulated in the Washington consensus was disseminated widely and aggressively over the 1980s and the 1990s, particularly across Latin America and the Caribbean, sub-Saharan Africa and eastern Europe. The 'structural adjustment' programmes of the international financial institutions (IFIs) – notably, the World Bank and the International Monetary Fund (IMF) – constituted the central mechanism by which this new thinking was implanted in domestic contexts. It was through their attachment to loans incorporating wide-ranging conditions stipulating the policy reforms that must take place – so-called 'conditionality' – that the IFIs were pivotal in propelling the domestic restructuring processes necessary to maintain the new global norms of high capital mobility and free trade. Their efforts with structural adjustment through the 1980s, which foreshadowed the Washington consensus, were marked by a 'one-size-fits-all' approach, under the guise of an 'apolitical' lending strategy, in which exactly the same reform agenda was promoted as suitable for all countries without attention to specific historical, political or socioeconomic contexts, and was, moreover, imposed without significant consultation or negotiation. This approach failed dramatically, particularly in preventing the resurgence of hyperinflation in Latin America and the continued stagnation of sub-Saharan African economies. The 'first-generation' trajectory of the neoliberal counter-revolution thus fell far short of its aspirations, with the result that, by the start of the 1990s, the Latin American and African regions were widely deemed to have experienced a 'lost decade' in terms of development performance.

It was the political explanation for these failures, especially the alleged inappropriateness of the 'one-size-fits-all' notion, which was seized upon by the IFIs in their reformulation of their strategies in the early 1990s. Their faith in the economic orthodoxy remained unshaken by the storm of criticism that had greeted the experiences of the 1980s. The World Bank rearticulated its central goal as one of 'build[ing] home-grown commitment mechanisms, rooted in domestic institutions', to be pursued through a more politically inclusive approach to negotiating its loan agreements (World Bank 1997: 60). The term 'structural adjustment' was dropped in favour of a new organising concept – that of 'good governance' – by which the Bank sought to assert a new focus on the centrality of institutions in economic reform and development processes (World Bank 1992; also Williams and Young 1994; Williams 1996; Tussie 2000; Doornbos 2001). The good governance approach was articulated in highly managerialist and administrative terms, focusing on public sector management, accountability, the legal framework, transparency and information, and civil society (World Bank 1992) – in short, an agenda for institution-building in the interests of providing 'an enabling environment for private sector growth and poverty reduction' (Williams 1996: 163). The World Bank's policy reform prescriptions thus shifted away from an exclusive focus on macroeconomic stabilisation and adjustment to the so-called 'second-generation' reform agenda, addressing fiscal reform, labour flexibilisation and the 'modernisation of the state' (World Bank 1997).

The implication of the new emphasis on good governance was that the former pretence of 'apoliticism' in the Bank's agenda was abandoned, the licence to intervene in highly political ways in developing countries was massively expanded, and the IFIs, powerful governments and associated agents of the neoliberal counter-revolution thus accrued 'an unprecedented capacity to shape the strategic direction of large parts of the world' (Payne 2005b: 59). Yet, in a different sense, the 'apolitical' thrust of neoliberal development strategies was maintained and perpetuated. The agenda of good governance rested on what Adrian Leftwich has called a 'technicist illusion' – that is, a misplaced conviction that there is always a technical, administrative or managerial 'fix' for development problems (Leftwich 2000: 107). Governance in this conception was deemed to be essentially about administrative capacity, presented as if it were 'detached from the turbulent world of social forces, politics and the structure and purpose of the state' (Leftwich 2000: 108). It was this universalising apoliticism which accounted for many of the subsequent woes of the good governance agenda and its failure to become securely implanted in the target political economies of the developing world.

We will pause here in our discussion of the neoliberal counter-revolution. It is time now to delve into the theoretical debates surrounding the spectacular growth performance of the 'late-industrialising' countries of East Asia and to consider the body of neostatist theory that emerged as the principal counterweight to the neoliberal counter-revolution from the 1970s onwards.

Neostatism and the Battle for the East Asian 'Miracle'

From the early 1960s to the early 1980s the Japanese economy grew at annual rates of around 7 per cent, the four NICs grew at annual rates of over 8 per cent, and the jumps made by these economies in the hierarchy of 'rich nations' over this time were collectively genuinely arresting. These trends constituted not only one of the 'biggest stories of the twentieth century' (Wade 1990: 34), but also one of the biggest stories in the evolution of development theory. Even the most sophisticated versions of dependency theory and its offshoots were left floundering for anything convincing to say on the question of East Asian development, having instead anticipated only the perpetuation of underdevelopment as the consequence of the obstacles to industrialisation that derived from the structural logic of capitalism. As underdevelopment theory thus beat a reluctant retreat, the debate was largely left to be fought out between exponents of the neoliberal counter-revolution and the proponents of neostatist theories of East Asian development, both of whom sought to lay claim to the East Asian 'miracle' as vindication of their respective approaches.

We noted earlier that an important part of the neoliberal assault on development economics rested on the performance of the East Asian economies, which were understood to have adopted outward-looking trade regimes and pursued export-oriented industrialisation featuring a heavy emphasis on manufactured exports. In short, they were deemed to have conformed to the principles of the free market and reaped the rewards. Such interpretations ranged from those neoclassical accounts which contended that the performance of the NICs was a direct consequence of minimal levels of government intervention in the economy and a heavy reliance on private markets (Galenson 1979) to others which inclined towards what Wade (1990) identified as a 'simulated free market theory of East Asian success'. This latter approach accommodated a perspective on the forms of government intervention that were associated with East Asian development strategies, but insisted nonetheless that these resulted in only small deviations from market prices and were concentrated in export promotion strategies designed to set in place 'neutral' trade regimes – that is, regimes in which biases towards the domestic market that resulted from government protection of certain sectors were offset by 'desirable' export promotion measures (Lal 1983: 46–7; Bhagwati 1988). The burden of these analyses therefore remained faithful to the contention that the East Asian NICs conformed to the principles of free markets, that growth was explained by the fact that governments 'got the prices right', and that the engine of growth in these economies was not the state but the private sector. These arguments were applied as much to Japan as to the four East Asian NICs (Calder 1993).

This neoliberal claim to the East Asian success story was reflected clearly in the evolution of the World Bank's official thinking, as, indeed, was the often very shaky line that its proponents sought to tread between the Washington-consensus version of neoliberal theory and the realities of the East Asian NICs. The Bank's annual *World Development Reports* over the 1980s drew systematically on the cases of the 'outward-oriented' East Asian economies to buttress the case for trade liberalisation. With the redefinition of its agenda in the late 1980s and early 1990s, the East Asian cases were again marshalled as supporting evidence: the new emphasis on 'market-friendly' government intervention in economies was justified by the experiences of these economies. On this basis the Bank published in 1993 its major report entitled *The East Asian Miracle: Economic Growth and Public Policy*, a landmark publication emblematic of the clumsy and faltering way in which the story of the East Asian miracle was 'spun' so as to remain within the parameters of the neoliberal orthodoxy. The publication of this report arose from a protracted dispute between the Japanese government and the World Bank (and by extension the US government), in which the Japanese government pressed trenchantly for greater accommodation of the achievements of East Asian development in the Bank's thinking, principally as a means of enhancing Japanese influence and leadership both in the Bank and more widely (Wade 1996). In the event, the report constituted the first acknowledgement of the *fact* of government intervention in East Asian successes and contained a series of very mealy-mouthed concessions to the benefits of 'selective interventions' in the areas of exports and credit. But it continued staunchly to defend the Bank's line against 'industrial policy' and marshalled an array of (for many, very dubious) pieces of evidence to insist on the underlying 'market-conforming' character of the East Asian development model (World Bank 1993; Wade 1996).

The approaches which came centrally to challenge the neoliberal claim to the East Asian 'miracle' had emerged in the 1960s and 1970s, more in tandem with the neoliberal counter-revolution than directly in response to it or for the purposes of engagement with it. These approaches were concerned centrally with the process of so-called 'late industrialisation' (or sometimes 'late-late industrialisation', to distinguish it from the earlier phases of 'catch-up' that had been given the same label), and specifically with the question of how late industrialisers could set themselves on development trajectories that would result in their 'catching up' with the more industrialised countries. In this sense, theories of East Asian development can be seen as the second generation of the 'catch-up' theories we surveyed in Chapter 2, motivated by a strongly nationalist conception of development and drawing on the legacy of the 'first-generation' theorists. What we see is the transformation of the ideas of Hamilton, List and others, particularly those associated with infant industry arguments, into contemporary versions of neostatist development theory. Equally, neostatist development theory did not only contribute to a protracted debate with neoliberalism: its central contention that there is more than one historical path to economic development, which was explicitly linked to Gerschenkron's understanding of late industrialisation, stood as a challenge to a range of other theories that proffered ahistorical and teleological models of development, such as the crudest Marxian versions of stages of history, Western modernisation theory, and the 'stages of growth' approach associated with Rostow and others (Pempel 1999a). The significance of neostatism for development theory was in this sense very much wider than the debate conducted with neoliberalism from the 1960s onwards. Furthermore, a very direct connection was established between contemporary versions of neostatist theory and bodies of theory associated with early industrialisation, in order to argue that the thrust of Japanese and East Asian development strategies mirrored the early industrial, trade and technology policies pursued by the 'now-developed' countries, including Britain in the eighteenth century, the United States in the nineteenth century, and Germany and Sweden in the late nineteenth and early twentieth centuries (Chang 2002).

The early emphasis was on the story of Japanese development from the 1950s to the 1980s. During this period Japan moved from a position of being the twentieth largest exporter in the world to being the third largest and, by the 1980s, represented by most indicators the most successful industrialised economy in the world (Pempel 1999a). It became the model for all the other countries of East Asia in their subsequent development strategies, including China (Johnson 1999), at the same time as its superior performance vis-à-vis the Anglo-American economies provoked a protracted, introspective debate about the perceived decline of US economic hegemony. The fact that the Japanese were 'flagrantly flouting all received principles of capitalist rationality' (Dore 1986) made more urgent the tasks of both charting and theorising the nature of Japanese growth and arriving at an understanding of the implications of the Japanese experience for both orthodox development theory and the associated international development policy framework.

One of the most influential early contributions to theorising Japanese development, and indeed to explaining divergence in national developmental trajectories, was made by the Japanese economist Kaname Akamatsu in the early 1960s. He famously conceived of Japanese industrialisation as being best represented by a pattern of 'wild geese flying'. Plotting on to the same axis indicators for imports, exports and production relating to the new industries that were introduced into the Japanese economy – such as cotton yarn, cotton cloth, and spinning and weaving machinery – he noticed that the resulting graphs depicted a shape similar to a line of flying geese. The dynamism in the model resulted from the evolution of these new industries: an increase in imports of particular industrial products was followed by a period of import substitution as the relevant industry became established in the national economy, which was in turn followed by a process of export expansion as the industries developed export bases. At that point, a new process of import substitution began for capital goods industries, which then themselves became export industries (Akamatsu 1961, 1962). The initiation of domestic production of imported consumer goods was therefore the 'take-off' stage in the flying geese model, occurring as a result of 'a struggle of economic nationalism' in which domestic consumer markets were created and promoted for the purposes of 'recover[ing] the home market from the hands of foreign industries' (Akamatsu 1961: 13). Such a process could then be replicated in countries wanting to begin their own industrialisation processes, seeking to replace imports from the early 'newly rising countries'; as a result, exports from the latter of basic consumer goods decline and industrial upgrading is in turn promoted (Akamatsu 1962: 17). The emphasis in Akamatsu's analysis was consequently on both appropriate intervention to create and stimulate domestic consumer goods markets and the prioritisation of intervention in those sectors in which growth and export potential was highest.

Yet Akamatsu had little to say about the political, social and institutional arrangements that were necessary for the forms of intervention he deemed to be central to Japanese industrialisation. It was not until some twenty years later that the concept which came to be most associated with explanations of Japanese and East Asian industrialisation – that of the 'developmental state' – was put forward by Chalmers Johnson in what is regarded as his seminal work, *MITI and the Japanese Miracle: The Growth of Industrial Policy, 1925–1975*, published in 1982. The theoretical lineage of this concept is to be found in the work of List and Hamilton and in the work of Marx and Poulantzas, as well as in the long tradition of statism in development economics associated with such figures as Rosenstein-Rodan, Scitovsky,

Gerschenkron, Baran and, more recently, Gunnar Myrdal and Simon Kuznets (see Chang 1999; Leftwich 2000). Johnson's work on Japan and East Asian states nevertheless constituted the first use of the term 'developmental state' and the first serious attempt to conceptualise it (Leftwich 2000).

Distinguishing the 'plan-rational' state associated with his conception of the developmental state from the 'plan-ideological' (or 'plan-irrational') state of Soviet-type command economies, and from the 'regulatory, or market-rational' state most associated with the earlier industrialising countries of the United States and Western Europe, Johnson (1982) set out the contours of the Japanese developmental state essentially as follows:

1. The first priority of the state is economic development – a priority maintained consistently by the Japanese government in both the pre-war and post-war periods. Economic development is defined in terms of growth, production and competitiveness, rather than consumption, distribution and welfare.
2. A 'small, inexpensive but elite' bureaucracy, recruited on the basis of merit, is responsible for selecting the industries to be developed (industrial structure policy), identifying the best means of developing these industries (industrial rationalisation policy) and supervising competition in the selected sectors to guarantee their economic effectiveness.
3. The legislative and judicial branches of government are restricted to the 'safety valve' functions of ensuring that the bureaucracy responds to the requirements of those groups in society on which the stability of the model rests, thus institutionalising consultation and coordination between bureaucratic and business elites (the private sector) as the basis for effective policy making. Put more pithily, 'the politicians reign and the bureaucrats rule' (Johnson 1981: 12).
4. State intervention in the economy is of a 'market-conforming' nature.
5. The bureaucracy is led by a 'pilot agency' – such as the Japanese Ministry of Trade and Industry (MITI), which formed the basis of Johnson's study – possessed of a

wide array of functions associated with controlling and directing the process of industrial transformation.

Johnson's work on Japan caused a storm of critical neoliberal reaction. Johnson reported in a later retrospective essay that the strength of this reaction had taken him by surprise, not having quite realised the extent to which his book was 'an ideological red flag to the bull of Anglo-American cold war orthodoxy about economic correctness' (Johnson 1999: 34). Yet it would be no exaggeration to say that the concept of the developmental state came to represent the cornerstone for all subsequent understandings of East Asian development in the neostatist tradition, notwithstanding inevitable disagreements with parts of the argument and modifications of the approach. The immediate influence of Johnson's work was on understandings of the trajectories of the East Asian NICs, in particular Korea and Taiwan, some the most influential studies of these two countries being associated with, respectively, Alice Amsden and Robert Wade.

Amsden's (1989, 1990) work on South Korea drew very directly on Johnson's concept of the developmental state. She marshalled evidence from the South Korean case to refute both the 'free-market' and 'simulated free-market' interpretations of its rapid growth, drawing attention to the highly politicised nature of export promotion and the dollar prices for exports, the nationalisation of the banking system in 1961 and the consequent consolidation of control by the government of Park Chung Hee over both domestic interest rates and the allocation of foreign loans. These loans were directed to the specific sectors targeted for development as well as specific firms. Other work on the Korean case similarly emphasised the control of finance as the single most important instrument of industrial policy (Woo 1991). Most importantly, contradicting neoliberal accounts, Amsden underlined the fact that governments in all the late-industrialising economies not only consistently failed to get the relative prices right, but in fact worked deliberately to get the prices *wrong* in order to stimulate investment and trade. Like Johnson, Amsden argued on this basis that 'an analysis of disparate growth rates among late-industrializing countries requires an institutional approach' (Amsden 1990: 7) and went on to provide a detailed account of the nature, extent and outcomes of state intervention in the South Korean case, emphasising the centrality of 'selectivity' in industrial policy, the distortion of prices for the purposes of directing economic activity towards greater investment and the strong disciplining of the private sector by the government. Rather than subsidising uncompetitive industries, as occurred in Western Europe and, indeed, as envisaged in the neoliberal case against state intervention, the South Korean government was instead stringent in penalising poorly performing firms and targeting its incentives and rewards to effective and efficient ones.

Wade (1990) used the case of Taiwan as the platform from which to argue for a 'governed market theory' of East Asian industrialisation. He drew substantially on Johnson's work, but took him to task for the descriptive rather than 'comparative-analytic' character of his developmental state concept and his lack of attention to the nature of policies and their impact on industrial performance. Wade instead understood the proximate causes of the superior performance of East Asian economies to be the following:

1. very high levels of productive investment, leading to the rapid transfer of new techniques into production processes (over the 1960–80 period, Japanese investment was equivalent on average to some 32.8 per cent of GDP, Taiwan's to 28.4 per cent and Korea's to 26.5 per cent);
2. more investment in certain key industries than would have occurred in the absence of government intervention;
3. the exposure of many industries to international competition, in foreign markets if not at home.

A second level of causation referred to the economic policies designed to bring about these three outcomes, policies which together amounted to the government's 'governing' of market processes of resource allocation. A third level of explanation rested on the types of organisation of the state and the private sector that facilitated these policies – that is, the 'corporatist and authoritarian' arrangements characteristic of East Asia that provided 'the basis for market guidance' (Wade

1990: 26–7). Echoing Amsden, therefore, Wade explored the manner in which intervention produced different sets of outcomes from those which would have prevailed in the absence of intervention, the deliberate distortion of prices so as to alter the signals to which market agents responded, and the political and institutional arrangements which supported these strategies and 'confer[red] sufficient autonomy on a centralized bureaucracy for it to influence resource allocation in line with a long-term national interest' (Wade 1990: 29, 298).

What we have in the early analyses of Japanese industrialisation, the developmental state approach and the 'revisionist' theories of East Asian industrialisation is thus a body of theory which located the determinants of developmental performance in the transformation of domestic political economies under state-driven, developmentalist regimes (also see Kohli 1999, 2004). Yet we must caution against caricaturing this body of theory as concerned with 'government intervention'. Indeed, as Wade points out, 'no serious scholar has argued that the difference between East Asia and elsewhere is to be explained mainly in terms of government intervention'. Rather, contradicting neoliberal accounts which posited that 'market-friendly policies plus export-push policies yield export-led growth', Wade encapsulates the East Asian story as one which relies on 'favourable initial conditions – especially human capital and infrastructure – plus investment-led growth' (Wade 1996: 26). In this conception exports are not the driving force behind economic growth. Rather, they are the result of higher investment, which leads to faster technical change and high import levels, which in turn generate higher exports – a formulation not dissimilar to Akamatsu's 'flying geese' model of industrialisation.

Put together, these perspectives acted as powerful rebuttals to the 'free-market' and 'simulated free-market' approaches to understanding East Asian development. These were denounced as fundamentally misunderstanding the political and institutional foundations of the Japanese and East Asian models, misrepresenting the nature and extent of government policies designed to foster particular patterns of resource allocation and bring about particular outcomes, and as being entirely unable to account for the rise of Japan and the East Asian NICs within their ideological and analytical frameworks. Had Japan conformed to the neoliberal model, as was claimed, and had it followed the prescriptions of the neoliberal economists of the 1960s, then at the most basic level the Japanese economy would have looked completely different by the 1980s and would have occupied a very different place in the world's hierarchy of powerful economies. It would have concentrated on its 'comparative advantage' in textiles and would not have developed a huge market share in steel or automobiles – the story of the rise of the Japanese car manufacturer Toyota being emblematic of the results achieved not by conforming with market principles, but by 'defying the market' (Chang 2007: 19–21, 210–12).

Looking back at our discussion thus far then, it is clear that neostatist theory displays a primary comparative concern with national development patterns and the characteristics of domestic political economy that give rise to them. Yet we should not imply that there was no attention in this body of theory to the structural context in which these economies were rooted, even though the international political and economic environment was neglected in favour of a focus on the domestic context (Pempel 1999a). In contrast to neoliberal theories, which, as we saw, prioritised a normatively globalist framework for development while attributing differences in national performance to domestic factors, neostatist theories located national patterns and processes within a global context, while maintaining a normatively nationalist frame of reference (Gore 1996). On one level, the emphasis on catch-up revealed a core concern with the insertion of these economies into the global economy, connected with a goal of achieving a global presence and influence which was formulated in strongly nationalist terms, especially explicitly in the Japanese context. On another level, there was due recognition of the role of the international environment in creating the conditions in which East Asian industrialisation could flourish. East Asian industrialisation occurred in the context of radical shifts in the organisation of the world economy, resulting in what was eventually called the 'new international division of labour' (NIDL) (Frobel et al. 1980). In the 1960s these shifts resulted in much greater access to international finance, more favourable access to the markets of the industrialised countries and the increasing relocation of productive activities to low-cost sites in what was then termed the 'periphery' of the world economy, notably to Asia (Wade 1990). Moreover, the East Asian NICs possessed the strength and autonomy to manage the impact of inflows of foreign capital on the local economies, in contrast to the 'dependent development' of Latin America on foreign multinational corporations (Evans 1979; Haggard and Cheng 1987). The geopolitical significance of the East Asian NICs in the context of a continuing 'Cold War' also meant that the United States intervened to favour the industrialisation of these economies, in a manner which has some importance – although it should not be exaggerated – in explaining why these four NICs enjoyed a relatively more favourable international environment than did many other industrialising economies in Asia and Latin America (Cumings 1984; also see Weiss and Hobson 1995).

Yet, notwithstanding these qualifications, overwhelmingly the most important contribution of neostatist theories of development was their understanding of the centrality of the developmental capacity of states and their strategic interventions in the economy in explaining the increasing differentiation between developing economies. A compelling explanation could be advanced on this basis for the relative underperformance of other developing economies, and an (unflattering) comparison on these grounds has often been made with Latin American political economies, where there has existed no endogenous technological core, where developmental capacity was not tapped prior to or independently of foreign capital flows, where there has been no consistent pattern of developmental institutionalisation within the state, and where elites have not been consistently nationalist nor of a determined developmental persuasion (Leftwich 2000; Phillips 2004; see also Hirschman 1968). While the Brazilian and Mexican cases have usually been taken as the best approximation of Latin American developmental states in comparative work, there are questions to be asked about the extent to which these (and indeed other) cases approximate a developmental state *per se*, as opposed to exhibiting developmentalist streaks in their policy orientation and ideological inclinations. Development strategies in a number of Latin

American economies (Brazil, Mexico, Chile) have arguably been characterised for limited periods of time by a certain developmentalist orientation, but the most that can be said of this effort is that it has represented a form of 'state developmentalism without a developmental state' (Kurtz 2001), at least of the type associated with the East Asian experience.

It is for this reason that the status of neostatist theory has been called somewhat into question, on the grounds that it is specific to East Asia and therefore unable to constitute a genuinely 'universalist' theory of development. The unique historical conditions in which East Asian industrialisation occurred have been taken as indicating a theory of narrow applicability and a development trajectory that cannot justifiably be called a 'model' which other states can emulate (Önis 1991). Others have argued that there are elements of the model which are amenable to replication elsewhere, or that initial institutional and cultural conditions are not as definitively 'binding' as is sometimes assumed, with 'policy ingenuity' therefore being of foremost importance (Wade 1990; Chang 2006). However, although its contemporary applicability is acknowledged to be quite specific to a number of East Asian economies, attempts have been made to broaden it to refer to a range of states outside Asia (Woo-Cumings 1999; Amsden 2001), including Brazil, Mexico, Chile, Argentina, France, India, China and Turkey. The inclusion of some of these cases (such as Argentina) seems tenuous at best and, on balance, the model of the developmental state has not travelled very well outside Asia. But the fact remains that the concept of the developmental state has become signally influential in development theory in general, not just in the study of East Asian political economy.

Nevertheless, both neoliberalism and neostatism came under significant pressure in the course of the 1990s, as economic and financial crises engulfed first Mexico and then much of the Asian region, as well as other economies such as those of Russia, Turkey, Brazil and Argentina by the start of the 2000s. The extent of the resulting disarray is revealed by the fact that, by this stage, obituaries had been written for both neoliberalism and the East Asian developmental state, at the same time as both bodies of theory battled to assert the continued vitality of their propositions. It is to these crises and the challenges they issued to neoliberalism and neostatism that we must now turn our attention.

The New Crisis of Development Theory in the 1990s

What was striking about the Washington consensus was that the speed with which it was elevated to the status of the 'common core of wisdom' (Williamson 1994: 18), and the vehemence with which it was disseminated, were matched only by the speed with which it was deemed to have spectacularly failed. The Latin American region was seen as the test-bed for the Washington-consensus version of the neoliberal agenda, and reform programmes were initiated across the region. In many countries they fell on fertile ground, given the policy space that had been opened up by the resurgence of hyperinflation, political instability and generalised economic crisis of the 1980s. Almost across the board, macroeconomic indicators in the early years of neoliberal reform were greeted with enthusiasm, inasmuch as trade and investment expanded rapidly, inflation sank to low levels, and in some cases (but not all) growth resumed – not at the extraordinary levels of the East Asian NICs, but at least for a couple of years at higher levels than those which had prevailed over the preceding decade. Given the effects on inflation in particular, for a short time the negative social consequences of privatisation and deregulation, particularly on employment and wages, were generally played down in favour of a rhetoric of economic stabilisation.

Yet by the middle of the 1990s the Washington consensus was in serious trouble across Latin America and the rest of the developing world. The onset of its swift deflation was seen as being marked by the Mexican 'peso crisis' of late 1994, occasioned by a speculative attack on the currency, a crisis which, together with the deteriorating performance of some of the 'poster child' economies in Latin America, was taken as evidence of the profound shortcomings of the neoliberal agenda. By the end of the 1990s the result of over a decade of neoliberal reform in Latin America had been a pattern of disappointing economic performance and increasing political tension across the region, leading many to speak of the second part of the 1990s as another 'lost half-decade' (ECLAC 2002). For the 1990s as a whole, per capita GDP grew more slowly than it had done between 1950 and 1980 and, by 2003, was 1.5 per cent lower than in 1997; unemployment had reached a regional average level of 10.7 per cent by the start of the 2000s, along with significant rises in underemployment and informal activity; and poverty levels were registered as encompassing 44 per cent of the region's total population by 2003. Inequality in Latin America also remained the highest in the world, revealing yet another sharp contrast with the East Asian NICs, where significant improvements had been rolled out in socioeconomic equality and living standards over the preceding decades. Economic performance in other regions, particularly sub-Saharan Africa, was similarly disappointing, most especially in the deepening of socioeconomic deprivation for huge sections of the region's populations.

Reaction to the disastrous results of the neoliberal agenda was predictably varied, but a rethinking of the dominant policy agenda was in evidence across the board. There was a significant movement away from the Washington consensus itself, even while the broad tenets of the neoliberal counterrevolution remained intact. The core characteristics of neoliberal development theory were apparent in orthodox reactions to the failures of the Washington consensus, inasmuch as the explanation was located purely in internal factors. Many placed emphasis on the incomplete implementation of neoliberal policy prescriptions as the root cause of continued development failures. John Williamson (2003) himself set out perhaps the clearest version of this argument. Others chose to see the Mexican crisis as a 'reality check' that was inevitable in view of the excessively optimistic expectations of economists and politicians with regard to what the Washington consensus would achieve. Their point was 'not that the policy recommendations that Williamson outlined are wrong, but that their efficacy – their ability to turn Argentina into Taiwan overnight – was greatly oversold' (Krugman 1995: 30). Going further, the World Bank summarised its reactions in a 2005 report entitled *Economic Growth in the*

1990s: Learning from a Decade of Reform, in which it drew the following conclusions (Rodrik 2006: 976–7): that insufficient attention had been paid to stimulating the dynamic forces that lie behind the growth process; that the objectives of economic reform did not translate into a single and unique set of policy prescriptions, but rather could be achieved in a number of ways; that solutions to development problems must be context-specific and the notion of 'models' for emulation was unhelpful; that rules had been set out in relation to government discretion in ways which introduced undue rigidities into economies and inflexibility into decision making; and that reform efforts needed to focus on the 'binding constraints' to development, rather than relying on a 'laundry list' of policy reforms that may or may not be appropriate.

Other reactions sought to modify this 'endogenist' diagnosis of these development failures, arguing that attention needed to be paid to the global economic context. For some, this was a question of how the dramatic liberalisation and deregulation of developing economies had been undertaken without mechanisms having been put in place to cope effectively with the consequences of globalisation, especially in relation to the impact on financial systems of the vast inflows of foreign investment (Naím 2000). Others drew attention to the nature of the global economy and the politics which shaped developing countries' participation in it, whether in relation to the workings of globalised financial markets, the barriers to developmentally effective participation in the world trade system, or the challenges for production of the shifting global division of labour (Phillips 2005b; Payne 2005a). Yet overwhelmingly the dominant reaction to development failures in countries that had experimented with versions of the Washington consensus was one which emphasised the deficiencies of domestic political economies and, by extension, the continuing validity of the neoliberal agenda.

At the time when the Washington consensus was beginning to implode in the mid 1990s, the perceived superiority of the East Asian model in producing positive developmental outcomes was able to remain relatively intact, both among those who had poured so much energy into claiming neoliberal credentials for East Asian development, and among those who sought to argue along neostatist lines for a very different understanding of it. But *both* neoliberalism and neostatism were thrown onto the back foot by the unfolding of the Asian financial crises from 1997 onwards, starting with the collapse of the Thai *baht* and spreading to Indonesia, South Korea, Malaysia and elsewhere in the region, and as well as to Latin America, Russia and Turkey. These crises were characterised by considerable falls in investment and output levels across East Asia, with severe social consequences. The incidence of poverty, for instance, was estimated by the World Bank to have increased by around 22 million (Glyn 2006a: 69).

The orthodox reaction was once again to account for the crisis by reference to internal factors. The most salient political explanation was summed up in the phrase 'crony capitalism', whereby the extent to which the private sector was organised and controlled by state patronage – in other words, that the state distorted the workings of markets – was presented as one of the key reasons for the collapse of economies (Henderson 1998; Pempel 1999b; Segal and Goodman 2000; also see Kang 2002). The culprit was therefore state intervention – an ironic twist in the story we have related here, given that the 'simulated free-market' approach, and, indeed, the World Bank's own pronouncements, had sought to play down the degree of state intervention in Asian economies in order to emphasise the 'market-conforming' character of development strategies, and indeed in order to present the East Asian experience as having the qualities of an economic 'miracle'. In many interpretations of the Asian financial crises, the strident defence of the market-driven character of East Asian growth was thus reversed with unseemly speed, and the key tenets of the neostatist interpretation were essentially accepted in wholesale fashion in order to make a set of new arguments about what was wrong with the East Asian model and what explained the implosion of East Asian economies at the end of the 1990s.

The other salient orthodox explanation identified the deficiencies of banking systems – not the workings of international financial markets, and certainly not economic 'openness' or 'export-oriented' growth – as being at the root of the financial crises. If openness was the problem, the argument went, a different set of economies, and also perhaps a larger number, would have also been in trouble: the Chilean financial system was considerably more 'open' at the time of the Asian crises than those of the East Asian NICs, at least in institutional terms, and only a small proportion of bank lending in the 1990s in the NICs was related to foreign-owned banks, while Chile had no restrictions on foreign access to ownership (*The Economist* 1998). Crucially as well, the countries worst affected by the crises were said to be those that had adopted only a lukewarm variant of the Washington consensus. It was no surprise, according to this interpretation, that in Latin America it should be Brazil and Venezuela that were most threatened by the contagion from the economic crisis, and not, for example, Chile (Higgott and Phillips 2000).

It was in this way that the orthodox neoliberal reaction to the Asian crises could tell a story that rested not on the fundamentals of a market-led development strategy or on the workings of the globalised financial markets, but on endogenous economic contradictions, institutional inadequacies and political distortions in the East Asian economies and those elsewhere in the world that were 'infected' by the contagion. Yet it had eventually to be accepted, even by the proponents of this interpretation, that macroeconomic distortions in the affected East Asian countries, with the possible exception of Indonesia, were simply not of a scale sufficient to warrant economic and financial chaos of such proportions. The orthodox response was largely to fall back, rather tenuously, on the political explanations noted above. These were challenged from other quarters, including those associated with neostatism. Forceful arguments were made to the effect that 'cronyism' was at best a minor contributing factor to the crises, having changed sufficiently in neither form nor extent to precipitate a crisis (Chang 2006). Others called for attention to be paid to the characteristics of 'globalisation', and especially the collective irrationality that resulted from the herd instincts in global financial markets, which in turn had produced the well-documented market panic (Wade 1998, 1999; Higgott and Phillips 2000). Others drew attention to the strategies of the IMF in pushing capital account liberalisation in East Asia which, combined with fixed exchange rates, encouraged reckless borrowing by banks and firms and the creation of 'moral hazard' by international creditors (Glyn 2006a; Chang 2006). The financial crises were thus deemed to have 'vividly demonstrated the risks of capital market liberalization' (Stiglitz 2004: 58), and their impact to have been compounded by the IMF's subsequent response.

In the midst of this vociferous debate, what can be clearly perceived is that, for neostatist development theory, the Asian financial crises generated a very awkward context for the continued defence of the developmental solidity of the East Asian model. One influential response to this difficulty was to attribute the crisis precisely to the partial acceptance of neoliberal principles in East Asia. In the case of Korea, for example, this was seen to have resulted in uncoordinated and excessive investments by the private sector, financial liberalisation which had led to the accretion of imprudent levels of debt, and a weakening of industrial policy (Chang et al. 1998). The call was therefore for a disavowing of these neoliberal principles, and many perceived the backlash emerging across Asia as pointing precisely in this direction. Such interpretations were met by others which perceived the Asian financial crises as signalling a turning point for the East Asian NICs, in which the developmental state was essentially finished and was in the process of being replaced by an emerging neoliberal or 'liberal-regulatory' state (Moon and Rhyu 1999; Jayasuriya 2005; Pirie 2005). These perspectives in turn yielded an emerging controversy with those who contended that, even in the midst of unquestionably significant changes in the direction of greater liberalisation, the East Asian NICs retained important continuity in the overall strategic thrust of their development project (Thurbon and Weiss 2006). In short, the key debate among students of East Asia came to be centred on the question of whether neoliberalism was now unquestionably in the theoretical and political ascendant, or whether a neostatist approach to development could be defended as a valid set of theoretical propositions and furthered as a form of development strategy.

Conclusion

In this chapter we have charted the deeply intertwined evolution of neoliberal and neostatist theories of development and argued that the debate between their contending propositions was pivotal to the shaping of development theory from the 1960s until the end of the 1990s. It is striking that, in good part, these bodies of theory were fighting over essentially the same ground – namely, the capacity to explain and claim superior theoretical purchase on the successes of development in Japan and East Asia, the increasingly pronounced differentiation between the developmental trajectories of developing economies, and, by extension, the ongoing failures of development in Latin America, sub-Saharan Africa and elsewhere. Both bodies of theory were driven in this sense by a commitment to providing genuinely 'globalist' theories of development.

It is tempting, in the light of what we have had to say about both of them, to contend that neoliberalism achieved this end in much more successful and influential fashion than neostatism, notwithstanding both the theoretical clumsiness and the huge empirical shortcomings of its attempts to claim neoliberal credentials for the East Asian miracle, as well as the disastrous social consequences of the neoliberal development agenda across the developing world. It is possible to argue, as many have, that neostatism remained essentially an approach to the study of East Asia. Indisputably also, neostatist contributions to development theory became considerably more muted with the onset of the Asian financial crises, whilst, by contrast, neoliberalism, albeit often on the shakiest of premises, was able to consolidate its hold on development strategies across the world. Yet this would be seriously to overlook the contributions of neostatism to longstanding debates in development theory which emphasise the importance of states, institutions and strategy in development processes. It is perhaps fairer to conclude that neoliberalism may well have been in the political ascendant across the globe by the end of the 1990s, but to note also that in the world of development theory it was still a good way from being theoretically hegemonic. Especially when taken out of their immediate associations with East Asia, evolving forms of neostatist theory continue to offer contributions to understanding the foundations of growth and development that are both widely credited and hotly contested.

At the same time, it would be wrong to suggest that this historical phase was marked only by the debate between neoliberalism and neostatism. In fact, a range of other theories of development developed in vibrant form over the same period, the bulk of which evolved as direct rejections of neoliberalism and sought to challenge the vision of development contained in the neoliberal counter-revolution. These other theories of development tended to draw not on traditions in development theory but rather on broader currents in social theory and, as such, represented innovative challenges to the mainstream debates we have surveyed in this chapter. We turn in the next chapter to a direct consideration of these 'alternative' theories and their contributions.

5
Alternative Theories

As neoliberalism was consolidating its ascendancy from the 1970s onwards, and as the contest between neoliberal and neostatist approaches was getting fully into its stride, a cluster of theoretical approaches began to emerge from other quarters. We term these approaches 'alternative' because they were consciously defined in terms of their challenge to the neoliberal 'mainstream' of development theory and the dominance of the rivalry between neoliberalism and neostatism. Specifically, their proponents sought to present 'alternative' visions of development in three spheres: What were the goals, objectives and values of 'development'? What or who were understood to be the agents of development? What were the methods by which development could and should be pursued? (Pieterse 1998: 346). If it can be said that there was a common theme running through these alternative approaches, then it was their collective rejection of the emphasis on economic growth – a longstanding characteristic of development economics in the post-war period, and one which continued to characterise mainstream approaches from the 1970s onwards. Such a rejection found an early cue in the work of, among others, the renowned development economist Dudley Seers. In 1969, he set out an emblematic argument for a redefinition of the very 'meaning of development':

> The questions to ask about a country's development are therefore: What has been happening to poverty? What has been

happening to unemployment? What has been happening to inequality? If all three of these have become less severe, then beyond doubt there has been a period of development for the country concerned. If one or two of these central problems have been growing worse, and especially if all three have, it would be strange to call the result 'development', even if per capita income had soared. (Seers 1969: 3–4)

The upshot was a flourishing of alternative approaches to development which proposed to supplant the established focus on growth with a more encompassing conception of development. This was characterised by a commitment to 'human' or 'people-centred' development – or, as it later came to be called, 'sustainable human development'. This was understood in a variety of ways in different approaches: as encompassing questions about the material, social and psychological well-being of individuals, captured in the influential proposition of notions of 'basic needs', 'capabilities' and 'freedoms' as the key goals of development (human development approaches); as focusing on questions of gender and gendered forms of inequality (gender approaches); as referring to the sustainability of human development in the context of the degradation of the natural environment and the depletion of natural resources (environmental approaches); and as questioning the compatibility between human development and modernisation (post-development approaches). Our discussion of the wide terrain of alternative development thinking will take these four approaches as its primary landmarks and explore the contributions of each in turn to the evolution of development theory and practice.

Human Development Approaches

The elaboration of the 'human development' approach aimed directly at inducing a significant rethinking of development in all three spheres mentioned above: the objectives and values of development, its agents, and the means by which it was to be pursued. The first incarnation was in the form of the 'basic needs' approach. This rested on a core recognition that across the world, and contrary to the predictions of neoclassical economics and the neoliberal orthodoxy, economic growth was clearly not associated with beneficial outcomes for the poor, either in incomes or in employment opportunities; consequently, the argument was put forward that special and comprehensive redistributive measures were required to target the poor and unemployed. The International Labour Organization (ILO) was at the forefront of this movement to instigate a special focus on poverty in the development agenda. Drawing on academic research appearing in the early 1970s (such as Chenery et al. 1974), it set out what became known as the basic needs approach in a key document entitled *Employment, Growth and Basic Needs: A One-World Problem* (ILO 1976).

The basic needs approach did not reject growth and modern industrialisation *per se*, but sought to move the development agenda beyond an exclusive focus on growth and a preoccupation with the material dimensions of development. Development was conceived as involving the opening of opportunities for the personal and social flourishing of individual human beings, the improvement of their life chances and the realisation of their human potential. In this spirit, the early basic needs approach placed emphasis on (a) the need for food, shelter, clothing and other necessities of survival, (b) the need for access to services such as clean drinking water, health care, sanitation, public transport, education facilities, and so on, and (c) the need for people to be able to participate in political and decision-making processes that affected their lives (ILO 1976; also see Streeten et al. 1982). The emphasis was as much on the political exclusion of the poor and unemployed as on their socioeconomic exclusion, and the two were seen to be connected and mutually reinforcing. The agenda that emerged was consequently one laden with a sense of moral imperative – that development should be, above all, about the satisfaction of the basic needs of all human beings, and that the development agenda should be re-oriented to prioritise this goal over the objectives of aggregate national growth and continued improvements in living standards in the rich countries of the world.

The 1976 report identified the year 2000 as the target date by which it should be possible to declare that the most essential basic needs should have been met in all societies, even while it appeared to concede that such a goal was quite simply unrealistic: first, it would involve the doubling of the income share of the poorest 20 per cent of households in all regions except Asia, and their trebling in Africa; and, second, everywhere except in the middle-income Latin American countries, 'the extent of redistribution that would be required would be such that social changes of this order of magnitude are unlikely to occur' (ILO 1976). The practical implementation of a basic needs agenda was in this sense a startlingly ambitious undertaking. The political obstacles to its early chances of taking root were also important. While early scholarly work on poverty and the contributions of the ILO generated considerable attention among the international development community in the 1970s, it was not embraced with any particular enthusiasm by governments in poor countries across the world. The sense was that this was yet another 'Northern' agenda which was unrealistic in its ambition and the extent of resources required for its implementation, as well as being open to political manipulation in the context of the Cold War and the North–South politics that prevailed at the time. Moreover, the preoccupation with the burgeoning debt crisis and the growing economic problems across the developing world served decisively to push this agenda to the sidelines, reinforced by the increasing dominance of neoliberal development strategies in the major IFIs (Martinussen 1997: 301). The shift of focus emphatically towards structural adjustment programmes throughout the 1980s reflected a dominant vision not of purposeful redistributive policies, but of freeing market forces as the most efficient means of allocating resources and reducing poverty.

Nevertheless, the focus on poverty and basic needs did not disappear, and indeed it gathered new momentum as the failures of structural adjustment and neoliberal strategies became increasingly apparent during the 1980s and 1990s. By the start of the 1990s it had come to occupy a position of some importance in the agendas of the IFIs and had acquired considerable intellectual stature, in no small part as a result of the work of Amartya Sen, an Indian-born economist who was awarded a Nobel prize in 1998 for his contributions to welfare economics. Sen's extensive work on poverty, inequality, relative deprivation, basic rights and inequalities arising from gender, particularly during the 1970s, was of key importance in defining an intellectual and practical agenda for human development. It led to the influential redefinition of development as the enlargement of people's choices and the development of people's 'capabilities' – the latter term constituting the cornerstone of Sen's approach as it crystallised in the 1980s (Sen 1985) and subsequently shaped a large body of work, notably that associated with Martha Nussbaum on gender (Nussbaum 1999).

By the end of the 1990s Sen's approach had shifted from a reliance on a notion of capabilities to the articulation of 'development as freedom' (Sen 1999). In some respects, the development as freedom framework was very similar to the capabilities approach, but it identified freedoms as the drivers of the enhancement of human capabilities and achievements, and the elimination of 'unfreedoms' as the focus of a strategy for achieving such an enhancement. It posited a definition of development as, stated in seductively simple terms, 'a process of expanding the real freedoms that people can enjoy' (Sen 1999: 3). Income and GNP growth could be important as a *means* in this process of expansion, Sen argued, but freedoms emanated from a range of other sources, including social and economic arrangements and political and civil rights. Freedoms were in this sense simultaneously the means and, moreover, the *ends* of development, and thus the approach called into question the orthodox focus only on some of the means which might be deployed to achieve them. At the same time, and critically, the 'freedom-centred' approach to development was presented as 'very much an agency-oriented view', in which equipping people with adequate social opportunities would lead to a situation in which they would become the primary agents of their own development (Sen 1999: 11).

The body of work that Sen produced over three decades, and the range of scholarly work and debate it inspired, were of pivotal importance in defining the human development approach as it evolved from an emphasis on basic needs to a more encompassing vision of development and development strategy. By the start of the 1990s the approach had been incorporated centrally into the agendas of the IFIs – a focus on poverty reduction and human development evolving alongside that other mascot of 1990s discourse, the good governance agenda. Thus the World Bank's *World Development Report* of 1990 set out an agenda for poverty reduction which rested on (a) the productive use of the labour of the poor – their most abundant asset – through the introduction of more labour-intensive technologies and other strategies to increase employment opportunities; (b) improved access to basic services such as nutrition, health care, primary education, family planning services, and so on; and (c) direct assistance to the very poorest in society (World Bank 1990). This agenda was far more limited, clearly, than the human development approach set out by Sen and others, which encompassed the entirety of human well-being. But it drew directly on the insights of the basic needs approach and its offshoots, particularly in the privileging of employment – that is, the opportunity for the poor to exploit their key endowment of labour – as the primary means to realising human development potential.

Perhaps the most salient landmark in the evolution of the human development approach was the launching by the United Nations Development Programme (UNDP) of the annual *Human Development Report* (HDR), first published in 1990. It was elaborated by a team of researchers led by the Pakistani economist Mahbub ul Haq, who, along with Sen and others, had been a pioneering influence in laying the foundations of the basic needs and human development approaches (ul Haq 1976, 1995; Haq and Ponzio 2008). The first HDR defined human development as 'a process of enlarging people's choices', including the ability to live a long and healthy life, to be educated and to enjoy a decent standard of living, political freedoms, human rights and self-respect, adding that: 'The process of development should at least create a conducive environment for people, individually and collectively, to develop their full potential and to have a reasonable chance of leading productive and creative lives according with their needs and interests' (UNDP 1990: 10, 1).

The centrepiece of the HDRs was the elaboration of a Human Development Index (HDI) intended to provide statistical indicators on aspects of development that were not captured by conventional economic indicators. The shortcomings of the latter were well recognised: the practice of measuring development in terms of per capita GNP, numbers of cars and telephones, and so on, was deficient 'not just because they represent averages and therefore tell us nothing about inequalities in their distribution, but also because they are insufficient to capture the wholeness of human development' (Benería 2003: 18). The HDI therefore set out a range of indicators relating to life expectancy, adult literacy, levels of educational enrolment and real GDP per capita, and later came to focus specifically on issues of gender inequality (UNDP 1995) – an aspect of the agenda which had been notably absent from the ILO's elaboration of the basic needs approach in the 1970s.

By the end of the 1990s the human development approach had thereby come to occupy a position of considerable visibility and influence. Even by 1992 the UNDP felt confident in declaring that human development had 'moved to the center of the global development debate', with the HDI seen to be an essential advance. In successive years it confirmed with arresting clarity the deficiencies of the mainstream approach in its reliance on conventional economic indicators as measures of development: a very wide range of countries in the developing world with high levels of per capita GNP consistently performed poorly on human development indicators, and vice versa. At the same time, the concept of human development attracted important criticisms. The HDI was itself subject to considerable critical scrutiny, including for its measurement of gender inequalities (Bardhan and Klasen 1999) and, more generally, for the 'fetishism of numbers' that it was seen to represent (Max-Neef 1991). From more radical quarters, some of which we will survey in the later part of this chapter, the human development approach was attacked as being nothing more than an adjunct to the neoliberal mainstream – an agenda which the latter was able to, and indeed did very successfully, appropriate in order to ensure its continued dominance. Human development was also deemed to have entirely missed the point, namely, that there is a fundamental tension between growth and what in these critiques was termed 'alternative development'. For this reason, the human development discourse was criticised for leading to a situation in which 'critical concerns are being instrumentalised short of the overhaul of the development-as-growth model, so that in effect development business-as-usual can carry on under a different umbrella' (Pieterse 1998: 358).

For radical versions of alternative development approaches, consequently, the human development approach simply would not do. As we will see, this was also a criticism directed at parts of the gender-based and environmental critiques emerging around the same time, in the sense that their parallel incorporation into neoliberal development theory and the global development agenda was seen to rob them too of their critical force and radical potential. Human development nevertheless represented a powerful intervention in development theory and practice, knitting together a wide and important range of perspectives that had previously been entirely neglected in the dominant debates.

Gender Approaches

Feminist and gender-based approaches to development had much in common with human development approaches, inasmuch as they proposed a re-focusing of the lenses through which we consider the meaning of development and the implications of development projects. The universe of gender-based analysis is a large and diverse one, and it is not possible to survey the whole of the terrain here. But the parts of it most relevant to our discussion are those associated with the early 'women in development' (WID) approach – the liberal feminist critique of development which crystallised in the 1970s – and its later evolution into the more materialist and critical 'gender and development' (GAD) approach, which came to form the backbone of gender-based and feminist critiques of the neoliberal orthodoxy through the 1980s and 1990s.

The WID approach emerged from the same concerns as the other alternative approaches we are exploring here – that is, from a recognition that the development optimism of the modernisation discourses of the 1960s was entirely at odds with the persistent and alarming levels of inequality and deprivation across the world. For feminists, the debate about the failures of development to bring about more egalitarian societies ignored the particular needs of women and an awareness of how development projects affected women in distinctive ways. Despite various post-war UN conventions relevant to the rights of women, and the UN General Assembly's commissioning in 1962 of a report on the role of women in development, it was not until well into the 1970s that questions about women and development were afforded substantive attention – most concretely with the 'discovery', four years after its original publication, of Esther Boserup's pioneering 1974 study *Women's Role in Economic Development* (Rai 2002: 60). Boserup advanced a forceful argument that women had been marginalised in both development policy and the productive economy, gaining less than men from their activities as workers in rural production. This marginalisation in turn affected women's social status, reinforcing patterns of exclusion and deprivation and leaving basic needs unsatisfied in very particular, gendered ways.

Boserup's study influenced a generation of WID scholars, whose work echoed the wider human development approach in its emphasis on employment and participation in the productive economy, alongside widening access to education and technology, as the key mechanisms by which women's needs could be met and gender inequalities addressed (Tinker 1976; Rogers 1980). The consequent benefits for development in general would be palpable. As Shirin Rai observed, '[t]his was an appeal to efficiency as much as to a better deal for women' (Rai 2002: 61), and one which assumed that modernisation was potentially a positive force for human development in its widest sense. Precisely for this reason, the influence of WID scholarship on the policy community was substantial. Its analysis and prescriptions could readily be absorbed into the mainstream without troubling established assumptions in any significant way, finding strong expression by the 1990s in the discourses of 'gender mainstreaming' and 'gender-sensitive' formulations of policy (Koczberski 1998; Pearson 2005; Ferguson 2007). The 'feminisation of poverty' thesis was also strongly represented in this discourse (Chant 2008).

The critique of WID scholarship centred precisely on its liberal bias and orientation to the mainstream. It was charged with failing to reflect adequately on the nature of capitalist accumulation and its impact on women of different classes, as well as on all human beings (Benería and Sen 1981). It was, in a famous and much-used phrase, an agenda to 'add women and stir' (Harding 1987), which left intact and unquestioned both social relations and the dominant model of accumulation. This critique, based on a theoretical under-standing of the implications of capitalist development for structures and politics of inequality, paved the way for the GAD approach. GAD analysis sought to move the focus away from 'women' (with strong reservations in any case about whether 'women' could be spoken of in such homogenised terms) and endeavoured instead to privilege enquiry into 'gender' and the social and power relations that determined the positions of women in society and forms of gender ine-quality (Marchand 1996; Waylen 1996; Rai 2002; Ferguson 2007). While the GAD field was quite a broad church, it was in the main a more overtly 'critical' and radical approach than WID, and was therefore less amenable to absorption by development agencies and planners (Moser 1993). Indeed, there was resistance to the idea that GAD approaches should be allowed to be co-opted by the neoliberal mainstream in the same ways as WID thinking had been (Rai 2002).

The shift that GAD represented was nevertheless partially evident in frameworks that informed development policy during the 1980s and 1990s. Perhaps the most salient of these was the 'gender needs' framework, associated with the work of Maxine Molyneux and Caroline Moser. Molyneux (1985) set out a twofold categorisation of 'gender interests': practical gender interests, which related to the satisfaction of basic needs, much as understood in the basic needs approach; and strategic gender interests, which related to the rectification of gender inequalities in such areas as political representation, educational achievement, employment conditions and wages, freedom of movement and mobility, expressions of sexuality, freedom from violence, freedom from exploitative relation-ships within the household, and so on. This framework was brought to the attention of development policy makers in Moser's (1989, 1993) further elaboration of this distinction, through which she set out an agenda for 'gender planning'. Replacing an early emphasis on 'equality' in development planning, what she identified as the 'empowerment' approach slowly achieved ascendance in the 1990s. Echoing the human development approach, this rested on strategies to increase women's ability to secure 'their own self-reliance and internal strength' (Moser 1989: 107) and led to innovations in development planning, particularly in the form of micro-credit, which came to be targeted particularly at women. Yet, in both versions of this framework, the underlying model of accumulation was not questioned. Issues relating to the intrinsically gendered nature of capitalist development were left to other strands of the GAD debate and, unsurprisingly, found only limited expression in policy debates.

Among the various contributions of GAD approaches, three deserve particular attention. The first relates to the GAD analysis of the highly gendered impact of neoliberal development strategies (especially structural adjustment policies [SAPs]) and the concomitant transformation of global and local labour markets. GAD theorists explored carefully the connections between the rise of export-oriented growth sectors and the transformation of the terms on which women's increased participation in the labour force was realised. Women were positioned as the primary source of cheap and flexible labour – the new, feminised 'ideal workers' – and their integration into the labour force was concentrated in low-wage, low-skill activities, particularly in manufacturing, export-processing and service sectors, despite the expansion of white-collar managerial and administrative jobs (Elson and Pearson 1981; Afshar and Dennis 1992; Pearson 1995). By the 1990s the central preoccupation was thus no longer the exclusion of women from the productive economy and their lack of access to employment opportunities, as it had been for Boserup and other exponents of the WID approach. Rather, it was the highly gendered and unequal terms on which the vast expansion of women's participation in global and local productive activity had occurred, and the complex and contradictory consequences of the feminisation of the labour force for women workers (Benería 2003; Marchand 1994, 1996).

Diane Elson's work was especially influential in this respect. She argued persuasively that, far from being gender neutral, there was a clear 'male bias' in structural adjustment processes. This bias was revealed in the ways in which increased unemployment and the removal of certain welfare provisions under SAPs generated greater pressure for women's participation in the labour force for the purposes of income generation, and concomitantly greater pressure on their time and energy in order to maintain the household (Elson 1989, 1992, 1995). The costs of structural adjustment were thus displaced from the market to the household – specifically, to 'the household's, and particularly women's ability to absorb the shocks of stabilization programs, through more work and "making do" on limited incomes' (Elson 1993: 241). The combination of women's increased role as workers outside the home and their continued (often exclusive) responsibility for the maintenance of the household meant that their labour became 'stretched unbearably', particularly in the context of the neoliberal rolling back of public social and welfare spending (Elson 1989; Rai 2002). The impact of SAPs and the restructuring of employment on domestic life and the provision of caring work in societies was thus understood as leading to a crisis of 'social provisioning'. Moser (1989) and others made the further point that children were often cared for by daughters as mothers went to work, which constrained the formers' educational opportunities and perpetuated a cycle of disadvantage and exclusion.

Second, digging deeper into the social and cultural structures that condition power relations in the home and outside it, an important critique was made of 'patriarchy' as the organising principle of societies and households by both exponents of the human development approach and by GAD theorists (Walby 1990). Countering the arguments put forward from the field of 'New Household Economics' that was emerging within neoclassical economics (Becker 1981), various scholars argued that households in many parts of the world were not organised according to an altruistic distribution of resources among their members; rather, trenchant structures of patriarchal power relations within families and societies meant that women's positions in both spheres were demeaned and adversely affected (Drèze and Sen 1989; Young 1992; Kabeer 1994; Folbre 1994, 1996; Sen 1999). Consistent with the emphasis on both employment and empowerment, some saw the solution as an enhancement of women's contribution to the household through paid work, which would give women more control over the total household resources (Drèze and Sen 1995: 178). GAD theorists adopted some of these insights, but in general were less sanguine about the potential for greater participation in the market economy to diminish the marginalisation of women and transform the patriarchal social relations that constructed these forms of marginalisation. Lucy Ferguson's (2007) work on tourism development in Central America, for instance, revealed a very complex co-existence between women's greater participation in the labour force and persistent, highly 'traditional' gender relations in homes and communities. Such findings reinforce the argument that women's increasing productive activity had not substantially disturbed the social and political relations governing their lives, but instead had simply stretched their finite time in ways inimical to sustainable human development.

Third, the debate surrounding unpaid work was central to the GAD and feminist project of making women visible in scholarly and policy approaches to development. This critique began to take root in the 1970s, propelled particularly by Marxian economists concerned with the ways in which women's unpaid labour and particular domestic divisions of labour were used to ensure the efficient reproduction of present and future generations of workers (Himmelweit and Mohun 1977). For their part feminist critics were concerned at the failure within these debates to ask the bigger questions about gender inequalities and reproduction, or to uncover the profoundly gendered relations behind domestic work (Molyneux 1979; Benería 1979, 2003). Subsequent contributions thus raised important considerations of social reproduction and its intrinsic connection to unpaid work performed primarily (but not exclusively) by women, and advanced a wider theoretical critique associated with the contention that unpaid work cannot be understood through the same lens as paid work in the market. As Benería put it: 'to the extent that unpaid work is not equally subject to the competitive pressures of the market, it can respond to motivations other than gain, such as nurturing, love, and altruism, or to other norms of behavior such as duty and religious beliefs and practices' (Benería 2003: 75). Hence alternative models of economic and development theory were needed, which would be based on assumptions of 'human cooperation, empathy and collective wellbeing' (Benería 2003: 76; see Ferber and Nelson 1993; Folbre 1994; Himmelweit 2000).

These debates also generated important insights into the ways in which unpaid labour was either omitted from or underestimated in national and international accounting systems. The problem was identified in the definition of 'work' that prevailed in both accounting practices and capitalist economic systems, which rested on an idea of remuneration and thus excluded unpaid work. As Marilyn Waring (1988) argued in her early and forceful statements to this effect, the failure to count unpaid work underpinned prevailing structures of gender inequality and contributed to the perpetuation of inadequate development strategies – a critique which was developed in insightful ways throughout the 1990s and beyond (Hoskyns and Rai 2007).

Environmental Approaches

Environmental approaches emerged as critiques of the view of the relationship between environment and development that had prevailed in post-war growth and modernisation theories, as well as neoliberal approaches. In these views, as in nineteenth-century development theories, natural resources were not considered to pose obstacles to economic growth and there was a general optimism that technical solutions would be found that allowed human beings to 'harness nature on an ever-larger scale' (Woodhouse 2002: 141). Critical counterpoints to this orthodoxy were advanced, notably by Karl Polanyi, who integrated questions of the natural environment into his seminal critique of the processes of commodification that were intrinsic to capitalist development. As early as 1944, he warned presciently that such processes would mean ultimately that 'nature would be reduced to its elements, neighbourhoods and landscapes defiled, rivers polluted, military safety jeopardised [and] the power to produce food and raw materials destroyed' (Polanyi 1944: 73). Yet a technological triumphalism defined the mood on both sides of the Cold War over the post-war period, and it was not until the early 1970s that debates about environment and development began to achieve some visibility.

The most significant stimulus to these debates was the publication in 1972 of a report commissioned by the Club of Rome, entitled *Limits to Growth* (Meadows et al. 1972). The report constituted a doom-laden critique of the emphasis on growth as the foundation of development, taking particular issue with the notions that economic growth could continue unabated and was consistent with the goals of sustainable human development. Its authors, alongside others of a 'catastrophist' persuasion (such as Erlich and Erlich 1970; Erlich 1972), advanced the arresting argument that the limits to growth could in fact be reached within the next century if trends in population growth, industrialisation, food production, natural resource depletion and environmental degradation continued. The arguments about how the collapse of human life could be avoided – namely, that material consumption levels needed to be reduced drastically and production techniques completely transformed – had become very familiar by the 1990s. But at the time they were greeted with no small degree of hostility. The sceptics asserted a continued faith in technological progress to increase efficiency in the extraction and consumption of natural resources and therefore to reduce prices for these commodities in world markets. A vehement (and equally catastrophist) defence of economic growth was also put forward: without it, according to one commentator, all the world could hope to see was 'continued poverty, deprivation, disease, squalor, degradation and slavery to soul-destroying toil for countless millions of the world's population' (Beckerman 1974: 9).

It was not until the mid 1980s that the scientific case for concern about the environmental consequences of growth became more firmly established – concretely, when it was verified that a hole was appearing in the ozone layer above the Antarctic, and that this was related directly to non-natural chemical emissions and modern consumption habits (Woodhouse 2002). These scientific discoveries were reinforced in the 1990s by work which indicated that resource depletion had occurred at a faster rate than had been anticipated in the 1970s (Meadows et al. 1992). The linkages between environment and development thus became a matter of global concern and moved belatedly, along with poverty and gender, to the centre of global development debates.

These environmental approaches, like others under the alternative heading, set out a critique of neoliberal theories which rested on various objections. The first related, as in other approaches, to their omission of non-economic factors from systematic consideration, and alluded to the highly utilitarian manner in which the natural environment was integrated into neoliberal understandings of development, where natural resources were identified as providing 'services' for production, the sustaining of life and aesthetic appeal. Natural resources were in this sense treated, in highly misleading ways, as a form of natural capital which could be accumulated or depleted in the same ways as other forms of capital (Woodhouse 2002: 143).

Second, and related, the focus in neoclassical economics on individual preferences was seen to lead to significant problems for this approach in aggregating those preferences into a collective valuing of the natural environment. It consequently becomes 'impossible to weigh the value that a society puts on the production and consumption of goods and services that damage the environment . . . vis-à-vis the value that society puts on environmental conservation' (Brohman 1995: 309). Parallel problems emerge in the core assumption of environmental economics, namely, that the depletion of resources is measurable in market prices. Conservation of a resource is presumed to result from the fact that scarcity will be reflected in increasing prices and therefore decreasing demand (Pearce et al. 1990; Dietz and van der Stratten 1992; Woodhouse 2002). The question of how both environmental costs *and* the benefits of human development can be expressed in market prices is thus one of the core problems which, critics argued, was not fully acknowledged in neoliberal approaches. To these problems we need to add another, which Garrett Hardin influentially identified in 1968 as the 'tragedy of the commons'. Natural resources which are not subject to private ownership do not carry market value, and are therefore rendered meaningless and value-less. The result is a lack of economic incentives for conservation and sustainable resource management; instead, there occurs a collective over-exploitation of these 'commons', such as the atmosphere, and consequently their degradation to the point of collapse or elimination (Hardin 1968). Without recourse to notions of private property and market value, exponents of neoliberal approaches are left floundering for politically feasible or effective ways of managing natural resources – a floundering which has been evident throughout the history of global environmental negotiations on such matters as air pollution, climate change and global warming.

Third, as in the case of unpaid work, environmental concerns were normally excluded from standard accounting practices which are based on measurements of market transactions. No account is taken of the kinds of depreciation that emerge from environmental degradation and the costs of natural resource exploitation (Helleiner 1989), not only in terms of physical damage and the limits that the costs of rectification imply for *future* growth, but also in matters of health or the destruction of livelihoods – that is, in terms of sustainable human development. In similar fashion the treatment of environmental costs as 'externalities' does not favour the elaboration of serious agendas for achieving sustainable human development.

Fourth, in arguments reminiscent of those put forward by GAD theorists, it was objected that neoclassical models entirely neglected the question of inequalities and imbalances of power within and among societies. As a result, 'dominant economic and political groups [are presented with] opportunities to put their individual and short-term interests ahead of the collective and long-term interest of a sustainable social and physical environment' and, besides, 'many poor and otherwise disadvantaged people may be virtually defenceless to prevent environmental damage resulting from pollution and other "diseconomies" generated by others' (Brohman 1995: 311).

Finally, the argument was widely made that neoliberal development agendas and environmental agendas alike tended to be imposed by the 'North' on the 'South' (Brohman 1995: 312). The question was whether an agenda driven by the North is or could be sufficiently sensitive and appropriate to the needs of human development in the 'South'. Indeed, global environmental negotiations were characterised by a very strong 'North–South' dimension as they evolved from the 1970s onwards (Williams 1993), even while it could be argued that the global environmental agenda unfolded 'on an ideological playing field that has been markedly more level' than in some other arenas of global politics, such as trade and finance (Payne 2005a: 228).

Environmental critiques of mainstream development theory thus gained ground in tandem with the basic needs, human development and gender critiques. Indeed, they took sustenance from debates in these other areas, particularly those relating to hunger, famine and food security (Sen 1981; Drèze and Sen 1989), and the need to ensure greater access to ownership of land and resources in the interests of conservation and sustainability. Likewise, by the end of the 1980s, environmental issues had also been incorporated squarely into the discourse of development practice, clothed in the concept of 'sustainable development'. The term, while not new in itself, entered into common parlance following the publication of a landmark report by the Brundtland Commission, *Our Common Future*, which was presented to the UN General Assembly in 1987. In that report sustainable development was defined famously as 'development that meets the needs of the present without compromising the ability of future generations to meet their own needs' (World Commission on Environment and Development 1987). To this end, the Commission called ambitiously for a reorientation of economic activity and development strategy to focus on human development and the needs of the poor, noting that unequal distribution of and access to resources, as well as vastly unequal patterns of resource consumption, contributed to both the perpetuation of poverty and the steady destruction of the global environment. As such, the Commission described sustainable development as 'contain[ing] within it two concepts: the concept of "needs", in particular the essential needs of the world's poor, to which overriding priority should be given; and the idea of limitations imposed by the state of technology and social organization in the environment's ability to meet present and future needs' (World Commission on Environment and Development 1987: 43). It is thus clear once again how the threads of the various alternative approaches were woven together as they were gradually, albeit partially and selectively, integrated into mainstream development thinking. The sustainable development agenda was endorsed formally by political leaders at the United Nations Conference on Environment and Development – the so-called 'Earth Summit' – held in Rio de Janeiro in 1992.

The concept of sustainable development inevitably attracted attention because of its growing prominence in global environmental and development debates. Echoing the critiques that emerged around the concept of human development, some of the most strident criticisms concerned the extent to which sustainable development could be seen as a significant, critical intervention in development theory. This was a reaction at least in part to its incorporation by the mainstream, as Bill Adams suggested in his contention that '[i]t is far from clear whether sustainable development offers a new paradigm, or simply a green wash over business-as-usual' (Adams 1993: 207). Critics had a point: the concept was elaborated and deployed not as a theoretical contribution to the study of development, but rather as a strikingly loose and accommodating concept which enabled the assertion of the value of integrating environmental concerns into the development agenda. In one view, sustainable development was thus nothing more than 'a fashionable phrase that everyone pays homage to but nobody can define' (Lélé 1991: 607). Its defenders did not disagree that the concept of sustainable development was vague and amorphous, although they exchanged these pejorative terms for others such as 'flexible' or 'open-textured' (Redclift 1987; Meadowcroft 2000). But they argued forcefully that these characteristics accounted precisely for its strength. Sustainable development was not intended to be 'either a logical construct or an operational maxim – but rather . . . a potentially unifying political metanarrative, with a suggestive normative core' (Meadowcroft 2000: 373). Moreover, it was precisely because of its connections with an overarching concern with human development that the concept could be said to constitute a serious contribution to development theory.

A further criticism of the approach set out in the Brundtland report was that it did not depart significantly from a focus on economic growth. It made all the right noises in terms of recognising that environmental issues were fundamentally issues of social relations and social practices, and that an environmental agenda was about enabling human development. But in reality it adopted the position we noted earlier in respect of the human development approach: growth was not abandoned as the overarching goal, rather the task was to render it compatible with other, broader goals. The more radical 'zero-growth' environmentalist approach was consequently not tolerated; indeed, it was the bypassing of these more radical interventions and the unwillingness to stray too far from mainstream terrain that ensured some of the success of the sustainable development agenda (Adams 1993). There was consequently no sense in which that agenda could be thought of as a genuinely alternative approach to development of the sort many would have liked to see. Instead, as with those of the human development approach, its insights were integrated selectively into the mainstream and served precisely to strengthen the latter's claim to legitimacy.

The sustainable development agenda was nevertheless assaulted systematically from a variety of radical quarters. These were loosely drawn together in an advocacy of local and participatory forms of environmental politics, and strongly connected with a broader approach which rejected not only a growth-led development agenda but, more broadly, the entire post-war 'project' of development. Such approaches have generally been grouped under the banner of 'post-development', and it is to these that we turn our attention in the final section of this chapter.

'Post-development' Approaches

> The idea of development stands like a ruin in the intellectual landscape. Delusion and disappointment, failures and crimes have been the steady companions of development and they tell a common story: it did not work. Moreover, the historical conditions which catapulted the idea into prominence have vanished: development has become outdated. But above all, the hopes and desires that made the idea fly are now exhausted: development has grown obsolete. (Sachs 1992: 1)

This often-quoted passage from Wolfgang Sachs offers a succinct statement of the starting point for post-development approaches. Over the 1980s and 1990s post-development evolved as a flag under which many ships were able to sail, setting off from a variety of intellectual ports. Post-development thinking featured strong debts to postmodernist and postcolonial thought, as well as social movements theory, and coalesced with radical ecological and feminist thinking to put forward a rejection of development theory in both its orthodox and its alternative guises.

The foundational contentions of post-development theory can be summarised as follows. First, the 'idea' of development was a political meta-narrative which constituted a Western project of intervention and reflected the interests of its practitioners. Development was seen to have become intimately connected with modernisation and a discourse of modernity and had been elaborated concretely as a project for extending Western control over the developing world. In influential work in this vein, Arturo Escobar (1992, 1995) traced and deconstructed the 'historically produced discourse' of development from the administration of US President Harry S. Truman onwards. In a similar vein to Edward Said's (1978) critique of 'Orientalism', Escobar understood development as constituting 'a mechanism for the production and management of the Third World' and 'organising the production of truth about the Third World' (Escobar 1992: 413–14). Such a strategy necessitated the professionalisation and institutionalisation of development and the proliferation of development 'experts', both in universities and in the web of international organisations devoted to the project of development. The project that emerged promoted a fundamentally modernist idea of development and privileged modernisation and production over traditional modes of social organisation. The result, for Escobar and other exponents of post-development, was the gamut of ills and evils associated with 'Westernisation': environmental destruction; a dehumanising experience of development for much of the world's population; and the continual reproduction of neo-imperialist, neo-colonialist and patriarchal structures of domination and exploitation (Constantino 1985; Friberg and Hettne 1985; Mies 1986; Shiva 1988; Kothari 1988; Ferguson 1990;

Alvares 1992; Cowen and Shenton 1996; Kothari 2005). As John Rapley described the position, '[a]ny improvements in living standards that follow from these [development] projects are epiphenomenal, even accidental, to the principal goal of building hegemony' (Rapley 2004: 351).

Second, post-development accounts rested on the contention that the post-war development project had been a failure of arresting proportions – a 'Frankenstein-type dream' (Escobar 1992: 419) – which revealed the economic, ecological and social impossibility of achieving middle-class living standards for the whole of the world's population (Dasgupta 1985; Andreasson 2005). For Gilbert Rist (1997), development had become akin to a religious faith to which its exponents and practitioners clung, regardless of the evidence all around them of vast inequalities, worsening poverty, environmental destruction and food crises. In the often-quoted words of Gustavo Esteva:

> [I]f you live in Mexico City today, you are either rich or numb if you fail to notice that development stinks ... The time has come to recognize development itself as the malignant myth whose pursuit threatens these among whom I live in Mexico ... [T]he 'three development decades' were a huge, irresponsible experiment that, in the experience of a world-majority, failed miserably. (Esteva 1985: 78)

Third, it was argued that the break with development must consequently come in the form of a 'different regime of truth and perception' (Escobar 1992: 414) and a new paradigm that would change the ways development was conceived (Rist 1997). Such a break would spring from 'localized, pluralistic grassroots movements' to constitute a radical challenge to imperialist, capitalist development (Escobar 1992: 431). The arguments to this effect were varied in their degree of radical traditionalism, but the dominant contention was that a 'development studies worth its salt should reflect on alternative accounts of the good life, and should not dismiss out of hand the claim that a good life is best lived locally, in contact with the soil, and in accord with Gandhian notions of beauty, fragility and simplicity' (Corbridge 1998: 139). The anti-modern discourse went on to reject forms of imperialist universalism that must be resisted in favour of 'traditional', 'local' cultural values (Esteva and Prakash 1998).

It is perhaps not surprising that post-development theory encountered a welter of criticism. Many found it to be not just a muddled and unhelpful intervention, but also unpalatable in its dogmatism and intolerance. One of the most trenchant critiques was made by Stuart Corbridge in a review of some of the most influential post-development tracts, where he condensed his attack into a pithy and eloquent summary:

> Proponents of post-development . . . often trade in non-sequiturs (the failure of development project A, B or C condemns development in all its manifestations), in unhelpful binaries (Modernity is bad, anti-modernity is good), in false deductions (the problems of poor countries are always and everywhere the result of a surfeit of capitalism or development and not their relative absence), in wobbly romanticism (only the rich get lonely, only the poor live hospitably and harmoniously), in self-righteousness (only the simple life is a good life), or in implausible politics (we can all live like the Mahatma, or would want to). (Corbridge 1998: 139)

Some of these points come together as a critique of the very starting points of post-development. On the one hand, the notion that development had failed was open to question. Could it really be the case that there was no space in a serious analysis of development for a recognition of both the complexity of development theory and the continual processes of contestation and experimentation that development necessarily involved? (Parfitt 2002). Was it really plausible, or indeed rigorous in scholarly terms, to think of, say, Walt Rostow and Robert Wade as cut from the same cloth, and homogenise the tremendously complex landscape of development theory into a single notion of 'development' against which post-development could be pitted? (Corbridge 1998: 145; Pieterse 1998: 363). The irony here is clear: post-development started out from a proposition asserting the impossibility of a single notion of development, but purposefully constructed this single, homogenised notion as the target of its critique. On the other hand, critics questioned the empirical validity of the contention that development had failed, and charged post-development theorists with wilfully ignoring 'the extraordinary accomplishments that have defined the Age of Development', such as unprecedented increases in life expectancy (Corbridge 1998: 145). While many could plausibly point to the failures of development to achieve many desirable goals, it was a leap indeed to allege that development *per se* had failed and stood in need of abandonment. It was also possible to contend that it was in fact an *absence* of development, or the presence of mal-development, that was responsible for persistent ills such as environmental destruction, poverty, food crises or exploitation and inequality (Corbridge 1998).

The perceived convenience in post-development's construction of its target was also evident in the fact that empirical attention was focused on Latin America, Africa and countries like India. Typically, the development experiences of East Asian NICs were entirely omitted. Parallel reservations were raised about the failure to understand the influence on development theory of the East Asian model of political economy or Japanese management and production techniques, or their significance in the panorama of global development (Pieterse 1998). Indeed, what was striking about post-development was its failure to engage carefully with any of the significant debates raging in development studies at the time. The tendency was instead either to ignore them (for some, in an entirely wilful manner) or to mould (for some, distort) them to fit the requirements of the favoured argument. For post-development theorists, development remained a product and project of the imperialist 'West', with no acknowledgement of the problematic nature of this category. The allegation that post-development not only glossed over the complexity of development but also presented a deeply flawed understanding of both development and contemporary political economy was thus seen by many as compelling.

The prescriptions extrapolated from the post-development approach drew equally withering criticisms. In one sense, it was argued that there were no prescriptions: '[t]here is no positive programme; there is critique but no construction' (Pieterse 1998: 366). While critique of development theory and contestation of the development agenda was absolutely warranted, critics contended that there was simply no point in a strategy of lambasting, rejecting and abandoning development without any clear idea about what kind of theory or practice might be put in its place. The prescriptions put forward by exponents of post-development instead constituted what were perceived to be acutely problematic assertions of the superiority of the local, traditional and 'simple' in accounts of the good life that human beings aspired to achieve. The dangers of romanticism at best and so-called 'ethnochauvinism' at worst were invoked in critical responses. In their idealisation of pre-modern communities and lifestyles, post-development approaches were depicted as the 'last refuge of the noble savage' (Kiely 1999), guilty of the absurdity of romanticising the traditional over the modern and blind to the kinds of exclusion, exploitation, abuse and domination that existed in 'traditional' societies quite as much as in modern capitalist ones (Parfitt 2002). Particular scorn was also reserved by Corbridge and others (such as Knippenberg and Schuurman 1994; Parfitt 2002) for the post-development attack on the discourse of human rights on the basis that it represented a Western modernist agenda that was an irrelevant and dangerous imposition on traditional and local values.

Finally, various critics argued that such a misplaced and dangerous idealism entirely misrepresented the complexity of people's lives and motivations. Social movements were recognised as being much more diverse than the sites of radical resistance they were mostly seen to be in idealised post-development understandings. Many movements, and indeed individual people, were clamouring for inclusion and participation in development and greater access to the trappings of a 'Western' lifestyle and the benefits of technology (Corbridge 1998; Pieterse 1998). Development in this view was associated at least in part with human beings' liberation from deprivation and discomfort, as in, for example, the benefits of electricity and heating or cooling technologies. It was also argued, even by sympathisers, that in their advocacy of pre-modern ways of living and dogmatic intolerance of alternatives, the most radical strands of post-development thought were just as authoritarian as they perceived modernist discourses to be (Cowen and Shenton 1996).

Much of this barrage of criticism inevitably took the most populist and traditionalist forms of post-development as its target, but it is important to reiterate that post-development was a label attached to a diverse collection of perspectives and approaches. While huddled together under the same umbrella, the most populist versions were associated more with an 'anti-development' position, but others took up a 'sceptical' position which 'does not deny globalization or modernity, but wants to find some ways of living with it and imaginatively transcending it' (Hoogvelt 2001: 172; Ziai 2004). To be sure, the dividing lines between these perspectives are difficult to draw, and many post-development texts offered a confusing mélange of arguments that could fit either part of this distinction. Their expressions in different parts of the world is perhaps easier to demarcate, especially with the help of Ankie Hoogvelt's (2001) contrasting of the anti-developmentalism of militant Islam and the post-developmentalism of Latin America, the latter being where much of the new thinking originated about social movements and civil society, along with hybrid forms of struggle and experimentations with alternative kinds of social and economic organisation. It is thus, perhaps not surprisingly, in post-development rather than anti-development perspectives that many located the contributions of these radical alternative approaches, particularly in their injection of real critical force into development theory debates and their contestation of the dominant development agenda. It was nevertheless a widely held view by the end of the 1990s that post-development approaches had failed to effect a theoretically cogent intervention in the study of development of the sort that might have dislodged or discomfited the mainstream and other alternative approaches.

Conclusion

It is clear that the clutch of alternative approaches that emerged from the 1970s onwards was too varied in orientation and substance to be thought of as a coherent body of development theory. The label 'alternative' is therefore merely a loose one which signifies, in essence, a group of approaches which sought to challenge the dominant understandings of development and forms of development policy that were consolidated over the post-war period, and from the 1970s onwards in the guise of neoliberalism. At the same time, we have underlined the ways in which insights from many of these approaches came to be incorporated into the neoliberal mainstream, such that, by the end of the 1990s, Jan Nederveen Pieterse could declare that '[t]he difference between mainstream and alternative . . . is a conjunctural difference, not a difference in principle, although it tends to be presented as such. In itself, "alternative" has no more meaning than "new" in advertising' (Pieterse 1998: 349). The more radical strands of post-development critique were never likely to leave much of a mark on mainstream debates inasmuch as, from the perspective of policy implementation and institutional acceptance, radical breaks with convention are much more difficult to effect and, ultimately, attempts to induce them are unlikely to prosper (ul Haq 1995; Pieterse 1998). Indeed, this was deemed to be precisely the reason why alternative development approaches of a radical persuasion were deemed by some, even by the middle of the 1990s, to have 'withered away' (Sanyal 1994).

Yet it would be hasty and unfair to dismiss alternative development approaches as having been subsumed by the mainstream or as having made little impact on development debates. To the contrary, the co-optation of certain perspectives into mainstream discourse was selective and instrumental, and vast swathes of alternative approaches took up and retained critical locations outside the parameters of the scholarly and policy mainstream. Influence is, in any case, not the same thing as co-optation, and it was perhaps the failing of more radical approaches to have conflated the two. Notwithstanding the diversity of the alternative theories surveyed in this chapter, it can be said that what they had collectively contributed by the end of the 1990s were extensive and provocative investigations into the full gamut of the forms, structures and politics of inequality within nations and between individuals and groups in societies. Questions of inequality had been placed squarely at the centre of development theory, altering in fundamental ways the terrain on which development debates had henceforth to be conducted.

6
Contemporary Theoretical Directions

The task in this final chapter is to bring our charting of development theories up to date and to consider some of the key contemporary directions in development debates. In Chapters 4 and 5 we broke off the story around the end of the 1990s, using the outbreak of the Asian financial crises as a rough point at which to signal the onset of what will be identified in this chapter as the 'contemporary' period. However, it will be apparent that this is only a very loose dividing device and, indeed, that it applies more naturally to the debate between neoliberalism and neostatism surveyed in Chapter 4 than to the alternative approaches discussed in Chapter 5.

To specify the end of the 1990s as an approximate cut-off point is not to suggest that any of the existing debates died away at that time; indeed, they continue to be central to the landscape of development theory and have evolved in important ways since the start of the twenty-first century. Yet the end of the 1990s can be taken as representing a juncture of sorts in the evolution of development debates. The collapse of the Asian 'miracle' economies and others around the world signalled a new direction in the debate between neoliberals and neostatists about the roles of markets, states and institutions in development processes. The theoretical and policy implications of the (re-)emergence in the world economy of China and other countries, such as India, began centrally to preoccupy students of development around this time. The ongoing traditions underpinning human development approaches were also evident in an acceleration of debates about poverty and inequality and their increasing centrality to development theory and practice. We also began to see the crystallisation of innovative frameworks which unfolded over the 1990s in order to capture in a theoretically sophisticated manner the 'globalised' or 'transnationalised' nature of development. Taken together, we consider these themes to constitute the major areas of contemporary debate in development theory, and will explore each of them in turn in what follows.

Neoliberalism: From the Washington Consensus to the Post-Washington Consensus

We addressed some of the reaction from both orthodox and neostatist quarters to the Asian financial crises towards the end of Chapter 4. While some critics had called attention to the deficiencies of the Washington consensus even in the mid 1990s (Krugman 1995), it was the collapse of economies across Asia in the late 1990s and the contagion which spread to Russia, Latin America and elsewhere that marked the demise of the consensus as the dominant framework for neoliberal development strategy. Many economists of formerly orthodox ilk came to be trenchantly critical of the failures of market reforms across the world, as well as of the IMF's handling of the financial crises. For instance, Jeffrey Sachs, the Harvard economist who was once an arch proponent of the 'shock therapy' reform agendas previously pressed upon a wide range of governments, particularly in Russia and eastern Europe, attacked the IMF for pursuing policies which turned liquidity crises into full-blown financial panics, and for having in effect 'screamed fire in the theatre' (Sachs 1998: 17). Still further cracks in the edifice of the neoliberal development consensus were introduced by the rift that manifestly opened up between the key IFIs – the World Bank and the IMF – in relation to how precisely to respond to the Asian and other financial crises.

In short, by the end of the 1990s the development consensus and the institutions which were central to its propagation were under severe strain, and discussion was well underway about what might take its and their place. The question of what to do with the IMF formed part of a wider debate about global financial markets and the need for reform of the 'international financial architecture'. This debate yielded rather little in the way of either agreement or concrete reform, and by the late 2000s it was not clear that much had been put in place that resembled a 'new' international financial architecture. Indeed, some argued that the agenda resembled nothing other than a reinvention of the Washington consensus (Soederberg 2001, 2002). By contrast, the question of how to reframe development thinking was 'resolved' reasonably quickly, at least in the minds of the neoliberal development community and those economists, some of whom we have already mentioned, who had come to position themselves just outside its boundaries as critical 'insider–outsider' voices. By far the most influential of these was the Nobel prize-winning economist Joseph Stiglitz, who served as the Chief Economist at the World Bank between 1996 and 1999 before being effectively dismissed from that post for his nonconformity with the orthodox tenets of the development thinking espoused by the Bank at that time. Stiglitz's public critique of the neoliberal (Washington) consensus was both damning in its substance and overtly ambitious in its ensuing recommendations. The failings of the Washington consensus were presented in catalogue form:

> That consensus all too often confused means with ends: it took privatization and trade liberalization as ends in themselves, rather than as means to more sustainable, equitable, and democratic growth ... It focused too much on price stability, rather than growth and the stability of output. It failed to recognize that strengthening financial institutions is every bit as important to economic stability as controlling budget deficits and increasingly the money supply. It focused on privatization, but paid too little attention to the institutional infrastructure that is required to make markets work, and especially to the importance of competition. (Stiglitz 1998a: 1)

The list went on. What was needed was nothing less than a 'new paradigm for development', to be found, in Stiglitz's view (1998b, 2001), in what he identified as the movement towards a 'post-Washington consensus' (PWC).

What was striking about the PWC was the way in which it stole at least some of the thunder of the neostatists. At its core was a statement of the importance of both micro-economic and macroeconomic interventions in economies in order to compensate for market failures and imperfections, and the centrality of institutions and regulation for this purpose. The foundations for such a statement had already been laid in parts of the thinking emanating from the World Bank from the early 1990s onwards, specifically in its preoccupation with 'governance' as a new framework for development thinking. But the movement away from the early, 'fundamentalist' versions of the neoliberal orthodoxy, and the concerted accommodation of questions of states and institutions at the centre of the dominant development agenda, was given decisive impetus in the rubric of the PWC. The PWC also purported to represent a 'development strategy [which] outlines an approach to the transformation of society' in which all aspects of society (including the state, the private sector, the family, community and individual) needed to be incorporated; it gave precedence to a focus on sustainable and equitable development; it developed the new 'buzzwords' of capacity-building, governance, participation, transparency, civil society, and so on, placing much greater emphasis on democratic governance than its predecessor; and it advocated reform of the IFIs and the 'global governance' of development. It also called for a greater degree of 'ownership' for developing countries of the development policies they pursued, and a correspondingly 'greater degree of humility' on the part of the international financial institutions – an acknowledgement that they 'do not have all the answers' (Stiglitz 1998b: 15).

The ambition of these early statements of the PWC is evident. But its contribution to development thinking attracted controversy. Of the very wide-ranging criticisms that were made, three stood out. First, Stiglitz's 'new development paradigm' was seen by many to be nothing of the sort. As observers like Guy Standing (2000) pointed out, the PWC failed adequately to acknowledge that such a critique had existed all along, and to incorporate any of the insights or 'nuances' generated by these longstanding debates. The 'discovery' of states and institutions was a case in point – the relevant debates and insights were not only those advanced by the neostatists concerned with East Asian development, but, as we have seen, reached well back into older phases of development theory.

Moreover, the PWC was seen not to represent any kind of significant departure from its predecessor. A jazzy new packaging did not conceal the way in which the PWC left intact the core of the Washington consensus. Jonathan Perraton (2005), for instance, observed that the only dimensions of the Washington consensus Stiglitz questioned related to capital account liberalisation, fiscal discipline and interest rates; Dani Rodrik (2002) dismissed the PWC as nothing more than an 'augmented Washington Consensus'. Certainly, the intellectual foundations of the PWC remained faithful to neoclassical economics and, as Ben Fine observed, the PWC itself retained a striking degree of 'intellectual narrowness and reductionism' in the way it simply, and problematically, replaced 'an understanding of the economy as relying harmoniously on the market by an understanding of society as a whole based on (informational) market imperfections' (Fine 2001a: 4). In a further step, praised by some as an important contribution (Önis and Şenses 2005), Stiglitz called attention to the ways in which markets and market-like mechanisms (particularly public–private competition and incentives structures) were important for the functioning of states, inverting the more common insistence on the importance of states in ensuring the effective functioning of markets. In PWC thinking, theories of both society and state thus rested on the extension of theories of the market.

Second, the PWC was perceived to suffer from its close association with a concept which had seized mainstream economics and social science over the course of the 1990s – that of social capital. The extent of the take-up of this concept across disciplines, in the policy world in general and in the neoliberal development community in particular, was, as many have observed, extraordinary (Harriss and de Renzio 1997; Woolcock 1998; Fine 2001b). By the mid 1990s the

World Bank had adopted the concept fully, echoing other academic and policy communities' identification of social capital as the 'missing link' in development theory, and going so far as to assemble an extensive website on the matter. Available definitions of social capital are unhelpfully plentiful, ranging from the resources relating to networks of social relations (Bourdieu 1980), levels of 'trust' between individuals in society (Coleman 1988), shared moral values (Fukuyama 1995), and the stocks of trust, norms and networks that allow people to solve common problems (Putnam 1993; see Schuurman 2003). The applications of the concept have been equally bewildering in their variety, social capital being the key variable in explaining situations as diverse as institutional underdevelopment, incidence of crime, propensity to migrate and vulnerability to dental disorders. Social capital is, for Fine, a 'totally chaotic concept, drawing its meanings from the more or less abstract studies or tidal wave of case studies on which it depends' (Fine 1999: 8). It can refer to anything at all, with 'the only proviso . . . that [it] should be attached to the economy in a functionally positive way for economic performance, especially growth' (Fine 1999: 5).

At the same time, as is often the case, its ambiguity has been one of its great attractions. The proponents of the PWC found in social capital a malleable concept which did not require any departures from the mainstream of neoclassical economics and provided an extremely convenient means of legitimising business-as-usual by attaching a notion of social imperfections to market imperfections, the former constituting both an explanation of and a remedy for the latter. Social capital in this sense represented the 'exact social and political counterpart' to Stiglitz's prospectus for a post-Washington economic consensus (Fine 1999: 10), and one which has been deemed to contribute centrally to the World Bank's project of 'depoliticising development' (Harriss 2002). Recalling our discussion in Chapter 4, the concept of social capital was also well suited to the neoliberal project of explaining development failures by reference to endogenous factors. In this scenario, it was the character of societies and social networks, and the nature of human interactions within them, that could be held responsible for the development performance of national economies.

The third deficiency of the PWC replicated the shortcomings of its predecessor: it lacked a sharp grasp of the nature and implications of globalisation and left untouched questions of the global structural and political context within which development strategies were articulated. The focus was instead on issues such as the sequencing of reforms, the means by which capital account liberalisation could be pursued effectively and the risks minimised, and the political, institutional and social requirements for effective reform and improved economic performance – all issues of domestic reform which were given clear priority over issues of global reform. Stiglitz and others did call attention to the problems of the international financial architecture and the apparent hazards of global financial liberalisation, but these concerns with financial flows were addressed in isolation from other dimensions of globalisation. This move to de-link trade from financial liberalisation, and then to distinguish between short-term and long-term capital flows as, respectively, potentially destabilising and highly desirable, was calculated in order to contain any possible backlash against globalisation (Gore 2000). The bigger, critical questions about development in the contemporary global economy, which the crises in effect put on the table, were thus avoided.

What we have in the PWC is therefore the expression of the (partial) co-optation and (selective) incorporation of insights from the approaches we reviewed in the two previous chapters. It is here that we see for the first time the full panoply of 'new' concerns not just with institutions, but also with 'human' development issues, living standards, sustainability, equity and equality, society, families, communities, participation, and so on. We may rightly say that the PWC represented a more humane approach to development than its neoliberal forerunners, and that its incorporation of many of these concerns and insights should be welcomed, notwithstanding the manifestly chaotic way in which they were thrown together. Yet the movement away from fundamentalist versions of neoliberal development theory must be understood as effected precisely in order to preserve the core principles of the neoliberal approach, rehabilitating it through a new obeisance to such factors as states, institutions, politics, the 'social', and so on, and attempting thus to ensure that the dominance of neoliberal development thinking was not mortally threatened by either the Asian crises or its association with the unpopular Washington consensus.

It was unsuccessful in doing so. Part of the reason for this can be found in the fracturing of a 'Western' consensus on development, for the first time since 1945, as a consequence of the particular approach to linking development with security and foreign policy strategies staked out by the administration of George W. Bush from 2001 onwards (Payne 2005a). But mostly it related to the deficiencies of the neoliberal approach itself, which were not convincingly addressed by the elaboration of a PWC. It is in this sense that we can see other areas of development theory as having advanced and evolved in much more dynamic ways than has the neoliberal mainstream since the late 1990s.

China and the Rise of the 'East'

As we saw in Chapter 4, the dust from the Asian financial crises settled more in favour of the neoliberal orthodoxy than the neostatist approach. The key debate among neostatist theorists came to revolve around whether neoliberalism was indisputably taking hold of the East Asian region by the early 2000s, displacing the developmental state model and initiating a march towards market reforms and neoliberal regulatory states, or whether the model was simply undergoing a period of transition, marked by important continuities in policy orientation if not institutional design. Few were willing to bow to the neoliberal contention that the financial crises had marked the end of a distinctive East Asian model, and continued to seek amidst the welter of market reforms that were pursued in the region evidence with which to discern the contours of a development model that could still be differentiated from the neoliberal orthodoxy and labelled 'East Asian'. For some, this involved a search for a sort of 'post-crisis paradigm' for the region, described in terms of a 'middle way' between the neoliberal and developmental state models (Park 2006), indicating perhaps a perceived necessity of calling a truce of sorts between neoliberal and neostatist perspectives.

Nevertheless, the role of Asian political economy as the thorn in the side of neoliberal orthodoxy was not relinquished. By the early 2000s, the force of the challenge emanated less from Japan and the NICs than from the spectacular growth of the Chinese and Indian economies since the late 1970s, accompanied by strong trends in some other parts of the region (see Nolan 2004a, 2004b; Winters and Yusuf 2007; Panagariya 2008). In one formulation, these dynamic emerging Asian economies were referred to collectively as the 'Asian drivers' (Kaplinsky 2006; IDS Asian Drivers Team 2006), pointing to their emergence as national and regional economies of considerable size and significance in the global economy. Yet, while the NICs could relatively comfortably be grouped together in earlier debates, the customary conflation of China and India, especially in popular debate and as reflected in the dreadfully jingoistic label 'Chindia', is very much less apposite. What unites China and India is their spectacular growth rates: in the case of China, average annual GDP growth of 9.5 per cent since the mid 1980s, and 10.7 per cent in 2006 (World Bank 2007); in the case of India, 6 per cent since the late 1980s, and 8.6 per cent in the 2003–7 period (Panagariya 2008). Equally, the political economies of both countries were marked by autarchic trade and investment policies until the late 1980s, with liberalisation processes initiated from that time. Beyond this, the comparison becomes stretched, not least in terms of the political systems which prevail in each country, the nature and extent of liberalisation that has taken place, and trends in poverty and inequality levels.

Notwithstanding the hazards of conflation, the questions posed by the emergence of China and India for the theorist of development are pressing. Are we witnessing the emergence of a new model of development of global significance? To what extent does the emergence of China represent a challenge to the ideological dominance of neoliberalism? And what does the emergence of China and India mean for development theory in general? In many respects it is still too early to be able to make pronouncements on any of these questions with full confidence. But we still need to consider each of them in order at least to sketch the contours of the emerging debate.

In relation to the first question, much was made in the early 2000s of the potential appeal of the Chinese experience as a model for the rest of world, and especially the countries of Africa and Latin America. The fact that extraordinary growth levels had been achieved without conformity to the neoliberal consensus led some to imagine that the rise of China could be translated as a 'model' which other countries and regions might adopt, especially given the widespread disenchantment with neoliberalism that had taken hold by the end of the 1990s. The boldest statement of such an argument was made by Joshua Ramo (2004) in his elaboration of what he called the 'Beijing consensus', self-consciously claiming with this title the same 'globalist' pretensions of the Washington consensus and other 'Western' development frameworks. In the substance of the 'Beijing consensus' one finds much that echoes not only theories of East Asian development but also the tenets of older 'catch-up' theories. First, the model 'reposition[ed] the value of innovation', prioritising 'bleeding-edge' innovation (fibre optics) over the sorts of 'trailing-edge' innovation (copper wires) that orthodox development theory deemed to be the starting point for catch-up processes. Second, it echoed some of the core arguments of human development theories, looking 'beyond' indicators such as per capita GDP to put in place a form of 'balanced development' which emphasised 'sustainability and equality' over luxuries. Third, it rested on a 'theory of self-determination' and 'the use of leverage to move big, hegemonic powers which might be tempted to tread on your toes' (Ramo 2004: 27). Ramo saw a model with considerable 'intellectual charisma', which was undoubtedly generating admiring attention from parts of Latin America and Africa.

But it became clear that the 'Beijing consensus' construct was something of a flash in the pan. It did not take hold with the force or durability of the other development consensuses that had emerged over the preceding decades, to the extent that by the late 2000s it had largely disappeared from development debates. Part of the reason for this relates to the difficulty with which a Chinese 'model' could possibly be exported to other countries, particularly in Latin America and Africa. At even a very basic level, both its political characteristics (a strong, controlling central state, with an

authoritarian socialist government) and its economic foundations (massive reserves, a huge ratio of investment to GDP)
are quite simply non-existent in those two regions, or indeed
elsewhere in the world. Thus, as a template for development
strategy, the contours of the Chinese experience can more
surely be seen as historically unique and not amenable to
replication, much like the East Asian developmental state in
its day.

The real significance of the rise of China has lain instead
in its forceful challenge to universalising theories of development and the neoliberal penchant for 'one-size-fits-all' development strategies. What Hubert Schmitz calls the 'find your
own way' strand of development studies (Schmitz 2007: 55)
– the notion that paths to development can be multiple and
are necessarily contingent – undoubtedly has received a boost
from the rise of China, India and the 'East' in general. The
ideological appeal of China's development experience derives
from precisely this challenge, coinciding as it has with political rejections in Latin America and elsewhere of universalist
policy impositions. Yet, clearly, the nature of this challenge
in itself militates against the universalisation of the Chinese
development strategy or its depiction as the foundation of an
emerging global consensus.

The second question of the extent to which the rise of
China and the 'East' has constituted a challenge to neoliberalism needs to be explored in two ways. First, the political
economy of Chinese development flies in the face of much
liberal and neoliberal development theory: the financial sector
remains tightly regulated and has not been significantly lib-
eralised; central and local governments have retained tight
control over the economic opening process and its political
implications; and economic opening has not been accompanied by political democratisation. Indeed, much scholarly
effort has been expended in trying to come to terms theoretically with the relationship between the market-oriented
economic strategy and the persistence of authoritarian socialist government, and to find appropriate labels for it. It is in
this sense that 'the most successful case of economic development in human history' (*Newsweek*, 6 March 2006, cited
in Schmitz 2007: 51) has been premised on theoretical and
policy foundations that are visibly at odds with the orthodox

development consensus. The challenge to contemporary versions of neoliberalism is thus potentially devastating.

Yet this does not mean that liberal theory should be deemed irrelevant. To the contrary, the rise of China has been interpreted as prompting a valuable re-reading of the ideas of Adam Smith. Giovanni Arrighi sees particular value in Smith's understanding of the kind of non-capitalist market economy which China represented before its incorporation into the European system of states in the sixteenth century, and which it 'might well become again in the twenty-first century under totally different domestic and world-historical conditions' (Arrighi 2007: 8). He goes on to make the provocative argument that the success of Chinese economic development and the implosion of the 'Western superiority of force', as a result of the failure of the US Project for a New American Century, 'have made the realization of Smith's vision of a world-market society based on greater equality among the world's civilizations more likely than it ever was in the almost two and a half centuries since the publication of *The Wealth of Nations*' (Arrighi 2007: 8–9). If this is so – and the argument is in many respects compelling – then the implications for the story of development theory which we have charted here are clearly of the highest significance and interest.

Second, the question of the challenge to neoliberalism has empirical dimensions. These relate to the ways in which, on the one hand, Chinese engagement in Africa and Latin America can be seen to be challenging the foothold of neoliberalism in those regions, and, on the other, China's participation in the institutions of global governance can be seen as altering the established rules of the game. Much attention has been devoted to China's incursions into other developing regions in its quest for the energy and other natural resources needed to sustain its industrialisation process. Africa has been the primary arena for these strategies, yielding vastly enhanced trade and investment links, and also substantial aid and development assistance (Tull 2006; Taylor 2006; Alden 2007). The relationship with Latin America has been more limited, but nevertheless significant for the speed of its growth, especially in the context of the traditional dominance of the United States in that region (Wise and Quiliconi 2007; Jenkins et al. 2008; Roett and Paz 2008; Phillips 2010). Particular attention has been directed to the implications of the Chinese regime's lack of concern for political issues in its trade, investment and aid strategies. Especially in the African case, Chinese loans have been designed explicitly to enable countries to avoid IMF conditionality, undoing Western development policy in order to gain a foothold in resource-rich regions (Gu et al. 2008). Equally, while not constituting a direct challenge to Western dominance of the WTO and the IFIs, China has been emerging over the 2000s as a significant actor in global governance, with the possibility that this participation in the future may act to fundamentally alter the rules of the game (Gu et al. 2008).

There are nevertheless critical questions to be asked about the consequences of the rise of China for development in regions like Latin America and Africa. While the opportunities for some resource-rich countries have been considerable, they carry the prospects of entrenching a development model based on Ricardian notions of comparative advantage and a reliance on resources and commodities for export. As we have seen, such a development strategy was roundly challenged by the East Asian NICs' industrialisation strategies from the 1960s onwards, based on what Chang called 'defying the market' (Chang 2007: 212). Its perpetuation in parts of Africa and Latin America holds out the prospect that many economies and sectors will remain situated in the lowest value-added niches of global production and trade systems. Equally, for other countries which established development strategies based on low-cost, export-oriented manufacturing in the 1970s and 1980s (such as Mexico and parts of Central America, the Caribbean and sub-Saharan Africa), the threat from the emergence of China has been profound to the extent that available 'development space' has been visibly squeezed (Mesquita Moreira 2006; Kaplinsky and Morris 2008; Phillips 2009a). Thus, even if it can be said that the rise of China and the 'East' challenges neoliberalism as the dominant development paradigm, it is questionable whether this should invite optimism about the development prospects of the African and Latin American regions.

What, then, can we say of the implications of all of this for development theory in general? The first point to make is obvious: these trends provide yet further evidence of the irrelevance of the terminology that has traditionally oriented the study of development. The rise of the East Asian NICs eroded the utility of established categories (Third World, developing world, and so on), but the emergence of China, India and other Asian economies has emphatically shut the lid on these terminological coffins. Second, the pretensions of universalising, globalist theories of development have been decisively undermined. Aspirations to replacing the Washington consensus with any other kind of neoliberal development consensus have become implausible, even though neoliberalism remains definitive of the contemporary world order. But theorists of development still have a great deal of work to do, not only in understanding the shifts in global development that are occurring as a result of the rise of these new political economies, but also in figuring out what kinds of theoretical constructs are now needed. Such a task constitutes the agenda for an important emerging strand of development theory.

Approaches to Poverty and Inequality

By the start of the 2000s we were witnessing another sea-change in both scholarly and policy-related development debates. The issues of poverty and inequality had genuinely taken the centre of the stage, reflecting an almost universal accommodation of the proposition that development could not be approached through theoretical lenses or policy frameworks which focused solely on growth. In this context, the central question for a large body of scholarship came to revolve around the relationship between globalisation, poverty and inequality – concretely, whether contemporary global economic and political forces perpetuate and/or increase levels of poverty and inequality across the world and, if so, how. What we see in these debates is thus a rehabilitation of critical enquiry into the nature of globalisation, a well-established preoccupation in earlier strands of development theory, but one which neoclassical economics and the neoliberal mainstream had done much to divert from the 1970s onwards.

The debate has been marked by fierce dispute about definitions and measurements. The most common measurement of 'absolute' poverty – that is, the absence of the basic necessities for human survival – relies on 'purchasing power parity' (PPP). This system calculates what a US dollar could buy at a given point in time, translates this into other currencies, and maps income levels across countries on this basis. The standard categorisation of absolute poverty is the proportion of the population existing on the PPP equivalent of US$1 per day. Using this system, the World Bank published a report in 2002 which traced trends over the 1990s. The main indications were that, while there had been a substantial increase in the number of people living below the PPP$1 per day line (864 million), world population growth over the same period meant that levels of global poverty had in fact fallen – from 27.9 per cent to 21.3 per cent of the world's population living on less than $1 per day, and 61.6 per cent to 52.8 per cent living on less than $2 per day. However, this improvement was almost entirely the result of the strong economic performance of East Asia, in particular China. The population living below the $1 per day poverty line increased significantly in most other parts of the world, and the recorded increase was even greater using the $2 per day measurement (World Bank 2002a; Kaplinsky 2005).

These figures have been challenged from various quarters. Some have contended that they represent a considerable overestimate of global poverty levels (Sala-i-Martin 2002) and others that they may be a substantial underestimate, not least because the PPP$1 per day line is considered absurdly low (Reddy and Pogge 2003; Wade 2004; Reddy 2008). It has nevertheless been conceded that there may be some merit in the argument that the *proportion* of the world's population living in absolute poverty has fallen since the 1980s (Wade 2004: 574). Further questions have been raised about the validity of treating the poor as a homogeneous group and failing to distinguish between 'chronic' poverty, 'transient' poverty and other permutations of the condition (Sen 1981; Hulme and Shepherd 2003).

Measurements of inequality have been beset by similar disagreements, but there has been rather more of a consensus that the trend in global levels of inequality has been sharply upwards, both within and between countries (Wade 2004; Kaplinsky 2005; Milanovic 2005; Edward 2006; Kiely 2007). As in the case of poverty, aggregate data have been shown to be skewed by the inclusion of China and India and measurements which rely on population weighting. It is also clear that the 'positive' influence on the aggregate data of fast incomes growth in these countries has been offset by the sharp increase in inequality *within* them (Wade 2004; Edward 2006). In short, widespread agreement has emerged that contemporary discrepancies among the world's population in income, wealth, living standards, opportunity and 'freedoms' are of grotesque proportions, 'without historical precedent and without conceivable justification – economic, moral or otherwise' (Pieterse 2002: 1024).

The force of the debate has therefore been directed at understanding the dynamics which have produced such an obscene development gap between and within countries. The orthodox view is that poverty is a 'residual' concept and the poor are those who have failed to engage with globalisation (Kaplinsky 2005: 50–1). The case is therefore made for an expansion of globalisation and the elaboration of strategies that will enable its benign forces to reach the world's poor more effectively (World Bank 2002a, 2002b; Dollar and Kraay 2002; Sala-i-Martin 2002). Branko Milanovic offers a pithy summary of this view:

> It is only a slight caricaturization . . . to state that its proponents regard globalization as a *deus ex machina* for many of the problems, such as poverty, illiteracy or inequality, that beset the developing world. The only thing that a country needs to do is to open up its borders, reduce tariff rates, attract foreign capital, and in a few generations if not less, the poor will become rich, the illiterate will learn how to read and write, and inequality will vanish as the poor countries catch up with the rich. (Milanovic 2003: 667)

The thrust of critical arguments has been that poverty is instead a 'relational' phenomenon (Kaplinsky 2005: 51; Bernstein 1990), generated and reinforced by globalisation processes. The task is therefore to understand how exactly this relationship works. The arguments of neoliberal economists have been scrutinised and found wanting, especially in terms of the causal arguments they seek to make in relation to the impact of liberalisation on reductions in poverty and inequality (Wade 2004). Sophisticated studies have gone about showing that, and theorising how, the global forces associated with the reorganisation of production (Kaplinsky 2005), finance (Wade 2006), labour markets (Glyn 2006a), and so on, and the global politics governing all of these arenas (Payne 2005a; Pieterse 2002), have contributed directly to at least a persistence of poverty and a pronounced widening of inequality between and within countries.

Crucially, many such studies note that widening inequality is not necessarily, or not only, the result of an increase in poverty and deprivation; rather, the acceleration and concentration of wealth accumulation in the richest sections of societies across the world has been far greater than any acceleration in the rate of absolute poverty, dramatically widening the gap between rich and poor. These trends are in ample evidence across the so-called developing world, but they are equally in evidence across the developed societies. Put slightly differently, the world's rich benefited disproportionately from global growth over the 1990s and the per capita consumption of the poor increased at only half the average global rate. As Peter Edward concludes, 'growth did help the poor, but it was much better for the rich' (Edward 2006: 1667).

Critical approaches have also injected new normative vigour into the question of why we should care about poverty and, in particular, inequality. The premise of the question responds directly to a neoliberal argument which posits not only the inevitability but also the benefits of inequality within and between societies. Inequality is seen to provide sets of incentives that encourage aspiration, effort and risk taking, and consequently improve efficiency – an argument made famously by Margaret Thatcher in her entreaties to us to 'glory in inequality' (Wade 2004: 582). Inequality is, in this view, a desirable situation, so long as there is equality of opportunity for individual betterment. It is also seen as questionable that inequality in itself should be a cause for moral concern. If a billionaire should move into a middle-class street, the argument goes, economic inequality would worsen dramatically, but nobody would be disadvantaged. There-fore, is it not appropriate to worry more about absolute poverty than inequality? And, if globalisation raises living standards across the board, is it not then irrelevant whether inequality increases as people get richer, so long as the cir-cumstances of the poor are also visibly improved? (Nel 2006).

The difficulties with these arguments will be evident to the student of development. As we know from the insights of human development theory, inequalities of opportunity are precisely the problem. There is no universal entitlement or access to such goods as welfare and education, and, recalling Sen's formulation, no equitable distribution of 'freedoms' or the possibility for achieving them. Second, socioeconomic inequality in most highly unequal countries is tightly attached to sociopolitical inequalities of influence, participation, access to justice, and so on, all skewed heavily towards the economi-cally privileged elites in ways which limit the opportunities and choices available to people in particular sections of society. In this context, inequality becomes not an incentive but a 'trap' that is transmitted down the generations (Nel 2006: 690–1).

Arguments about why we should worry about inequality are also made in instrumental terms: inequality slows economic growth by slowing demand, is associated with higher poverty levels, drives migration, and produces a range of social 'bads', such as crime and violence, corruption, reactionary global movements, and so on (Wade 2004). Increasing inequality between countries also encourages the relocation of capital to labour-rich, low-wage countries such as China, with potentially dramatic consequences for workers and prosperity in affluent parts of the world (Glyn 2006b). A concern with poverty and inequality as moral and ethical issues has resulted in vigorous arguments for framing the issues as fundamental questions of human rights (Pogge 2007, 2008), contrary to the neoliberal concern with the impact of poverty (and its reduction) on the ability of global capitalism to prosper.

How have these debates been reflected in development practice? Reflecting the gradual co-optation of human devel-opment perspectives, poverty became the centrepiece of the global development agenda from the late 1990s onwards. The new agenda was encapsulated in two key policy innovations: the poverty reduction strategy papers (PRSP) approach and the Millennium Development Goals (MDGs). The former was adopted in 1999 as a comprehensive, 'locally-owned' approach to poverty reduction, oriented around three key components: (a) 'promoting opportunity' and pursuing 'pro-poor growth'; (b) 'facilitating empowerment', particularly by promoting 'good governance'; and (c) 'enhancing [human] security', involving such areas as health, education and some-times 'social safety nets' or 'social protection measures' (Craig and Porter 2003: 53–4). They have been widely seen, by sup-porters and detractors, as integral to a PWC-type approach to development. Critiques of the PRSP approach have also echoed directly the critiques of the PWC, depicting it as a 're-morphing of neoliberal approaches, a new convergence in which governments and agencies of various stripes in both liberal OECD and developing countries are focusing on opti-mizing economic, juridical and social governance in order to create ideal conditions for international finance and investment' (Craig and Porter 2003: 54).

The MDGs were in turn announced to great fanfare in September 2000 at a meeting of the world's heads of state. They too put forward a wide-ranging set of concerns, articu-lated as concrete goals, designed to comprise the global devel-opment agenda for the twenty-first century. Of the eight goals – poverty, education, gender equality, child mortality, mater-nal health, HIV/AIDS and other diseases, environment and global partnership – poverty was ostentatiously at the helm. The MDGs have thus been seen by many to be the concrete practical expression of the human development approach as articulated by the UNDP, expanded to embrace also the World Bank's income poverty monitoring measures (Saith 2006; see Fukuda-Parr 2004).

Amidst the profusion of critiques of the MDGs, there are three issues that we should highlight here. The first is that the emphasis fell on absolute poverty, with questions of inequal-ity entirely absent. The reasons for such an 'omission' lie in the profoundly political nature of the issue of inequality. For, as we noted above, inequality is an issue as much about wealth as about poverty and, as such, raises the shadow of questions about distribution and redistribution. The matter of inequality is therefore highly contentious, politically difficult to handle in a global capitalist and neoliberal order, and much less amenable to global political consensus than absolute poverty. The focus on poverty in the MDGs was thus a means of dissipating the political charge of questions about inequality and reducing global development strategy to a set of 'technical' and 'technocratic' issues. In Pieterse's summary, 'the object of concern is not global inequality but global poverty, the instrument of analysis is economic data processing, and the bottom-line remedy is freeing up market forces, now with a human face' (Pieterse 2002: 1033).

Second, the MDG prospectus for global development remained rooted in the rich-country development community – precisely the much-criticised characteristic of the Washington consensus. It was 'a donor-country interpretation of the key issues, for a donor-country audience' (Nelson 2007: 2041). Moreover, the focus on absolute poverty contributed to the perpetuation of the longstanding view that development is about the 'developing world'. The MDGs asserted an apparently benevolent concern for the world's poor, so long as the poor are resident in other, poor countries. This focus diverted the need to address issues of poverty and inequality within the 'developed' countries from which the MDG agenda emanated, or to conceive of poverty and inequality as genuinely 'global' problems.

Finally, unsurprisingly, there was no mention in the MDG framework of those issues relating to globalisation, global politics and unequal power structures that have formed the backbone of many parts of the various poverty and inequality debates. Rather, poverty is emphatically the 'residual' concept that we described earlier, to be eradicated through a global concert of governments and institutions in conjunction with sustained market reforms in the relevant national contexts.

'Global' Theories of Development

Threads from the debates about both the rise of the 'East' and poverty and inequality are woven into the final body of development theory to be considered. We term these approaches 'global', inasmuch as they are concerned directly with the implications of contemporary globalisation for understandings and theories of development. Their various strands are pulled together in the contention that we need to dispense with the two core characteristics of development theory as it has evolved since the mid eighteenth century, namely, its entrenched 'methodological nationalism' and overt state-centrism. The former refers to the tenacious attachment to the nation-state as the primary unit of analysis in the study of development: theory is framed around the assumption that what develops is a country or national economy; the concept of development is strongly 'territorialised'; the relevant statistics are national ones. The latter further highlights the centrality of national states across development theory and practice: states are the agents of development; development strategy is formulated and implemented by states in defined national contexts; the target agents of the global development agenda are national states. For 'global' theories of development, these pervasive and entrenched inclinations have been rendered obsolete by the acceleration of globalisation and the associated reorganisation of the world capitalist system. In short, globalisation has thrown development studies into a 'paradigmatic quagmire' (Robinson 2002: 1047).

For our purposes, the approaches that have evolved in response can best be captured by exploring two key areas of debate. The first is associated with perspectives on the contemporary reorganisation of the global economy driven by changes in the form and strategies of global capital, and specifically with perspectives grouped under the banner of the 'global production network' (GPN) approach to the analysis of economic development. The second is built around a core concern with development as an intrinsically 'social' phenomenon, positing the necessity of conceptualising poverty and inequality through transnational (rather than national) lenses and moving 'from a territorial to a social cartography' of development (Robinson 2002). These areas of enquiry are closely related, are strongly rooted in perspectives drawn from sociology and economic geography, and advance a broad agenda of (re-)theorising development in a manner that responds appropriately to the contemporary juncture in the historical evolution of the global economy.

The GPN approach and its relatives find their intellectual roots in earlier phases of development theory. Over the 1990s a highly influential body of scholarship developed in the form of global commodity chain (GCC) analysis, which took its cue from two theoretical traditions. The first was the version of WST associated with Immanuel Wallerstein, which we encountered in Chapter 3. Wallerstein integrated the concept of a commodity chain into his theoretical work on world systems as an 'analytical device' designed to illuminate further the distribution of surplus value between the core and periphery of the world economy (Heron 2003: 3; see Wallerstein 1974, 1983; Hopkins and Wallerstein 1986). Yet the primary theoretical concerns of WST did not make much of a showing in GCC analysis, despite initial pronouncements that it was intended to breathe new life into this body of theory (Gereffi et al. 1994). Instead, the much greater intellectual debt was to a second body of thought, namely, the 'new international division of labour' (NIDL) school, which was which was mentioned in Chapter 4 as referring to the reorganisation of the global economy that resulted from the shift of productive activities to the 'periphery' and the concomitant restructuring of economic activity in the 'core'. The contribution of GCC analysis was to recognise that empirically observed patterns of global economic reorganisation were much more complex than the NIDL theorists had predicted, and that the centrality of labour costs to the NIDL appeared overstated as a determinant of corporate investment strategies. It also dispensed with the static and discredited categories of core, periphery and semi-periphery associated with both WST and NIDL theory. Instead, its proponents argued that 'capitalism today . . . entails the detailed disaggregation of stages of production and consumption across national boundaries, under the organizational structure of densely networked firms or enterprises' (Gereffi et al. 1994: 1). On this basis, Gary Gereffi and his colleagues set out a definition of GCCs as 'sets of interorganizational networks clustered around one commodity or product, linking households, enterprises, and states to one another in the world economy', thereby highlighting the 'social embeddedness of economic organization' (Gereffi et al. 1994: 2; Gereffi 1996). The focus was thus on firms, rather than states, as the primary drivers of the emerging 'global' (as opposed to international) division of labour.

The concept of the GPN took its cue from these insights, but its proponents argued for a concept of a 'network' as an improvement on the essentially linear and vertical character of the 'chain' metaphor. Production networks, defined as 'the nexus of interconnected functions and operations through which goods and services are produced, distributed and consumed', were seen to have become both organisationally more complex and more 'global' in their reach (Henderson et al. 2002: 445). The GPN approach was set out as a framework capable of capturing these changing forms of global economic reorganisation and understanding their developmental consequences. As an influential statement put it:

> [W]e have foregrounded the ways in which companies organize and control their global operations, the ways in which they are (or can be) influenced by states, trade unions, NGOs and other institutions in particular locations, and the implications that the resulting combinations of agents and processes might have for industrial upgrading, higher value added etc. and ultimately for the prospects of poverty reduction and/or generalized prosperity in those locations. (Henderson et al. 2002: 457–8)

Development is thus not primarily a matter of state strategy, as understood in the bulk of development theory, but rather the result of complex economic and social forces driving the globalisation of the world economy. 'Nationalist' approaches to the study of development are thus rendered inadequate: the idea of a 'national economy' is no longer revealing of the nature of production and consumption, and ideas of 'national' development strategy have lost meaning. As Philip McMichael explains:

> The global production system depends on a technical division of labor among specialized processes located in different world sites. Instead of countries specializing in an export industry (manufacturing or agriculture), world production sites specialize as part of a production chain linking several

countries. . . . The change was essentially from producing a national product to producing a world product. (McMichael 2000: 92)

The implications of these insights can be illustrated by returning to the debate about the rise of China. When approached from this perspective, understanding and theorising Chinese development involves moving the debate away from the narrow preoccupation with states, institutions and government policy which characterised the stand-off between the neoliberals and neostatists. Instead, analysis needs to be consciously located in a global context; in so doing the limitations of methodologically nationalist development theory are immediately revealed. According to this perspective, the story of the emergence of 'China' is one of a particular phase in global capital accumulation driven by mobile transnational capital. Transnational capital has 'landed' in parts of coastal China as a result of particular sets of factor endowments, facilitated by the internal economic reforms undertaken by the Chinese government from the late 1970s onwards. Equally, the growth pattern has been fuelled primarily by the production and investment strategies of companies in the advanced industrialised economies, which in turn are premised largely on demand in these markets (Breslin 2005). It is consequently misleading to talk about the development of 'China' as a national unit – rather, we are seeing the consolidation of a contemporary phase in the evolution of global production networks and value chains, which is manifested in certain spatial sites within the territorial boundaries of the Chinese state. William I. Robinson captured this well in his reference to China as not just the 'industrial workhouse of the world' but, moreover, the 'workhouse of transnational capital' (Robinson 2006).

The other key benefit of GPN analysis is seen to lie in its purchase on global inequalities. This framework and other cognate approaches, such as those associated with 'global value chains' (GVCs) (Gereffi and Kaplinsky 2001; Gereffi et al. 2005; Gibbon et al. 2008), have been mobilised for the purposes of explaining exactly *how* and *why* the distribution of gains from global production and exchange have been so markedly unequal (Kaplinsky 2000, 2005). Particular attention is afforded to the political and social embeddedness of global production and exchange, and the forms of power relations that facilitate or block participation in networks and chains which drive economic development processes. Explanations for global inequalities are thus sought in the workings of the global economy, echoing but modifying some of the insights of earlier bodies of theory that also situated the study of inequality in the world system of capitalism. In terms of the discussion of the last section, inequality in this perspective is clearly understood as a 'relational' phenomenon, disputing the orthodox view of its 'residual' character.

The concern with inequality in GPN and GVC analysis links directly to the second strand of 'global' development theory. This advances a conceptualisation of development as an intrinsically social process, and an understanding of global social inequalities as intrinsically 'transnationalised' rather than territorially bounded. The point of departure has been cogently articulated by Robinson as follows:

> Development connotes a social rather than a geographic, spatial or territorial process: we need to reconceive of development not in terms of nations but in terms of social groups in a transnational setting ... Here the focus becomes how accumulation processes that are no longer coextensive with specific national territories determine levels of social development among a population stratified increasingly along transnational class and social lines rather than along national lines. (Robinson 2002: 1062)

The processes which have generated this 'transnationalisation' of social inequality are associated with the restructuring of the global economy. As an integral dimension of globalisation processes and complex GPNs, labour markets have become increasingly transnationalised and people participate in these markets in highly differentiated and segmented ways. Crucially, as Robinson goes on to suggest, '[it] is the nature of participation in global production, through transnationalised labour markets, not through membership of nation-states, that determines the social development of groups' (Robinson 2002: 1065). Social groups are in this perspective constituted by their members' position in a global social hierarchy, not by their nationality or geographical location.

Affluent groups of the world's consumers (the 'developed' population) exist alongside the various strata of the poor and underprivileged (the 'underdeveloped' population), and indeed depend on their labours. These social hierarchies exist within cities, countries and regions. It is when one grasps that 'underdevelopment' is a social concept with no clear geographical significance, the argument goes, that we can begin properly to understand the nature of global inequalities and offer appropriate theoretical lenses for the study of development.

The processes which arguably best illustrate the need for such a theoretical shift are those associated with global migration. Migration processes emerge as functions of global inequalities, propelled by massive discrepancies in socioeconomic conditions and opportunities among the world's population, and enabled by the transnationalisation of labour markets. These labour markets do not rest entirely on migration; rather, they are shaped by the unequal participation of workers regardless of whether people have physically moved from one place to another. But migrant labour is increasingly central to their constitution. Mobility is strongly associated with membership of a global professional elite, as labour markets and recruitment networks for highly skilled, highly paid workers become increasingly globalised. Mobility is equally associated with the transformation of labour markets for workers at the bottom ends of the skill and wage spectrum, and migration among these workers is directly associated with the constitution of an ultra-flexible, highly exploitable global labour force (Sassen 2001; Bauder 2006; Phillips 2009b).

The acceleration of global migration generates huge difficulties for nationalist and state-centric development theory. Debates about poverty and inequality continue to rely on nation-states and national societies as the focus of their enquiries, taking national statistics as the points of measurement and comparing the situations of people who share a nationality or citizenship and are resident in the same national territory. Thus, as Anja Weiss (2005) and many others have pointed out, a homemaker in Texas is compared with an unemployed person in Chicago simply because they happen to live in the same country, whilst a Polish domestic worker working illegally in Germany is *not* compared with her German employer. Equally, a Romanian migrant worker in the UK who does not have UK citizenship is not included in the relevant statistics for that country, and is not included either in national statistics for Romania. Especially given high levels of illegal migration, the result is that large parts of the world's population are simply unaccounted for in conventional measures of poverty and inequality. For this reason, nation-state-centric approaches are deemed unable to capture either the empirical extent or the moral and ethical significance of global inequalities. Instead, it is suggested that we should focus on the material and social conditions of individual people without reference to nationality, national averages or, indeed, migration status. In other words, we are deemed to require a conception of global inequality as 'transnationalised', in the terms set out by Robinson, and an understanding of the social, not territorial, bases of global stratification.

A challenge is thus issued from these 'global' theories to the whole enterprise of development studies as it has been defined and articulated over the post-war period. How meaningful can it be to talk about 'national development' when large parts of productive economic activities exist only as dimensions of global production networks or are located in other territorial sites? What meaning can 'national development' retain when large proportions of the resident labour force are citizens of other countries? The emphasis in earlier development theories on fixed sets of factor endowments, including labour, as the determinants of a country's developmental potential has arguably been undermined by contemporary globalisation processes. The case is therefore made for a reworking – a 'globalisation', as it were – of development theory.

Notwithstanding the obvious force of their arguments, by the end of the 2000s these 'global' theories of development have not led to an appreciable loosening of the analytical and theoretical attachment to the national state in the bulk of development theory. Transnational perspectives had become well established in the social sciences, attracting wide-ranging debate and critique, notably for a certain 'overegging of the pudding' in their arguments against nation-state-centrism.

States, and indeed countries, were deemed to remain more important than theorists of transnationalism often permitted in their analyses. Among development theorists more specifically, it is tempting to say simply that old habits die hard. But perhaps a salient reason for indifference or hostility to these perspectives in some quarters has been that transnational perspectives present huge difficulties for a development theory which seeks to bridge scholarly and policy debates, inasmuch as it is unclear how a transnational perspective on inequality could translate into development strategy or practice, or indeed who the agents of that strategy would be. To this extent, particularly for the orthodox development policy community, these vibrant scholarly debates have been not only theoretically and politically unpalatable, but also unappealing in a practical policy sense. For these and other reasons, the success of transnationalist efforts in dislodging traditional emphases on the nation-state across the bulk of development theory had been rather limited at the end of the 2000s, even as their intellectual impact on political economy and the social sciences more broadly had been marked.

Conclusion

We conclude here our history of the concept of development. The evolution of theories and debates in the contemporary period has revealed a vigorous scholarly enterprise around the study of development. In all of the contemporary directions surveyed here, we have seen the legacy of bodies of development theory from previous periods and, in this respect, we recognise a strong element of theoretical continuity in the study of development even as the force of distinct theories and concepts has waxed and waned over time. But we have also revealed clearly the contemporary condition of uncertainty to which we alluded in the introduction. There is a striking lack of agreement or convergence on the basic questions of how we should define, understand, theorise and 'do' development. It would not be an exaggeration to say that the proliferation of approaches and the extent of divergence and contention between them are greater in this period than in any of the others we have described and analysed. In public discourse as well, development has become more widely used than possibly ever before, but the content of this discourse has been chaotic, often lacking in rigorous substance, and usually deeply conservative within the mainstream orthodoxy.

Our survey of contemporary directions has also highlighted the incipient turning point at which we appear now to have arrived. The rise of China and India is generally accepted to augur a very significant reordering of the global economy and processes of global development and, as we have suggested here, necessarily implies a shaking up of the enterprise of studying development. The longer-term significance of these changes for distinct bodies of theory remains to be seen. Is the challenge to the neoliberal mainstream devastating, or will the orthodoxy find ways to protect itself and preserve its dominance? Does the emergence of China and India breathe new life into neostatist debates? Are we returning to a nation-state-focused development studies in our concern with these two economies, or does their development experience offer sustenance to those 'global' theories which argue for a fundamental refocusing of our theoretical lenses? How do we, and should we, think about poverty and inequality in this context? In short, all the theories and concepts we have surveyed thus far find themselves illuminated and exposed by the changing global economic and political order. The challenge for development theory in general is to go on responding imaginatively to these changing realities.

Conclusion

We started this book by contending that the study of development stands on uncertain ground. The concept of development has become more widely used than ever before in its long history, and yet there remains a striking, and continuing, lack of agreement among theorists and practitioners about what it can be taken to mean. In some cases, this is the result of a failure even to reflect on the question of meaning, deploying the term 'development' glibly as a 'buzzword' which is deemed hardly to need defining. In others, it is the result of accepting unquestioningly a set of established assumptions about the concept without reflecting critically on their adequacy. In others still, it is the result of a vibrant debate which *does* seek to interrogate the concept and reflect on the implications of ascribing to it particular meanings, but in which no common ground has been found between the many contending approaches about what it is, exactly, that theorists of development are trying to do.

Our survey of theories of development in this book has revealed at once the centrality of the concept of development to a long and, at times, illustrious tradition of scholarship in the social sciences, and the uncertainty which has crept into the post-1945 enterprise of 'development studies' and gradually stifled its potential for continued vibrancy. Clearly, the field of development studies has found few paths to overcoming the 'impasse' that David Booth identified in the 1980s.

Yet the reality is that the study of development not only has been capable of retaining enormous validity – the extent of the early twenty-first century's preoccupation with it is sufficient testament to its ongoing resonance – but also has the potential to become the centrepiece of the wider intellectual enterprise of political economy in which it used, at least, to be squarely rooted. Moreover, it requires precisely this relocation within the broader field of political economy in order to advance fruitfully over the coming decades. We seek to justify this contention by returning to the approach we outlined in the Introduction and highlighting here what our exploration of development theory in the ensuing chapters has further revealed about the three distinguishing features of our approach.

First, we indicated our understanding of development as an object of strategy. The discussion demonstrated that one of the defining characteristics of development theory until the late twentieth century was its focus on national states as the primary agents of development, responsible for assembling and executing national development strategies. In other words, the study of development has historically been marked by both a strong methodological nationalism and an overt state-centrism in the ways that the parameters of enquiry were set. Questions of strategy have always been central to the study of development, with specialists and students always alert to the importance of agency. The point is that both strategy and agency were tied tightly to nation-states. What has changed is that theorists (and practitioners) have become increasingly sensitive to the ways in which globalisation has challenged the idea of 'national development' and the extent to which, as a consequence, this particular formulation of how strategy can be made can stay the central preoccupation of the contemporary study of development. There has emerged a global economy within which development is driven, and the possibilities for development are conditioned, by the strategies and activities of a range of economic and other actors beyond national states. Many of these strategies do not serve a set of goals associated with 'national' development, but, rather, are articulated in a range of different socio-spatial contexts that no longer correspond solely with territorial borders.

Conceptualisations of both strategy and agency vary between the approaches we have explored. In those approaches which emphasise the spatial reorganisation of development – that is, the idea that development occurs in spaces that are not (only) national but also sub-, supra- and trans-national or 'global' – there has emerged a new emphasis on the ways in which actors at sub- and supra-national arenas have been drawn into the development discourse and are engaged in formulating different kinds of development strategy. Institutions of global governance, regional organisations, city-level bodies and civil society organisations are examples. We saw that theorists who approach development through the lenses of globalisation, particularly those associated with GPN, GVC and other such transnational perspectives, have been pivotal in understanding the spatial reorganisation of the global economy and the new 'economic geography' of development. They also situated firms at the centre of their analyses, advancing understandings of the ways in which development is conditioned by the sets of social, political and power relations that are embedded in particular GPNs and GVCs. Other approaches, of course, offer different and perhaps more traditional perspectives and it is right to emphasise that national states do still seek to pursue development and are driven to do so often by good democratic impulses, namely, the perceived needs of their peoples.

Yet in the study of development there is clearly an ongoing tendency to focus too much on 'formal' agents, particularly institutions and organisations, and to perceive development strategy in this light as primarily a 'top-down' phenomenon. If we are to take seriously the insights that result from a focus on globalisation, then we must consider the ways in which social groups and individual people are also positioned as the agents of development, and indeed the architects of development strategies. Perhaps the most vivid contemporary version of this argument is the new-found fascination, particularly among national governments and in the official global development community, with the role of migrants and diasporic communities in development processes. In this public discourse, the development process is still conceived as national, but the preoccupation is with the ways in which diasporas can act as the agents and drivers of national development, most especially as senders of remittances. In other words, migrants are themselves situated not only as the drivers of their own 'development', if the argument can be so expressed, but also as key agents of national development in their home countries. The point is that, whether development is defined in traditional national terms or in the newer terms associated with human development and the opportunities available to particular social groups, it will no longer do to think of national states as the sole or even predominant entities that devise development strategy. An emphasis on the diverse strategies that shape the development prospects of the world's population, articulated by a variety of social and institutional actors in different spatial settings, is now indispensable.

Second, we highlighted the importance of uncovering the contested ideological terrain of development. We suggested at the start that there is no longer a consensus on either the meaning of development or its core normative agenda, and our discussions have revealed the extent of this contestation between different views of what development should entail. Development means different things to and for different groups of people across the world, and contending theoretical approaches reflect these divergent visions. Many older versions of development theory did not fully grasp the significance of this lack of consensus, nor its political implications. In part, this was because development theory was developed in the so-called 'North' for the supposed benefit of the so-called 'South', and the meanings that were ascribed to development, along with their normative assumptions, were distinctively 'Northern', 'Western', and so on. It was in fact often assumed that we knew what development was, and that it was simply a matter of figuring out how to bring it about. Development was thus widely defined as the process of 'catch-up' with the 'West' – in other words, as the achievement of modernity and the processes by which 'developing' countries became economically, politically and culturally similar to the so-called 'developed countries'. This emphasis on 'catch-up' informed earlier phases of development theory, but took a firm hold in the post-1945 period as a field called 'development studies' grew up around a presumed core distinction between the 'developed' zone and the rest of the world that was aspiring to achieve this status. Indeed, even when and where the national focus has been discarded or downplayed in some contemporary theories, the notion of catch-up is still evident in approaches concerned with the mitigation of social inequalities and the discrepancies in living standards and opportunities among the world's population.

This conception of development as catch-up has become redundant for two reasons. First, the rise of China, India and the 'East' generally has fundamentally shaken up all of the categories and assumptions that were integral to traditional notions of catch-up. The pace of growth and industrialisation in China, in particular, has far exceeded the levels of performance achieved by any early industrialising country at a similar stage. Moreover, the rise of Asia has decisively undermined the monopoly on a condition of 'development' that the 'West' has claimed for itself over several centuries and on which the enterprise of 'development studies' was founded. This accounts for a good part of the contemporary crisis of the field. Second, it has become abundantly clear to many observers that catch-up, defined as convergence on the levels of prosperity in the richest societies, is quite simply impossible to achieve on a global scale as a result of the planet's environmental and resource constraints (Humphrey 2007). At a time when the world is coming to terms with the environmental consequences of massive population growth, burgeoning greenhouse gas emissions and a looming food crisis, it is widely recognised that the goal of mitigating global inequalities can no longer be about the achievement of 'Western'-style prosperity and consumption for the whole of the world's population, but must focus on effecting convergence on living standards at a level of material well-being that is much lower than that enjoyed in the richest countries and among the richest parts of all societies (Sachs 2007).

The consequent challenge to most meanings of 'development' is arresting in its proportions. The emphasis on sustainability advanced by both environmental and human development perspectives has apparently been adopted in the global development community with no appreciation of the sense in which 'sustainable development' cannot but imply a restriction of consumption and growth for parts of the world's population. In this perspective, development can no longer be seen as a process of the continual improvement in people's material conditions, and the mitigation of inequalities cannot be pursued by attention solely to improving the lot of the world's poor and disadvantaged. Instead, development comes to be as much about mitigating levels of wealth and consumption patterns among the world's rich as it does about poverty alleviation *per se*. For this combination of reasons, many have come to the emphatic view that 'development as a project of catch-up is dead in the water' (Harriss-White 2007: 50).

The loosening of the grip of what were traditionally 'Western' ideas about development has thus contributed substantially to the increasing ideological contestation that surrounds development and development strategies. The disintegration of consensus from the early 2000s onwards among the 'Western' governments associated with these ideas has also played a part in putting in place a situation in which the content of development is far more *open to* and *available for* contestation than at many other points in history. Equally, new ideas about development have crystallised around the rise of Asia and had a substantial early impact on development debates. It may be, as John Humphrey observes, that 'perhaps for the first time, we are seeing Southern policy agendas that are backed up by financial muscle . . . the credibility that goes with rapid growth, and the intellectual and policymaking capacity to shape global agendas' (Humphrey 2007: 18). Conceivably, even bigger changes can be expected as Chinese, Indian and other new theorists begin to set out on the global stage their particular visions of development.

The third dimension of the approach we outlined in the Introduction constituted an insistence on the ways in which all development theories have been historically conditioned. It emerged clearly in the subsequent chapters that attempts to define development in some scientific sense are ill-conceived and fruitless, and that the meanings ascribed to development instead change over time in accordance with particular sets of historical circumstances, and are thus always profoundly political. Attempts to define development in ways that transcend historical contexts and historical events are therefore misplaced. We saw the difficulties with such perspectives most clearly in relation to neoliberal theories of development, which put forward universalist perspectives on the world's development problems, and advanced universalising solutions for them, without paying sufficient attention to the specificities of time and place. Yet it is possible to argue that we have not yet taken the importance of historicised development theory sufficiently on board in the contemporary period, and that sophisticated theorisations of development in an era of globalisation remain rather thin on the ground. We see this to be the result of what Robert Bates (1998: 6) has called the continued 'bondage' of development studies in comparative analysis, marked by a failure to engage seriously with theories of global change and bring comparative perspectives into the central endeavour of understanding the contemporary historical juncture and its consequences for development. It is perhaps significant in this regard that the most notable contributions to 'global' development theories have generally been advanced by scholars who associate themselves with the study of development within wider traditions in political economy, including sociologists and economic geographers, rather than those who adhere more rigidly to the traditions of a narrower field of 'development studies'.

On the basis of these observations, we can begin to assemble a conception of development that is appropriate for its study in the contemporary historical context of globalisation. It has four central ingredients.

- A methodologically nationalist and state-centric conception of development needs to be extended into one which gives precedence to a broader notion of development, in which what 'develops' are understood to be social groups. Such an understanding can of course accommodate continuing attention to how development is organised within the territorial borders of states, to inequalities between and within states, and so on. But our enquiries must at the same time be much wider in scope, focusing not (only) on groups linked by geographical location or nationality, but also on those linked by particular sets of material and social circumstances that cut across territorial boundaries.

- Equally, an exclusive focus on states and governments as the key 'agents' of development needs to be abandoned in favour of a recognition of the diverse strategies that are pursued by a wide range of formal and informal actors, and which shape development processes across the world. In that sense, the field of study has again to grow so as to incorporate fully and comfortably this more extensive list of key agents.

- Questions of poverty and inequality need to be central to this mode of enquiry and to debates about the substantive and normative content of development. For inequalities block possibilities for development for some social groups and facilitate the improvement of living standards and the expansion of opportunities for others. This means that the study of development needs to abandon its concern solely with poor(er) people. We need instead a conception of development which is widened to accommodate questions of wealth as well as poverty, which explores the connections between the two, and which is consequently capable of offering a more comprehensive understanding of sustainability in this context.

- Finally, the identification of development with traditional notions of 'area studies' or 'Third World' studies needs at last decisively to be abandoned. The assumption which has underpinned the enterprise of post-1945 'development studies' – namely, that there is something 'different' about developing countries which requires different theoretical approaches and, indeed, a separate sub-field – has surely been shown to be redundant. What is needed is a 'globalised' conception of development, advanced by vibrant theoretical debate and serious empirical research.

Such a prospectus for a reworked conception of development leads us to propose that the time has now come to move away from a specialist field of 'development studies', and instead to (re)locate the study of development squarely within the intellectual project of political economy and the diverse theoretical traditions associated with it. Indeed, we believe that this is the only way of advancing the study of development according to the parameters outlined above, and the only viable way of generating theoretical debates and empirical analyses that are rooted within a serious understanding of contemporary global change. Our contention that a history of development theory needs to start not in 1945, with the post-Second World War crystallisation of 'development studies' and the associated development project, but in the classical theories of the eighteenth and nineteenth centuries is the vital first step that needs to be taken in this direction, necessitating as it does engagement with the main intellectual traditions in classical political economy. As we noted in the Introduction, the key classical political economists (Marx, Smith, Ricardo, Weber, and so on) were fundamentally theorists of development. Equally, thinkers whom we identified as the figureheads of later development theories, such as Wallerstein, Friedman, Hayek and others, are also identified as the key thinkers of their relevant traditions in political economy more broadly. In short, classical political economy was concretely synonymous with the study of development and, notwithstanding the separatism of the post-1945 'development studies' project, development theory has continued to evolve in tandem with theories of political economy (Phillips 2005a). Yet this is also a two-way street, inasmuch as development studies produced many of the theoretical frameworks and vocabularies – such as those relating to dependency, world systems, imperialism, structuralism, and so on – that have left a deep imprint on political economy and remain of central importance in its critical strands (Harrison 2004).

This proposed re-grounding of the study of development in political economy therefore rests on strong historical and theoretical foundations. We suggest furthermore that it is the emergence of particular critical currents in contemporary political economy – what in the Introduction we called 'new political economy' – that creates an especially hospitable terrain for this project. The particular perspective that new political economy scholarship has offered on the relationship between structure and agency, and how methodologically we can build an approach which integrates a due emphasis on agency with the institutional and historical analysis of structures, resonates strongly with the prospectus that we have set out for the study of development. It is also a framework that is self-consciously rooted in the study of global change, concerned with questions of 'world order' and preoccupied with the key relationships that emerge at particular historical junctures between the prevailing world order, states and social forces (Cox 1981). As such, it offers notably fertile ground on which to pursue the project of locating the study of development firmly within an understanding of global change and the constellation of economic, social and political forces that constitute the contemporary era of globalisation. Finally, a core concern with ideological and ideational factors is injected centrally into the study of development, adding another dimension to our understanding of the power relations which shape the prospects for development of the world's population.

We suggest, on this basis, that re-grounding the study of development in the wider intellectual tradition of political economy, and particularly within new political economy approaches of the sort outlined above, offers a way to rescue it from its increasing marginalisation from key debates in the social sciences. When hived off into a sub-field called 'development studies', and premised on a notion that the study of certain parts of the world and certain sections of the world's population require separate treatment, both the concept of development and the core issues of poverty and inequality become visibly sidelined in other parts of the wider study of the social and political order. By reworking development into a concept that is genuinely of global relevance, oriented to the study of historical processes of global change and their consequences for the material and social conditions in which human beings live, we can move the concept of development to the very centre of a vibrant new political economy.

Bibliography

Adams, B. (1993) 'Sustainable Development and the Greening of Development Theory', in F. J. Schuurman (ed.) *Beyond the Impasse: New Directions in Development Theory* (London: Zed Books), pp. 207–22.

Afshar, H. and Dennis, C. (eds) (1992) *Women and Adjustment Policies in the Third World* (Basingstoke: Macmillan).

Akamatsu, K. (1961) 'A Theory of Unbalanced Growth in the World Economy', *Weltwirtschaftliches Archiv*, No. 86, pp. 196–215.

——(1962) 'A Historical Pattern of Economic Growth in Developing Countries', *The Developing Economies*, Vol. 1, No. 1, pp. 3–25.

Alden, C. (2007) *China in Africa* (London: Zed Books).

Almond, G. A. (1970) *Political Development: Essays in Heuristic Theory* (Princeton NJ: Princeton University Press).

Almond, G. A. and Coleman, J. (eds) (1960) *The Politics of the Developing Areas* (Princeton NJ: Princeton University Press).

Almond, G. A. and Powell, C. B. (1965) *Comparative Politics: A Developmental Agenda* (Boston MA: Little, Brown).

Alvares, C. (1992) *Science, Development and Violence: The Revolt Against Modernity* (Oxford: Oxford University Press).

Amin, S. (1976) *Unequal Development: An Essay on the Social Formulation of Peripheral Capitalism* (New York: Monthly Review Press).

Amsden, A. (1989) *Asia's Next Giant: South Korea and Late Industrialization* (New York: Oxford University Press).

——(1990) 'Third World Industrialization: "Global Fordism" or a New Model?', *New Left Review*, No. 182, pp. 5–31.

——(2001) *The Rise of the Rest: Challenges to the West from Late-industrializing Economies* (New York: Oxford University Press).

Andreasson, S. (2005) 'Orientalism and African Development Studies: The "Reductive Repetition" Motif in Theories of African Underdevelopment', *Third World Quarterly*, Vol. 26, No. 6, pp. 971–86.

Apter, D. (1965) *The Politics of Modernization* (Chicago IL: University of Chicago Press).

Arblaster, A. (1984) *The Rise and Decline of Western Liberalism* (Oxford: Basil Blackwell).

Arndt, H. W. (1987) *Economic Development: The History of an Idea* (Chicago IL: University of Chicago Press).

Arrighi, G. (1994) *The Long Twentieth Century: Money, Power, and the Origins of our Times* (London: Verso).

——(2007) *Adam Smith in Beijing: Lineages of the Twenty-First Century* (London: Verso).

Avineri, S (1968) *Karl Marx on Colonialism and Modernization* (New York: Doubleday).

Bairoch, P. (1993) *Economics and World History – Myths and Paradoxes* (Brighton: Harvester Wheatsheaf).

Balassa, B. (1982) *Development Strategies in Semi-Industrial Economies* (Baltimore MD: Johns Hopkins University Press).

Baran, P. (1973) [1957] *The Political Economy of Growth* (Harmondsworth: Penguin).

Baran, P. and Sweezy, P. (1966) *Monopoly Capital* (New York: Monthly Review Press).

Bardhan, K. and Klasen, S. (1999) 'UNDP's Gender-Related Indices: A Critical Review', *World Development*, Vol. 27, No. 6, pp. 985–1010.

Barnett, V. (2001) 'Marx, Karl Heinrich (1818–83), in R. J. B. Jones (ed.), *Routledge Encyclopedia of International Political Economy* (London: Routledge), pp. 987–95.

Bates, R. (1998) 'The Future in Comparative Politics', *Journal of Chinese Political Science*, Vol. 4, No. 2, pp. 1–18.

Bauder, H. (2006) *Labor Movement: How Migration Regulates Labor Markets* (New York: Oxford University Press).

Bauer, P. (1972) *Dissent on Development* (London: Weidenfeld and Nicolson).

Becker, G. (1981) *A Treatise on the Family* (Cambridge MA: Harvard University Press).

Beckerman, W. (1974) *In Defence of Economic Growth* (London: Jonathan Cape).

Beetham, D. (1985) *Max Weber and the Theory of Modern Politics* (Cambridge: Polity Press).

Bendix, R. (1959) *Max Weber: An Intellectual Portrait* (London: Methuen).

Benería, L. (1979) 'Reproduction, Production and the Sexual Division of Labor', *Cambridge Journal of Economics*, Vol. 3, No. 3, pp. 203–25.

——(2003) *Gender, Development, and Globalization: Economics As If All People Mattered* (New York: Routledge).

Benería, L. and Sen, G. (1981) 'Accumulation, Reproduction, and Women's Role in Economic Development: Boserup Revisited', *Signs*, Vol. 7, No. 2, pp. 279–98.

Bernstein, H. (ed.) (1990) *The Food Question: Profits vs. People* (London: Earthscan).

Bhagwati, J. (1988) 'Export-promoting Trade Strategy: Issues and Evidence', *World Bank Research Observer*, Vol. 3, No. 1, pp. 27–57.

Billington, M. O. (1992) 'Hamilton Influenced Sun Yat-Sen's Founding of the Chinese Republic', *Executive Intelligence Review*, 3 January.

Binder, L., Coleman, J. S., LaPalombara, J., Pye, L. W., Verba, S. and Weiner, M. (1971) *Crisis and Sequences in Political Development* (Princeton NJ: Princeton University Press).

Blomström, M. and Hettne, B. (1984) *Development Theory in Transition: The Dependency Debate and Beyond: Third World Responses* (London: Zed Books).

Blaug, M. (1986) *Economic Theory in Retrospect* (Cambridge: Cambridge University Press).

Bock, K. (1979) 'Theories of Progress, Development, Evolution', in T. B. Bottomore and R. Nisbet (eds), *A History of Sociological Analysis* (London: Heinemann), pp. 39–79.

Booth, D. (1985) 'Marxism and Development Sociology: Interpreting the Impasse', *World Development*, Vol. 13, No. 7, pp. 761–87.

Boserup, E. (1970) *Women's Role in Economic Development* (London: Allen and Unwin).

Bourdieu, P. (1980) 'Le Capital Social: Notes Provisoires', *Actes de la Recherche en Sciences Sociales*, Vol. 31, pp. 2–3.

Brenner, R. (1977) 'The Origins of Capitalist Development: A Critique of Neo-Smithian Marxism', *New Left Review*, No. 104, pp. 27–92.

Breslin, S. (2005) 'Power and Production: Rethinking China's Global Economic Role', *Review of International Studies*, Vol. 31, No. 4, pp. 735–53.

Brohman, J. (1995) 'Economism and Critical Silences in Development Studies: A Theoretical Critique of Neoliberalism', *Third World Quarterly*, Vol. 16, No. 2, pp. 297–318.

Brookfield, H. (1975) *Interdependent Development* (London: Methuen).

Bukharin, N. (1979) [1928] 'Notes of an Economist', *Economy and Society*, Vol. 8, No. 4, pp. 473–500.

Calder, K. (1993) *Strategic Capitalism: Private Business and Public Purpose in Japanese Industrial Finance* (Princeton NJ: Princeton University Press).

Caporaso, J. A. and Levine, D. P. (1992) *Theories of Political Economy* (Cambridge: Cambridge University Press).

Cardoso, F. H. (1977) 'The Consumption of Dependency Theory in the United States', *Latin American Research Review*, Vol. 12, No. 3, pp. 7–24.

Cardoso, F. H. and Faletto, E. (1979) *Dependency and Development in Latin America* (Berkeley CA: University of California Press).

Carr, E. H. (1941) *The Twenty Years' Crisis, 1919–1939* (London: Macmillan).

Chang, H-J. (1999) 'The Economic Theory of the Developmental State', in M. Woo-Cumings (ed.) *The Developmental State* (Ithaca NY: Cornell University Press), pp. 182–99.

——(2002) *Kicking Away the Ladder: Development Strategy in Historical Perspective* (London: Anthem Press).

——(ed.) (2003) *Rethinking Development Economics* (London: Anthem Press).

——(2006) *The East Asian Development Experience: The Miracle, the Crisis and the Future* (New York: Zed Books).

——(2007) *Bad Samaritans: Rich Nations, Poor Policies and the Threat to the Developing World* (London: Random House Business Books).

Chang, H-J., Park, H-J. and Yoo, C. G. (1998) 'Interpreting the Korean Crisis: Financial Liberalisation, Industrial Policy and Corporate Governance', *Cambridge Journal of Economics*, Vol. 22, No. 3, pp. 110–31.

Chant, S. (2008) 'The "Feminisation of Poverty" and the "Feminisation" of Anti-Poverty Programmes: Room for Revision?', *Journal of Development Studies*, Vol. 44, No. 2, pp. 165–97.

Chenery, H., Bowen I. and Svikhart, B. (1974) *Redistribution with Growth: Policies to Improve Income Distribution in Developing Countries in the Context of Economic Growth* (Oxford: Oxford University Press).

Chilcote, R. H. (1984) *Theories of Development and Underdevelopment* (Boulder CO: Westview Press).

Cohn, S. H. (1970) *Economic Development in the Soviet Union* (Lexington MA: D. C. Heath).

Colclough, C. (1982) 'Lessons from the Development Debate for Western Economic Policy', *International Affairs*, Vol. 58, No. 3, pp. 489–500.

——(1991) 'Structuralism versus Neo-liberalism: An Introduction', in C. Colclough and J. Manor (eds) *States or Markets? Neoliberalism and the Development Policy Debate* (Oxford: Clarendon Press), pp. 1–25.

Coleman, J. (1988) 'Social Capital in the Creation of Human Capital', *American Journal of Sociology*, Vol. 94, supplement, pp. S95–S120.

Collins, R. (1980) 'Weber's Last Theory of Capitalism', *American Sociological Review*, Vol. 45, No. 6, pp. 925–42.

Constantino, R. (1985) *Synthetic Culture and Development* (Quezon City: Foundation for Nationalist Studies).

Corbridge, S. (1998) ' "Beneath the Pavement Only Soil": The Poverty of Post-Development', *Journal of Development Studies*, Vol. 34, No. 6, pp. 138–48.

Cowen, M. P. and R. W. Shenton (1996) *Doctrines of Development* (London: Routledge).

Cox, R. W. (1981) 'Social Forces, States and World Orders: Beyond International Relations Theory', *Millennium: Journal of International Studies*, Vol. 10, No. 2, pp. 126–55.

Craig, D. and Porter, D. (2003) 'Poverty Reduction Strategy Papers: A New Convergence', *World Development*, Vol. 31, No. 1, pp. 53–69.

Crane, G. T. (1998) 'Economic Nationalism: Bringing the Nation Back In', *Millennium: Journal of International Studies*, Vol. 27, No. 1, pp. 55–75.

Cumings, B. (1984) 'The Origins and Development of the Northeast Asian Political Economy: Industrial Sectors, Product Cycles, and Political Consequences', *International Organization*, Vol. 38, No. 1, pp. 1–40.

Dasgupta, S. (1985) *Towards a Post Development Era* (London: Mittal).

Desai, M. (1982) 'Homilies of a Victorian Sage: A Review Article on Peter Bauer', *Third World Quarterly*, Vol. 4, No. 2, pp. 291–7.

Dietz, F. and van der Stratten, J. (1992) 'Rethinking Environmental Economics: Missing Links between Economic Theory and Environmental Policy', *Journal of Economic Issues*, Vol. 29, No. 1, pp. 27–51.

Dollar, D. and Kraay, A. (2002) 'Spreading the Wealth', *Foreign Affairs*, Vol. 81, No. 1, pp. 120–33.

Domar, E. (1947) 'Expansion and Employment', *American Economic Review*, Vol. 37, No. 1, pp. 34–55.

Doornbos, M. (2001) ' "Good Governance": The Rise and Decline of a Policy Metaphor?', *Journal of Development Studies*, Vol. 37, No. 6, pp. 93–108.

Dore, R. (1986) *Flexible Rigidities: Industrial Policy and Structural Adjustment in the Japanese Economy, 1970–1980* (Stanford CA: Stanford University Press).

Dos Santos, T. (1970) 'The Structure of Dependence', *American Economic Review*, Vol. 60, No. 2, pp. 231–6.

——(1977) 'Dependence Relations and Political Development in Latin America: Some Considerations', *Ibero-Americana*, Vol. 7, No. 1.

Doyle, M. W. (2001) 'Adam Smith (1723–90)', in R. J. Barry Jones (ed.), *Routledge Encyclopedia of International Political Economy* (London: Routledge), pp. 1403–10.

Drèze, J. and Sen, A. (1989) *Hunger and Public Action* (Oxford: Clarendon Press).

——(1995) *India: Economic Development and Social Opportunity* (Oxford: Oxford University Press).

ECLAC (United Nations Economic Commission for Latin America and the Caribbean) (2002), *Preliminary Overview of the Economies of Latin America and the Caribbean, 2002* (Santiago: United Nations).

Edward, P. (2006) 'Examining Inequality: Who Really Benefits from Global Growth?', *World Development*, Vol. 34, No. 10, pp. 1667–95.

Elson, D. (1989) 'How is Structural Adjustment Affecting Women?', *Development*, No. 1, pp. 67–74.

——(1992) 'Male Bias in Structural Adjustment', in H. Afshar and C. Dennis (eds) *Women and Adjustment Policies in the Third World* (London: Macmillan), pp. 46–68.

——(1993) 'Gender-aware Analysis and Development Economics', *Journal of International Development*, Vol. 5, No. 2, pp. 237–47.

——(ed.) (1995) *Male Bias in the Development Process* (Manchester: Manchester University Press).

Elson, D. and Pearson, R. (1981) 'Nimble Fingers Make Cheap Workers: An Analysis of Women's Employment in Third World Manufacturing', *Feminist Review*, No. 7, pp. 87–107.

Emmanuel, A. (1972) *Unequal Exchange: A Study of the Imperialism of Trade* (New York: Monthly Review Press).

Erlich, A. (1960) *The Soviet Industrialization Debate 1924–28* (Cambridge MA: Harvard University Press).

Erlich, P. (1972) *The Population Bomb* (London: Ballantine).

Erlich, P. and Erlich, A. (1970) *Population, Resources and Environment: Issues in Human Ecology* (New York: W. H. Freeman).

Escobar, A. (1992) 'Reflections on "Development": Grassroots Approaches and Alternative Development in the Third World', *Futures*, Vol. 24, No. 5, pp. 411–36.

——(1995) *Encountering Development: The Making and Unmaking of the Third World* (Princeton NJ: Princeton University Press).

Esteva, G. (1985) 'Beware of Participation', *Development: Seeds of Change*, Vol. 3, pp. 77–9.

Esteva, G. and Prakash, M. S. (1998) *Grassroots Post-modernism: Remaking the Soil of Cultures* (London: Zed Books).

Evans, P. B. (1979) *Dependent Development: The Alliance of Multinational, State and Local Capital in Brazil* (Princeton NJ: Princeton University Press).

Ferber, M. and Nelson, J. (eds) (1993) *Beyond Economic Man* (Chicago: University of Chicago Press).

Ferguson, J. (1990) *The Anti-Politics Machine: Development, Depoliticization and Bureaucratic Power in Lesotho* (Cambridge: Cambridge University Press).

Ferguson, L. (2007) *Production, Consumption and Reproduction in the Global Political Economy: The Case of Tourism Development in Central America*, unpublished PhD thesis, University of Manchester.

Fine, B. (1999) 'The Developmental State Is Dead – Long Live Social Capital', *Development and Change*, Vol. 30, No. 1, pp. 1–19.

——(2001a) 'Neither the Washington nor the Post-Washington Consensus: An Introduction', in B. Fine, C. Lapavitsas and J. Pincus (eds), *Development Policy in the Twenty-First Century: Beyond the Post-Washington Consensus* (London: Routledge), pp. 1–27.

——(2001b) *Social Theory versus Social Capital: Political Economy and Social Science at the Turn of the Millennium* (London: Routledge).

Folbre, N. (1994) *Who Pays for the Kids?* (London: Routledge).

——(ed.) (1996) *The Economics of the Family* (Cheltenham: Edward Elgar).

Foster-Carter, A. (1974) 'Neo-Marxist Approaches to Development and Underdevelopment', in E. de Kadt and G. Williams (eds), *Sociology and Development* (London: Tavistock), pp. 67–105.

——(1976) 'From Rostow to Gunder Frank: Conflicting Paradigms in the Analysis of Underdevelopment', *World Development*, Vol. 4, No. 3, pp. 167–80.

——(1978) 'The Modes of Production Controversy', *New Left Review*, No. 107, pp. 47–77.

Fox-Genovese, E. (1976) *The Origins of Physiocracy: Economic Revolution and Social Order in Eighteenth Century France* (Ithaca NJ: Cornell University Press).

Frank, A. G. (1967) *Capitalism and Underdevelopment in Latin America* (New York: Monthly Review Press).

——(1969) *Latin America: Underdevelopment or Revolution?* (New York: Monthly Review Press).

Friberg, M. and Hettne, B. (1985) 'The Greening of the World – Towards a Nondeterministic Model of Global Process', in H. Addo, S. Amin, G. Aseniero, A. Gunder Frank and F. M. Friberg (eds) *Development as Social Transformation: Reflections on the Global Problematique* (London: Hodder and Stoughton), pp. 204–70.

Frieden, J. A. and Lake, D. A. (1991) *International Political Economy: Perspectives on Global Power and Wealth* (London: Unwin Hyman).

Friedman, M. (1962) *Capitalism and Freedom* (Chicago IL: University of Chicago Press).

Friedman, M. and Schwartz, A. J. (1963) *Monetary History of the United States, 1867–1960* (Princeton NJ: Princeton University Press).

Frobel, F., Heinrichs, J. and Kreye, O. (1980) *The New International Division of Labor: Structural Unemployment in Industrialized Countries and Industrialization in Developing Countries* (Cambridge: Cambridge University Press).

Fukuda-Parr, S. (2004) 'Millennium Development Goals: Why They Matter', *Global Governance*, Vol. 10, No. 4, pp. 396–402.

Fukuyama, F. (1995) 'Social Capital and the Global Economy', *Foreign Affairs*, Vol. 74, No. 5, pp. 89–103.

Furtado, C. (1964) *Development and Underdevelopment* (Berkeley CA: University of California Press).

——(1969) *Economic Development in Latin America* (Cambridge: Cambridge University Press).

Galenson, W. (ed.) (1979) *Economic Growth and Structural Change in Taiwan: the Postwar Experience of the Republic of China* (Ithaca NY: Cornell University Press).

Gamble, A. (1995) 'The New Political Economy', *Political Studies*, Vol. 43, No. 3, pp. 516–30.

——(2001) 'Neo-Liberalism', *Capital and Class*, No. 75, pp. 127–34.

Gamble, A., Payne, A., Hoogvelt, A., Dietrich, M. and Kenny, M. (1996) 'Editorial: New Political Economy', *New Political Economy*, Vol. 1, No. 1, pp. 5–11.

Gereffi, G. (1996) 'Global Commodity Chains: New Forms of Coordination and Control Among Nations and Firms in International Industries', *Competition and Change*, Vol. 1, No. 4, pp. 427–39.

Gereffi, G., Humphrey, J. and Sturgeon, T. (2005) 'The Governance of Global Value Chains', *Review of International Political Economy*, Vol. 12, No. 1, pp. 78–104.

Gereffi, G. and Kaplinsky, R. (eds) (2001) *The Value of Value Chains: Spreading the Gains from Globalisation*, special issue of *IDS Bulletin*, Vol. 32, No. 3.

Gereffi, G., Korzeniewicz, M. and Korzeniewicz, R. P. (1994) 'Introduction: Global Commodity Chains', in G. Gereffi and M. Korzeniewicz (eds) *Commodity Chains and Global Capitalism* (London: Praeger), pp. 1–14.

Gerschenkron, A. (1962) *Economic Backwardness in Historical Perspective* (Cambridge MA: Harvard University Press).

Gerth, H. H. and Mills, C. W. (eds) (1947) *From Max Weber: Essays in Sociology* (London: Kegan Paul, Trench, Trubner and Co.).

Gibbon, P., Bair, J. and Ponte, S. (2008) 'Governing Global Value Chains: An Introduction', *Economy and Society*, Vol. 37, No. 3, pp. 315–38.

Giddens, A. (1971) *Capitalism and Modern Social Theory: An Analysis of the Writings of Marx, Durkheim and Weber* (Cambridge: Cambridge University Press).

——(1972) *Politics and Sociology in the Thought of Max Weber* (London: Macmillan).

Gill, S. and Law, D. (1988) *The Global Political Economy: Perspectives, Problems and Policies* (Hemel Hempstead: Harvester Wheatsheaf).

Gill, S. and Law, D. (1989) 'Global Hegemony and the Structural Power of Capital', *International Studies Quarterly*, Vol. 33, No. 1, pp. 475–99.

Gilpin, R. (1987) *The Political Economy of International Relations* (Princeton NJ: Princeton University Press).

——(2001) *Global Political Economy* (Princeton NJ: Princeton University Press).

Glyn, A. (2006a) *Capitalism Unleashed: Finance, Globalization, and Welfare* (Oxford: Oxford University Press).

——(2006b) 'Will Marx Be Proved Right?', *Oxonomics*, Vol. 1, No. 1, pp. 13–16.

Goody, J. (1996) *The East in the West* (Cambridge: Cambridge University Press).

Gopalakrisnan, P. K. (1959) *Development of Economic Ideas in India, 1880–1950* (New Delhi: People's Publishing House).

Gore, C. (1996) 'Methodological Nationalism and the Misunderstanding of East Asian Industrialisation', *European Journal of Development Research*, Vol. 8, No. 1, pp. 77–122.

——(2000) 'The Rise and Fall of the Washington Consensus as a Paradigm for Developing Countries', *World Development*, Vol. 28, No. 5, pp. 789–804.

Grossman, G. (1963) 'Notes for a Theory of the Command Economy', *Soviet Studies*, Vol. 15, No. 2, pp. 101–23.

Gu, J., Humphrey, J. and Messner, D. (2008) 'Global Governance and Developing Countries: The Implications of the Rise of China', *World Development*, Vol. 36, No. 2, pp. 274–92.

Gurrieri, A. (1987) 'The Validity of the State-as-planner in the Current Crisis', *CEPAL Review*, No. 31, pp. 193–209.

Haggard, S. and Cheng, T.-J. (1987) 'State and Foreign Capital in the East Asian NICs', in F. Deyo (ed.) *The Political Economy of the New Asian Industrialism* (Ithaca NY: Cornell University Press), pp. 84–135.

Hamilton, A. (1966) [1791] 'Report on the Subject of Manufactures', in H. C. Syrett (ed.), *The Papers of Alexander Hamilton* (New York: Columbia University Press), Vol. X, pp. 230–340.

Haq, K. and Ponzio, R. (2008) *Pioneering the Human Development Revolution: An Intellectual Biography of Mahbub ul Haq* (Delhi: Oxford University Press).

Hardin, G. (1968) 'The Tragedy of the Commons', *Science*, No. 162, pp. 1243–8.

Harding, S. (ed.) (1987) *Feminism and Methodology* (Bloomington IN: Indiana University Press).

Harlen, C. M. (1999) 'A Reappraisal of Classical Economic Nationalism and Economic Liberalism', *International Studies Quarterly*, Vol. 43, No. 4, pp. 733–44.

Harrison, D. (1988) *The Sociology of Modernization and Development* (London: Unwin Hyman).

Harrison, G. (2004) 'Introduction: Globalisation, Governance and Development', *New Political Economy*, Vol. 9, No. 2, pp. 155–62.

Harriss, J. (2002) *Depoliticizing Development: The World Bank and Social Capital* (London: Anthem Press).

Harriss, J. and de Renzio, P. (1997) ' "Missing Link" or Analytically Missing? The Concept of Social Capital: An Introductory Bibliographic Essay', *Journal of International Development*, Vol. 9, No. 7, pp. 919–37.

Harriss-White, B. (2007) 'Development Research and Action: Four Approaches', *IDS Bulletin*, Vol. 38, No. 2, pp. 46–50.

Harrod, R. F. (1939) 'An Essay in Dynamic Theory', *Economic Journal*, Vol. 49, No. 1, pp. 14–33.

Harvey, D. (2005) *A Brief History of Neoliberalism* (New York: Oxford University Press).

Heckscher, E. (1935) *Mercantilism* (London: George Allen and Unwin).

Helleiner, E. (2002) 'Economic Nationalism as a Challenge to Economic Liberalism? Lessons from the 19th Century', *International Studies Quarterly*, Vol. 46, No. 3, pp. 307–29.

Helleiner, G. K. (1989) 'Conventional Foolishness and Overall Ignorance: Current Approaches to Global Transformation and Development', *Canadian Journal of Development Studies*, Vol. 10, No. 1, pp. 107–20.

Henderson, C. (1998) *Asia Falling: Making Sense of the Asian Crisis and its Aftermath* (New York: McGraw-Hill).

Henderson, J., Dicken, P., Hess, M., Coe, N. and Yeung, H. W-C. (2002) 'Global Production Networks and the Analysis of Economic Development', *Review of International Political Economy*, Vol. 9, No. 3, pp. 436–64.

Henderson, O. W. (1983) *Friedrich List: Economist and Visionary, 1789–1846* (London: Frank Cass).

Henley, K. (1989–90) 'The International Roots of Economic Nationalist Ideology in Canada, 1846–85', *The Journal of Canadian Studies*, Vol. 24, pp. 107–21.

Heron, T. (2003) 'Commodity Chains and Global Capitalism: A Theoretical Critique', mimeo, University of Sheffield.

Hettne, B. (1995) *Development Theory and the Three Worlds: Towards an International Political Economy of Development* (Harlow: Longman).

Higgott, R. and Phillips, N. (2000) 'Challenging Triumphalism and Convergence: The Limits of Global Liberalisation in Asia and Latin America', *Review of International Studies*, Vol. 26, No. 3, pp. 359–79.

Himmelweit, S. (ed.) (2000) *Inside the Household: From Labour to Care* (Basingstoke: Palgrave Macmillan).

Himmelweit, S. and Mohun, S. (1977) 'Domestic Labor and Capital', *Cambridge Journal of Economics*, Vol. 1, No. 1, pp. 15–31.

Hirschman, A. O. (1958) *The Strategy of Economic Development* (New Haven CT: Yale University Press).

——(1961) (ed.) *Latin American Issues: Essays and Comments* (New York: Twentieth Century Fund).

——(1968) 'The Political Economy of Import Substitution Indus-trialization in Latin America', *Quarterly Journal of Economics*, Vol. 82, No. 1, pp. 1–32.

——(1981) *Essays in Trespassing: Economics to Politics and Beyond* (Cambridge: Cambridge University Press).

Hobsbawm, E. (1994) *Age of Extremes: The Short Twentieth Century, 1914–1991* (London: Michael Joseph).

Hobson, J. M. (2004) *The Eastern Origins of Western Civilization* (Cambridge: Cambridge University Press).

Hoogvelt, A. (1978) *The Sociology of Developing Societies* (London: Macmillan).

——(1982) *The Third World in Global Development* (London: Macmillan).

——(2001) *Globalization and the Post-colonial World: The New Political Economy of Development*, second edition (Basingstoke: Palgrave).

Hopkins, T. and Wallerstein, I. (1986) 'Commodity Chains in the World Economy Prior to 1800', *Review*, Vol. 10, No. 1, pp. 157–70.

Hoselitz, B. F. (1952) (ed.) *The Progress of Underdeveloped Areas* (Chicago IL: University of Chicago Press).

——(1960) *Sociological Aspects of Economic Growth* (Glencoe IL: The Free Press).

Hoskyns, C. and Rai, S. M. (2007) 'Recasting the Global Political Economy: Counting Women's Unpaid Work', *New Political Economy*, Vol. 12, No. 3, pp. 297–317.

Hsu, L. S. (1933) *Sun Yat-Sen's Political and Social Ideas: A Source-book* (Los Angeles CA: University of Southern California Press).

Hulme, D. and Shepherd, A. (2003) 'Conceptualizing Chronic Poverty', *World Development*, Vol. 31, No. 3, pp. 403–23.

Humphrey, J. (2007) 'Forty Years of Development Research: Trans-formations and Reformations', *IDS Bulletin*, Vol. 38, No. 2, pp. 14–19.

Huntington, S. P. (1968) *Political Order in Changing Societies* (New Haven CT: Yale University Press).

——(1971) 'The Change to Change: Modernization, Development and Politics', *Comparative Politics*, Vol. 3, No. 3, pp. 283–322.

IDS Asian Drivers Team (2006) 'The Impact of Asian Drivers on the Developing World', *IDS Bulletin*, Vol. 37, No. 1, pp. 3–11.

ILO (International Labour Organization) (1976) *Employment, Growth and Basic Needs: A One-World Problem* (Geneva: ILO).

Inkeles, A. and Smith, D. H. (1974) *Becoming Modern: Individual Change in Six Developing Countries* (Cambridge MA: Harvard University Press).

Jayasuriya, K. (2005) 'Beyond Institutional Fetishism: From the Developmental to the Regulatory State', *New Political Economy*, Vol. 10, No. 3, pp. 381–7.

Jenkins, R., Dussel Peters, E. and Mesquita Moreira, M. (2008) 'The Impact of China on Latin America and the Caribbean', *World Development*, Vol. 36, No. 2, pp. 235–53.

Johnson, C. (1981) 'Introduction: The Taiwan Model', in J. S. Hsiung (ed.) *Contemporary Republic of China: The Taiwan Experience, 1950–1980* (New York: Praeger), pp. 9–18.

——(1982) *MITI and the Japanese Miracle: The Growth of Industrial Policy, 1925–1975* (Stanford CA: Stanford University Press).

——(1999) 'The Developmental State: Odyssey of a Concept', in M. Woo-Cumings (ed.), *The Developmental State* (Ithaca NY: Cornell University Press), pp. 32–60.

Johnson, C. and Keehn, E. B. (1994) 'A Disaster in the Making: Rational Choice and Asian Studies', *The National Interest*, No. 36, pp. 14–22.

Jones, P. and Skinner, A. (eds) (1992) *Adam Smith Reviewed* (Edinburgh: Edinburgh University Press).

Kabeer, N. (1994) *Reversed Realities: Gender Hierarchies in Development Thought* (London: Verso).

Kang, D. (2002) *Crony Capitalism: Corruption and Development in South Korea and the Philippines* (Cambridge: Cambridge University Press).

Kaplinsky, R. (2000) 'Globalisation and Unequalisation: What Can Be Learned from Value Chain Analysis?', *Journal of Development Studies*, Vol. 37, No. 2, pp. 117–46.

——(2005) *Globalization, Poverty and Inequality* (Cambridge: Polity).

——(ed.) (2006) 'Asian Drivers: Opportunities and Threats', special issue of *IDS Bulletin*, Vol. 37, No. 1.

Kaplinsky, R. and Morris, M. (2008) 'Do the Asian Drivers Undermine Export-oriented Industrialization in SSA?', *World Development*, Vol. 36, No. 2, pp. 254–73.

Kay, C. (1989) *Latin American Theories of Development and Underdevelopment* (London: Routledge).

Keynes, J. M. (1936) *The General Theory of Employment, Interest and Money* (New York: Harcourt Brace).

Kiely, R. (1999) 'The Last Refuge of the Noble Savage? A Critical Assessment of Post-development Theory', *European Journal of Development Research*, Vol. 11, No. 1, pp. 30–55.

——(2007) 'Poverty Reduction Through Liberalization, or Intensified Uneven Development?: Neo-liberalism and the Myth of

Global Convergence', *Review of International Studies*, Vol. 33, No. 3, pp. 415–34.

Kitching, G. (1982) *Development and Underdevelopment in Historical Perspective: Populism, Nationalism and Industrialization* (London: Methuen).

Knippenberg, L. and Schuurman, F. (1994) 'Blinded by Rainbows: Anti-modernist and Modernist Deconstructions of Development', in F. Schuurman (ed.) *Current Issues in Development Studies: Global Aspects of Agency and Structure* (Saarbrücken: Entwicklungspolitik Breitenbach), pp. 90–106.

Koczberski, G. (1998) 'Women in Development: A Critical Analysis', *Third World Quarterly*, Vol. 19, No. 3, pp. 395–409.

Kohli, A. (1999) 'Where Do High-Growth Political Economies Come From? The Japanese Lineage of Korea's "Developmental State"', in M. Woo-Cumings (ed.) *The Developmental State* (Ithaca NY: Cornell University Press), pp. 93–136.

——(2004) *State-Directed Development: Political Power and Industrialization in the Global Periphery* (Cambridge: Cambridge University Press).

Kothari, R. (1988) *Rethinking Development: In Search of Humane Alternatives* (Delhi: Ajanta).

Kothari, U. (2005) 'From Colonial Administration to Development Studies: A Post-Colonial Critique of the History of Development Studies', in U. Kothari (ed.) *A Radical History of Development Studies: Individuals, Institutions and Ideologies* (London: Zed Books), pp. 47–66.

Kozul-Wright, R. (1995) 'The Myth of Anglo-Saxon Capitalism: Reconstructing the History of the American State', in H-J. Chang and R. Rowthorn (eds), *The Role of the State in Economic Change* (Oxford: Clarendon Press), pp. 81–113.

Krueger, A. (1980) 'Trade Policy as an Input to Development', *American Economic Review*, Vol. 70, pp. 288–92.

Krugman, P. (1995) 'Dutch Tulips and Emerging Markets', *Foreign Affairs*, Vol. 74, No. 4, pp. 28–44.

——(2007) 'Who Was Milton Friedman?', *New York Review of Books*, Vol. LIV, No. 2, 15 February, pp. 27–30.

Kurtz, M. (2001) 'State Developmentalism Without a Developmental State: The Public Foundations of the "Free Market Miracle" in Chile', *Latin American Politics and Society*, Vol. 43, No. 2, pp. 1–25.

Laclau, E. (1971) 'Feudalism and Capitalism in Latin America', *New Left Review*, No. 67, pp. 19–38.

——(1979) *Politics and Ideology in Marxist Theory* (London: Verso).

Lal, D. (1983) *The Poverty of 'Development Economics'* (London: Institute of Economic Affairs).

Larrain, J. (1989) *Theories of Development: Capitalism, Colonialism and Dependency* (Cambridge: Polity).

Leftwich, A. (2000) *States of Development: On the Primacy of Politics in Development* (Cambridge: Polity).

Lélé, S. (1991) 'Sustainable Development: A Critique', *World Development*, Vol. 19, No. 6, pp. 607–21.

Lenin, V. I. (1916) *Imperialism, the Highest Stage of Capitalism* (London: Lawrence and Wishart).

——(1960–70) *Collected Works* (Moscow: Progress Publishers).

Lerner, D. (1972) 'Modernization: Social Aspects', in D. Sills (ed.), *International Encyclopedia of the Social Sciences*, Vol. 9 (New York: Collier Macmillan).

Levi-Faur, D. (1997a) 'Economic Nationalism: From Friedrich List to Robert Reich'. *Review of International Studies*, Vol. 23, No. 3, pp. 359–70.

——(1997b) 'Friedrich List and the Political Economy of the Nation-state', *Review of International Political Economy*, Vol. 4, No. 1, pp. 154–78.

Levy, M. J. (1952) 'Some Sources of the Vulnerability of the Structures of Relatively Non-industrialised Societies to Those of Highly Industrialised Societies', in B. F. Hoselitz (ed.), *The Progress of Underdeveloped Areas* (Chicago IL: University of Chicago Press), pp. 113–25.

Lewin, M. (1968) *Russian Peasants and Soviet Power* (London: Allen and Unwin).

Lewis, W. A. (1950) 'The Industrialisation of the British West Indies', *Caribbean Economic Review*, No. 2, pp. 1–61.

——(1954) 'Economic Development with Unlimited Supplies of Labour', *The Manchester School of Economic and Social Studies*, Vol. 22, No. 2, pp. 139–91.

——(1955) *The Theory of Economic Growth* (London: George Allen and Unwin).

Leys, C. (1975) *Underdevelopment in Kenya: The Political Economy of Neo-colonialism* (London: Heinemann).

——(1977) 'Underdevelopment and Dependency: Critical Notes', *Journal of Contemporary Asia*, Vol. 7. No. 1, pp. 92–107.

——(1996a) *The Rise and Fall of Development Theory* (Oxford: James Currey).

——(1996b) 'The Crisis in "Development Theory"', *New Political Economy*, Vol. 1, No. 1, pp. 41–58.

List, F. (1909) [1827] 'Outlines of American Political Economy', in M. E. Hirst (ed.), *The Life of Friedrich List and Selections from His Writings* (London: Smith, Elder).

——(1991) [1885] *The National System of Political Economy* (New York: Augustus M. Kelley).

Love, J. L. (1980) 'Raúl Prebisch and the Origins of the Doctrine of Unequal Exchange', *Latin American Research Review*, Vol. 15, No. 1, pp. 45–72.

Luthin, R. (1944) 'Abraham Lincoln and the Tariff', *The American Historical Review*, Vol. 49, No. 4, pp. 610–29.

Luxemburg, R. (1951) [1913] *The Accumulation of Capital* (London: Routledge).

McClelland, D. C. (1961) *The Achieving Society* (Princeton NJ: Van Nostrand).

——(1966) 'The Achievement Motive in Economic Growth', in B. F. Hoselitz and W. E. Moore (eds), *Industrialization and Society* (Paris: UNESCO-Mouton), pp. 74–96.

McLellan, D. (1971) *The Thought of Karl Marx* (London: Macmillan).

McMichael, P. (2000) *Development and Social Change: A Global Perspective*, second edition (Thousand Oaks CA: Pine Forge Press).

Marchand, M. (1994) 'Gender and New Regionalism in Latin America: Inclusion/Exclusion', *Third World Quarterly*, Vol. 15, No. 1, pp. 63–76.

——(1996) 'Reconceptualising "Gender and Development" in an Era of "Globalisation"', *Millennium: Journal of International Studies*, Vol. 25, No. 3, pp. 577–603.

Martinussen, J. (1997) *Society, State and Market: A Guide to Competing Theories of Development* (London: Zed Books).

Marx, K. (1964) [1844] *Early Writings*, translated and edited by T. B. Bottomore (New York: McGraw-Hill).

——(1968) 'Preface to *A Contribution to the Critique of Political Economy*', in K. Marx and F. Engels, *Selected Works in One Volume* (London: Lawrence and Wishart).

——(1970) *Capital: A Critique of Political Economy*, Vol. 1 (London: Lawrence and Wishart).

Marx, K. and Engels, F. (1965) *The German Ideology*, edited by S. Ryazanskaya (London: Lawrence and Wishart).

——(1975) *Selected Correspondence* (Moscow: Progress Publishers).

——(1985) *The Communist Manifesto* (Harmondsworth: Penguin).

Max-Neef, M. A. (1991) *Human-scale Development* (New York: Apex Press).

Meadows, D. H., Meadows, D. L. and Randers, J. (1992) *Beyond the Limits: Global Collapse or a Sustainable Future?* (London: Earthscan Publications).

Meadows, D. H., Meadows, D. L., Randers, J. and Behrens, W. W. (1972) *The Limits to Growth* (New York: Universe Books).

Meadowcroft, J. (2000) 'Sustainable Development: A New(ish) Idea for a New Century?', *Political Studies*, Vol. 48, No. 2, pp. 370–87.

Meier, G. M. (2005) *Biography of a Subject: An Evolution of Development Economics* (Oxford: Oxford University Press).

Meier, G. M. and Seers, D. (eds) (1984) *Pioneers in Development* (Oxford: Oxford University Press).

Melotti, U. (1977) *Marx and the Third World* (London: Macmillan).

Mesquita Moreira, M. (2006) 'Fear of China: Is There a Future for Manufacturing in Latin America?', *World Development*, Vol. 35, No. 3, pp. 358–9.

Mies, M. (1986) *Patriarchy and Accumulation on a World Scale: Women in the International Division of Labour* (London: Zed Books).

Milanovic, B. (2003) 'The Two Faces of Globalization: Against Globalization As We Know It', *World Development*, Vol. 31, No. 4, pp. 667–83.

——(2005) *Worlds Apart: Measuring International and Global Inequality* (Princeton NJ: Princeton University Press).

Mill, J. S. (1848) *The Principles of Political Economy with Some of Their Applications to Social Philosophy* (London: John W. Parker).

Molyneux, M. (1979) 'Beyond the Domestic Labour Debate', *New Left Review*, No. 115, pp. 3–28.

——(1985) 'Mobilization Without Emancipation? Women's Interests, the State, and Revolution in Nicaragua', *Feminist Studies*, Vol. 11, No. 2, pp. 227–54.

Moon, C-I. and Rhyu, S-Y. (1999) 'The State, Structural Rigidity, and the End of Asian Capitalism', in R. Robison, M. Beeson, K. Jayasuriya and H-R. Kim (eds), *Politics and Markets in the Wake of the Asian Crisis* (London: Routledge), pp. 77–98.

Morris-Suzuki, T. (1989) *A History of Japanese Thought* (London: Routledge).

Moser, C. (1989) 'Gender Planning and Development: Meeting Practical and Strategic Needs', *World Development*, Vol. 17, No. 11, pp. 1799–825.

——(1993) *Gender Planning and Development: Theory, Practice and Training* (London: Routledge).

Myint, H. (1977) 'Adam Smith's Theory of International Trade in the Perspective of International Development', *Economica*, Vol. 44 (n.s.), pp. 231–48.

Myrdal, G. (1957) *Economic Theory and Underdeveloped Regions* (London: Duckworth).

Naím, M. (2000) 'Washington Consensus or Washington Confusion?', *Foreign Policy*, No. 118, pp. 86–103.

Nairoji, D. (1962) [1901] *Poverty and un-British Rule in India* (Delhi: Government of India).

Nel, P. (2006) 'Review Article: The Return of Inequality', *Third World Quarterly*, Vol. 27, No. 4, pp. 689–706.

Nelson, P. (2007) 'Human Rights, the Millennium Development Goals, and the Future of Development Cooperation', *World Development*, Vol. 35, No. 12, pp. 2041–55.

Nisbet R. (1969) *Social Change and History: Aspects of the Western Theory of Development* (Oxford: Oxford University Press).

Nolan, P. (2004a) *Transforming China: Globalization, Transition and Development* (London: Anthem).

——(2004b) *China at the Crossroads* (Cambridge: Polity).

Notz, W. (1925) 'Friedrich List in America', *American Economic Review*, Vol. 16, No. 2, pp. 249–65.

Nove , A. (1964) *Was Stalin Really Necessary?* (London: Allen and Unwin).

——(1969) *An Economic History of the U.S.S.R.* (London: Allen Lane).

——(1975) *Stalinism and After* (London: Allen and Unwin).

Nussbaum, M. (1999) 'Women and Equality: The Capabilities Approach', *International Labour Review*, Vol. 138, No. 3, pp. 227–45.

O'Brien, D. C. (1972) 'Modernization, Order and the Erosion of a Democratic Ideal', *Journal of Development Studies*, Vol. 8, No. 3, pp. 49–76.

O'Brien, P. J. (1975) 'A Critique of Latin American Theories of Dependency', in I. Oxaal, T. Barnett and D. Booth (eds), *Beyond the Sociology of Development* (London: Routledge), pp. 7–27.

Oliver, I. J. (2001) 'Weber, Max (1864–1920)', in R. J. B. Jones (ed.), *Routledge Encyclopedia of International Political Economy* (London: Routledge), pp. 1676–87.

Önis, Z. (1991) 'Review: The Logic of the Developmental State', *Comparative Politics*, Vol. 24, No. 1, pp. 109–26.

Önis, Z. and Şenses, F. (2005) 'Rethinking the Emerging Post-Washington Consensus', *Development and Change*, Vol. 36, No. 2, pp. 263–90.

Ormerod, P. (1994) *The Death of Economics* (London: Faber).

Palma, G. (1978) 'Dependency: A Formal Theory of Underdevelopment or a Methodology for the Analysis of Concrete Situations of Underdevelopment?', *World Development*, Vol. 6, No. 7–8, pp. 881–924.

Panagariya, A. (2008) *India: The Emerging Giant* (Oxford: Oxford University Press).

Parfitt, T. (2002) *The End of Development: Modernity, Postmodernity and Development* (London: Pluto Press).

Park, Y. C. (2006) *Economic Liberalization and Integration in East Asia: A Post-Crisis Paradigm* (Oxford: Oxford University Press).

Parsons, T. (1951) *The Social System* (London: Routledge).

Payne, A. J. (2004) 'Rethinking Development inside International Political Economy', in A. J. Payne (ed.), *The New Regional Politics of Development* (Basingstoke: Palgrave Macmillan), pp. 1–28.

——(2005a) *The Global Politics of Unequal Development* (Basingstoke: Palgrave Macmillan).

——(2005b) 'The Study of Governance in a Global Political Economy', in N. Phillips (ed.), *Globalizing International Political Economy* (Basingstoke: Palgrave Macmillan), pp. 55–81.

Pearce, D., Barbier, E. and Markandya, A. (1990) *Sustainable Development: Economics and Environment in the Third World* (Aldershot: Edward Elgar).

Pearson, R. (1995) 'Male Bias and Women's Work in Mexico's Border Industries', in D. Elson (ed.) *Male Bias in the Development Process* (Manchester: Manchester University Press), pp. 13–63.

——(2005) 'The Rise and Rise of Gender and Development', in U. Kothari (ed.) *A Radical History of Development Studies: Individuals, Institutions and Ideologies* (London: Zed Books), pp. 157–79.

Pempel, T. J. (1999a) 'The Developmental Regime in a Changing World Economy', in M. Woo-Cumings (ed.), *The Developmental State* (Ithaca NY: Cornell University Press), pp. 137–81.

——(ed.) (1999b) *The Politics of the Asian Financial Crisis* (Ithaca NY: Cornell University Press).

Perraton, J. (2005) 'Review Article: Joseph Stiglitz's *Globalisation and its Discontents*', *Journal of International Development*, Vol. 16, No. 6, pp. 897–906.

Petras, J. (1978) *Critical Perspectives on Imperialism and Social Class in the Third World* (New York: Monthly Review Press).

Phillips, A. (1977) 'The Concept of Development', *Review of African Political Economy*, Vol. 4, No. 8, pp. 7–20.

Phillips, N. (2004) *The Southern Cone Model: The Political Economy of Regional Capitalist Development in Latin America* (London: Routledge).

——(2005a) 'Whither IPE?', in N. Phillips (ed.), *Globalizing International Political Economy* (Basingstoke: Palgrave Macmillan), pp. 246–69.

——(2005b) 'Latin America in the Global Political Economy', in R. Stubbs and G. Underhill (eds) *Political Economy and the Changing Global Order*, third edition (Oxford: Oxford University Press), pp. 332–43.

——(2009a) 'Consequences of an Emerging China: Is Development Space Disappearing for Latin America and the Caribbean?', in A. F. Cooper and J. Heine (eds) *Which Way Latin America? Hemispheric Politics Meets Globalization* (Tokyo: United Nations University Press).

——(2009b) 'Migration as Development Strategy? The New Political Economy of Dispossession and Inequality in the Americas', *Review of International Political Economy*, Vol. 16, No. 2, pp. 231–59.

——(2010, forthcoming) 'China and Latin America', in L. Dittmer and G. Yu (eds) *China and the World of Development* (Boulder CO: Lynne Rienner).

Pieterse, J. N. (1998) 'My Paradigm or Yours? Alternative Development, Post-Development, Reflexive Development', *Development and Change*, Vol. 29, No. 2, pp. 343–73.

——(2002) 'Global Inequality: Bringing Politics Back In', *Third World Quarterly*, Vol. 23, No. 6, pp. 1023–46.

Pirie, I. (2005) 'The New Korean State', *New Political Economy*, Vol. 10, No. 1, pp. 25–42.

Pogge, T. (ed.) (2007) *Freedom from Poverty as a Human Right: Who Owes What to the Very Poor?* (Oxford: Oxford University Press).

——(2008) *World Poverty and Human Rights*, second edition (Cambridge: Polity Press).

Polanyi, K. (1944) *The Great Transformation: The Political and Economic Origins of Our Time* (Boston: Beacon Press).

Pollock, D. H. (1978) 'Some Changes in United States' Attitudes towards CEPAL over the Past 30 Years', *CEPAL Review*, No. 6, pp. 57–80.

Prebisch, R. (1950) *The Economic Development of Latin America and its Principal Problems* (New York: United Nations).

Preobrazhensky, E. (1965) [1926] *The New Economics* (Oxford: Clarendon Press).

Preston, P. W. (1996) *Development Theory: An Introduction* (Oxford: Basil Blackwell).

Putnam, R. (1993) *Making Democracy Work: Civic Traditions in Modern Italy* (Princeton NJ: Princeton University Press).

Rai, S. (2002) *Gender and the Political Economy of Development* (Cambridge: Polity).

Ramo, J. (2004) *The Beijing Consensus* (London: The Foreign Policy Centre).

Rapley, J. (2004) 'Development Studies and the Post-development Critique', *Progress in Development Studies*, Vol. 4, No. 4, pp. 350–4.

Redclift, M. (1987) *Sustainable Development: Exploring the Contradictions* (London: Methuen).

Reddy, S. (2008) 'The World Bank's New Poverty Estimates – Digging Deeper into a Hole', working paper, Institute for Social Analysis, Columbia University, available at http://www.columbia.edu/~sr793/response.pdf

Reddy, S. and Pogge, T. (2003) 'How Not to Count the Poor', working paper, Institute for Social Analysis, Columbia University, version 6.2, 29 October.

Ricardo, D. (1981) [1819] *Principles of Political Economy* (Cambridge: Cambridge University Press).

Rist, G. (1997) *The History of Development: From Western Origins to Global Faith* (London: Zed Books).

Robinson, W. I. (2002) 'Remapping Development in Light of Globalisation: From a Territorial to a Social Cartography', *Third World Quarterly*, Vol. 23, No. 6, pp. 1047–71.

——(2006) 'Latin America, State Power and the Challenge to Global Capital: An Interview with William I. Robinson', *Focus on the Global South*, 21 November (http://www.focusweb.org).

Rodrik, D. (2002) 'After Neoliberalism, What?', paper presented to the conference on 'Alternatives to Neoliberalism' sponsored by the New Rules for Global Finance Coalition, 23–24 May, available at http://www.new-rules.org/docs/afterneolib/rodrik.pdf

——(2006) 'Goodbye Washington Consensus, Hello Washington Confusion: A Review of the World Bank's *Economic Growth in the 1990s: Learning from a Decade of Reform*', *Journal of Economic Literature*, Vol. 44, No. 4, pp. 973–87.

Roett, R. and Paz, G. (eds) (2008), *China's Expansion into the Western Hemisphere: Implications for Latin America and the United States* (Washington DC: Brookings Institution).

Rogers, B. (1980) *The Domestication of Women: Discrimination in Developing Societies* (London: Kogan Page).

Rosenstein-Rodan, P. N. (1943) 'Problems of Industrialization of Eastern and South-Eastern Europe', *Economic Journal*, Vol. 53, No. 210/11, pp. 202–11.

——(1961) 'Notes on the Theory of the Big Push', in H. S. Ellis and H. C. Wallich (eds), *Economic Development for Latin America* (London: Macmillan), pp. 57–67.

Rostow, W. W. (1960) *The Stages of Economic Growth: A Non-Communist Manifesto* (Cambridge: Cambridge University Press).

Roxborough, I. (1979) *Theories of Development* (London: Macmillan).

Sachs, J. (1998) 'The IMF and the Asian Flu', *American Prospect*, March–April, pp. 16–21.

Sachs, W. (ed.) (1992) *The Development Dictionary: A Guide to Knowledge as Power* (London: Zed Books).

——(2007) 'Global Challenges: Climate Chaos and the Future of Development', *IDS Bulletin*, Vol. 38, No. 2, pp. 36–9.

Said, E. W. (1978) *Orientalism* (London: Penguin).

Saith, A. (2006) 'From Universal Values to Millennium Development Goals: Lost in Translation', *Development and Change*, Vol. 37, No. 6, pp. 1167–99.

Sala-i-Martin, X. (2002) 'The Disturbing "Rise" in Income Inequality', NBER Working Paper No. 8904, April.

Sanyal, B. (1994) 'Ideas and Institutions: Why the Alternative Development Paradigm Withered Away', *Regional Development Dialogue*, Vol. 15, No. 1, pp. 23–35.

Sassen, S. (2001) *The Global City: New York, London, Tokyo* (Princeton NJ: Princeton University Press).

Schmitz, H. (2007) 'The Rise of the East: What Does It Mean for Development Studies?', *IDS Bulletin*, Vol. 38, No. 2, pp. 51–8.

Schuurman, F. J. (1993) (ed.) *Beyond the Impasse: New Directions in Development Theory* (London: Zed Books).

——(2003) 'Social Capital: the Politico-Emancipatory Potential of a Disputed Concept', *Third World Quarterly*, Vol. 24, No. 6, pp. 991–1010.

Seers, D. (1963) 'The Limitations of the Special Case', *Bulletin of the Oxford Institute of Economics and Statistics*, Vol. 25, No. 2, pp. 77–98.

——(1969) 'The Meaning of Development', *International Development Review*, Vol. 11, No. 4, pp. 2–6.

——(ed.) (1981) *Dependency Theory: A Critical Reassessment* (London: Pinter).

Segal, G. and Goodman, D. (eds) (2002) *Towards Recovery in Pacific Asia* (London: Routledge).

Sen, A. K. (1981) *Poverty and Famines: An Essay on Entitlement and Deprivation* (Oxford: Oxford University Press).

——(1983) 'Development: Which Way Now?', *Economic Journal*, Vol. 93, No. 372, pp. 745–62.

——(1985) *Commodities and Capabilities* (Oxford: Oxford University Press).

——(1999) *Development as Freedom* (Oxford: Oxford University Press).

Shannon, T. R. (1989) *An Introduction to the World-System Perspective* (Boulder CO: Westview Press).

Shils, E. (1963) 'On the Comparative Study of the New States', in C. Geertz (ed.), *Old Societies and New States* (New York: The Free Press), pp. 1–26.

Shiva, V. (1988) *Staying Alive: Women, Ecology and Development* (London: Zed Books).

Singer, H. W. (1950) 'The Distribution of Gains between Investing and Borrowing Countries', *American Economic Review*, Vol. 40, No. 2, pp. 473–85.

Smith, A. (1969) [1759] *The Theory of Moral Sentiments*, introduced by E. G. West (Indianapolis IN: Liberty Classics).

——(1976) [1776] *An Inquiry into the Nature and Causes of the Wealth of Nations*, Glasgow edition, edited by R. H. Campbell and A. S. Skinner (Oxford: Clarendon Press).

Soederberg, S. (2001) 'The Emperor's New Suit: The New International Financial Architecture as a Reinvention of the Washington Consensus', *Global Governance*, Vol. 7, No. 4, pp. 453–67.

——(2002) 'On the Contradictions of the New International Financial Architecture: Another Procrustean Bed for Emerging Markets?', *Third World Quarterly*, Vol. 25, No. 2, pp. 607–20.

Solow, R. (1956) 'A Contribution to the Theory of Economic Growth', *Quarterly Journal of Economics*, Vol. 70, No. 10, pp. 65–94.

Spiegel, H. (1971) *The Growth of Economic Thought* (Englewood Cliffs NJ: Prentice Hall).

Stalin, J. V. (1976) [1931] 'The Tasks of Economic Executives', in J. V. Stalin, *Problems of Leninism* (Peking: Foreign Language Press), pp. 519–31.

Standing, G. (2000) 'Brave New Worlds? A Critique of Stiglitz's World Bank Rethink', *Development and Change*, Vol. 31, No. 4, pp. 737–63.

Staniland, M. (1985) *What is Political Economy? A Study of Social Theory and Underdevelopment* (New Haven CT: Yale University Press).

Stewart, F. (1985) 'The Fragile Foundations of the Neo-classical Approach to Development', *Journal of Development Studies*, Vol. 21, No. 2, pp. 282–92.

Stiglitz, J. (1998a) 'Towards a New Paradigm for Development: Strategies, Policies and Processes', The 1998 Prebisch Lecture at UNCTAD, Geneva, 19 October.

——(1998b) 'More Instruments and Broader Goals: Moving Toward the Post-Washington Consensus', The 1998 World Institute for Development Economic Research Annual Lecture, Helsinki, 7 January.

——(2001) 'An Agenda for Development in the Twenty-First Century', in A. Giddens (ed.), *The Global Third Way Debate* (Cambridge: Polity), pp. 340–57.

——(2004) 'Capital Market Liberalisation, Globalisation and the IMF', *Oxford Review of Economic Policy*, Vol. 20, No. 1, pp. 57–71.

Streeten, P., with Burki, S. J., ul Haq, M., Hicks, N. and Stewart, F. (1982) *First Things First: Meeting Basic Human Needs in Developing Countries* (New York: World Bank/Oxford University Press).

Sunkel, O. (1969) 'National Development Policy and External Dependency in Latin America', *Journal of Development Studies*, Vol. 1, No. 1, pp. 23–48.

——(1973) 'Transnational Capitalism and National Disintegration in Latin America', *Social and Economic Studies*, Vol. 22, No. 1, pp. 132–76.

Szporluk, R. (1988) *Communism and Nationalism: Karl Marx versus Friedrich List* (Oxford: Oxford University Press).

Taylor, I. (2006) *China and Africa: Engagement and Compromise* (London: Routledge).

Taylor, J. G. (1979) *From Modernization to Modes of Production: A Critique of the Sociologies of Development and Underdevelopment* (London: Macmillan).

Thatcher, I. D. (2000) 'Alec Nove, Soviet Planning and Market Reform, and the Need for Relevant Economics', *New Political Economy*, Vol. 5, No. 2, pp. 269–80.

The Economist (1998), 'Two Kinds of Openness', 12 September.

Thurbon, E. and Weiss, L. (2006) 'Investing in Openness: The Evolution of FDI Strategy in South Korea and Taiwan', *New Political Economy*, Vol. 11, No. 1, pp. 1–22.

Tinker, I. (1976) 'The Adverse Impact of Development on Women', in I. Tinker and M. Bramsen (eds) *Women and World Development* (New York: Praeger), pp. 22–34.

Tipps, D. C. (1973) 'Modernization Theory and the Comparative Study of Societies: A Critical Perspective', *Comparative Studies in Society and History*, Vol. 15, No. 2, pp. 199–226.

Toye, J. (1991) 'Is there a New Political Economy of Development?', in C. Colclough and J. Manor (eds) *States or Markets? Neo-liberalism and the Development Policy Debate* (Oxford: Clarendon Press), pp. 320–38.

——(1993) *Dilemmas of Development*, second edition (Oxford: Blackwell).

Trebilcock, C. (1981) *The Industrialization of the Continental Powers 1780–1914* (Harlow: Longman).

Tribe, K. (1988) 'Friedrich List and the Critique of "Cosmopolitical Economy"', *The Manchester School*, Vol. 56, No. 1, pp. 17–36.

Tull, D. (2006) 'China's Engagement in Africa: Scope, Significance and Consequences', *Journal of Modern African Studies*, Vol. 44, No. 3, pp. 459–79.

Tussie, D. (ed.) (2000) *Luces y sombras de una nueva relación: El Banco Interamericano de Desarrollo, el Banco Mundial y la sociedad civil* (Buenos Aires: Grupo Editorial Temas).

ul Haq, Mahbub (1976) *The Poverty Curtain: Choices for the Third World* (New York: Columbia University Press).

——(1995) *Reflections on Human Development* (New York: Oxford University Press).

UNDP (United Nations Development Program) (1990) *Human Development Report 1990* (New York: Oxford University Press).

——(1995) *Human Development Report 1995* (New York: Oxford University Press).

United Nations (1951) *Measures for the Economic Development of Underdeveloped Countries* (New York: United Nations).

Vaggi, G. and Groenewegen, P. (2003) *A Concise History of Economic Thought: From Mercantilism to Monetarism* (Basingstoke: Palgrave Macmillan).

Valdés, J. G. (1995) *Pinochet's Economists: The Chicago School in Chile* (Cambridge: Cambridge University Press, 1995).

Viner, J. (1950) *The Customs Union Issue* (New York: Carnegie Endowment for International Peace).

Wade, R. (1990) *Governing the Market: Economic Theory and the Role of Government in Taiwan's Industrialization* (Princeton NJ: Princeton University Press).

——(1996) 'Japan, the World Bank, and the Art of Paradigm Maintenance: The East Asian Miracle in Political Perspective', *New Left Review*, No. 217, pp. 3–36.

——(1998) 'The Asian Debt-and-Development Crisis of 1997–?: Causes and Consequences', *World Development*, Vol. 26, No. 8, pp. 1535–53.

——(1999) 'Gestalt Shift: From "Miracle" to "Cronyism" in the Asia Crisis', *Cambridge Journal of Economics*, Vol. 30, No. 1, pp. 134–50.

——(2004) 'Is Globalization Reducing Poverty and Inequality?', *World Development*, Vol. 32, No. 4, pp. 567–89.

——(2006) 'Choking the South', *New Left Review*, No. 38, pp. 1–13.

Walby, S. (1990) *Theorizing Patriarchy* (Cambridge: Polity).

Walicki, A. (1969) *The Controversy over Capitalism: Studies in the Social Philosophy of the Russian Populists* (Oxford: Clarendon Press).

Wallerstein, I. (1974) *The Modern World System*, Vol. I (New York: Academic Press).

——(1979) *The Capitalist World Economy* (Cambridge: Cambridge University Press).

——(1980) *The Modern World System*, Vol. II (New York: Academic Press).

——(1983) *Historical Capitalism* (New York: Norton).

Ward, C. (1998) (ed.) *The Stalinist Dictatorship* (London: Arnold).

Waring, M. (1988) *Counting for Nothing: What Men Value and What Women Are Worth* (Auckland: Allen and Unwin).

Warren, B. (1973) 'Imperialism and Capitalist Industrialization', *New Left Review*, No. 81, pp. 3–44.

——(1980) *Imperialism: Pioneer of Capitalism* (London: Verso).

Watson, M. (2005) *Foundations of International Political Economy* (Basingstoke: Palgrave Macmillan).

Waylen, G. (1996) *Gender in Third World Politics* (Buckingham: Open University Press).

Weber, M. (1958) *The Protestant Ethic and the Spirit of Capitalism*, translated and edited by T. Parsons (New York: Charles Scribner's Sons).

Weiss, A. (2005) 'The Transnationalization of Social Inequality: Conceptualizing Social Positions on a World Scale', *Current Sociology*, Vol. 53, No. 4, pp. 707–28.

Weiss, L. and Hobson, J. M. (1995) *States and Economic Development: A Comparative Historical Analysis* (London: Polity).

Wells, A. (2002) *The Political Thought of Sun Yat-Sen: Development and Impact* (Basingstoke: Palgrave Macmillan).

Williams, M. (1993) 'Re-articulating the Third World Coalition: The Role of the Environmental Agenda', *Third World Quarterly*, Vol. 14, No. 1, pp. 7–29.

Williams, D. G. (1996) 'Governance and the Discipline of Development', *European Journal of Development Research*, Vol. 8, No. 2, pp. 157–77.

Williams, D. and Young, T. (1994) 'Governance, the World Bank and Liberal Theory', *Political Studies*, Vol. 42, No. 1, pp. 84–100.

Williamson, J. (1990) 'What Washington Means by Policy Reform', in J. Williamson (ed.) *Latin American Adjustment: How Much Has Happened?* (Washington DC: Institute of International Economics), pp. 8–17.

——(1993) 'Democracy and the "Washington Consensus"', *World Development*, Vol. 21, No. 8, pp. 1329–36.

——(1994) *The Political Economy of Policy Reform* (Washington DC: Institute of International Economics).

——(2003) 'Overview: An Agenda for Restarting Growth and Reform', in J. Williamson and P-P. Kuczynski (eds) *After the Washington Consensus: Restarting Growth and Reform in Latin America* (Washington DC: Institute for International Economics), pp. 1–19.

Winch C. (1998) 'Listian Political Economy: Social Capitalism Conceptualised?', *New Political Economy*, Vol. 3, No. 2, pp. 301–16.

Winch, D. (1996) *Riches and Poverty: An Intellectual History of Political Economy in Britain 1750–1834* (Cambridge: Cambridge University Press).

Winters, L. A. and Yusuf, S. (eds) (2007) *Dancing With Giants: China, India and the Global Economy* (Washington DC: World Bank).

Wise, C. and Quiliconi, C. (2007) 'China's Surge in Latin American Markets: Policy Challenges and Responses', *Politics and Policy*, Vol. 35, No. 3, pp. 410–38.

Woo, J. (1991) *Race to the Swift: State and Finance in Korean Industrialization* (New York: Columbia University Press).

Woo-Cumings, M. (1999) 'Introduction: Chalmers Johnson and the Politics of Nationalism and Development', in M. Woo-Cumings (ed.) *The Developmental State* (Ithaca NY: Cornell University Press), pp. 1–31.

Woodhouse, P. (2002) 'Development Policies and Environmental Agendas', in U. Kothari and M. Minogue (eds) *Development Theory and Practice: Critical Perspectives* (Basingstoke: Palgrave Macmillan), pp. 136–56.

Woolcock, M. (1998) 'Social Capital and Economic Development: Toward a Theoretical Synthesis and Policy Framework', *Theory and Society*, Vol. 27, No. 2, pp. 151–208.

World Bank (1989) *Sub-Saharan Africa: From Crisis to Sustainable Growth: A Long-Term Perspective Study* (Washington DC: IBRD).

——(1990) *World Development Report 1990: Poverty* (New York: Oxford University Press).

——(1991) *World Development Report 1991: The Challenge of Development* (New York: Oxford University Press).

——(1992) *Governance and Development* (Washington DC: IBRD).

——(1993) *The East Asian Miracle: Economic Growth and Public Policy* (Washington DC: IBRD).

——(1997) *World Development Report 1997: The State in a Changing World* (New York: Oxford University Press).

——(2002a) *Globalization, Growth, and Poverty: Building an Inclusive World Economy* (Washington DC: World Bank).

——(2002b) *Global Economic Prospects and the Developing Countries 2002: Making Trade Work for the World's Poor* (Washington DC: World Bank).

——(2005) *Economic Growth in the 1990s: Learning from a Decade of Reform* (Washington DC: IBRD).

——(2007) *East Asia and Pacific Update: Ten Years After Asia's Financial Crisis*, April (http://siteresources.worldbank.org).

World Commission on Environment and Development (1987) *Our Common Future* (Oxford: Oxford University Press).

Worsley, P. (1982) *Marx and Marxism* (Milton Keynes: Open University Press).

Young, K. (1992) 'Household Resource Management', in L. Ostergaard (ed.) *Gender and Development: A Practical Guide* (London: Routledge), pp. 135–64.

Zeitlin, I. (1968) *Ideology and the Development of Sociological Theory* (New York: Prentice Hall).

Ziai, A. (2004) 'The Ambivalence of Post-development: Between Reactionary Populism and Radical Democracy', *Third World Quarterly*, Vol. 25, No. 6, pp. 1045–60.

Index